Women and Work in
Preindustrial Europe

# WOMEN and
# WORK in
# PREINDUSTRIAL
# EUROPE

EDITED BY

*Barbara A. Hanawalt*

Indiana University Press

BLOOMINGTON

Manufactured in the United States of America

Library of Congress Cataloging-in-Publication Data
Main entry under title:

Women and work in preindustrial Europe.

Bibliography: p.
Includes index.
1. Women—Employment—Europe—History—Addresses,
essays, lectures. 2. Women—Europe—Economic
conditions—Addresses, essays, lectures. 3. Europe—
Occupations—History—Addresses, essays, lectures.
I. Hanawalt, Barbara.
HD6059.5.E85W65   1986        331.4'094        85-42829
ISBN 0-253-36610-0
ISBN 0-253-20367-8 (pbk.)
1   2   3   4   5   90   89   88   87   86

# Contents

7. *Kathryn L. Reyerson*
   Women in Business in Medieval Montpellier              117
8. *Maryanne Kowaleski*
   Women's Work in a Market Town: Exeter in the Late
   Fourteenth Century                                     145

**PART V: Is There a Decline in Women's Economic Position
          in the Sixteenth Century?**               165

9. Natalie Zemon Davis
   Women in the Crafts in Sixteenth-Century Lyon          167
10. Martha C. Howell
    Women, the Family Economy, and the Structures of Market
    Production in Cities of Northern Europe during the Late Middle
    Ages                                                  198

    Contributors                                          223
    Index                                                 225

# Introduction

## *Barbara A. Hanawalt*

In a recent survey of women's history for the early modern period, Olwen Hufton commented upon the marked paucity of literature on women's work. As she observes, "We all *know* that women in pre-industrial society worked. . . . Yet we have very little detailed modern research bearing on the nature and importance of their labour."[1] The contributions to this volume address that lacuna, for they all bear on the subject of women's participation in the economy and labor force from the thirteenth through the sixteenth centuries. These essays have raised issues that have broad implications for current debates in women's history. The first is Hufton's deceptively simple question: What exactly was women's work in preindustrial Europe? The essays in this volume have gone far to answer that question and provide rich descriptive literature on both rural and urban women's work. But the authors have raised further and more profound questions about women in preindustrial Europe. Did women have an economic role outside the family or was their productive labor limited to the context of the domestic environment? Could a single woman be economically independent and successful, or was the only route open to her that of a domestic in a home other than her natal one? How did women's labor fit in with their usual life cycle of unmarried young womanhood, marriage and children, maturity and adult children, and widowhood? And finally, the authors raise once again the question that Alice Clark addressed in *Working Life of Women in the Seventeenth Century*. Were women more economically valued and independent in preindustrial, precapitalist Europe than they were afterward?[2]

The working women in this volume represent a wide diversity of stations in life, ranging from slaves and servants to respectable widows and professional midwives. Through a variety of sources including notarial records, wills, contracts, private account books, and city, manorial, and state court records, their work patterns come to life. The women studied lived in

Ragusa (Dubrovnik), Florence, Lyon and Montpellier, Exeter and rural England, Cologne, Leiden, and Nuremberg. With such a variety of work experiences, locations, and centuries separating their lives, a remarkable continuity of circumstances and options nevertheless emerges.

Working women were homebodies. Their participation in the economy rarely necessitated their leaving their quarter of a city or their village. At most they went to markets several miles from their household or came from surrounding villages to find work as domestics or laborers in nearby towns. The most widely traveled working women were the slaves that Susan Mosher Stuard has studied. Their roots were in the mountainous regions outside of Ragusa. Brought to the city, they were trained in domestic service or household crafts; if they learned well, they were sold to Italian merchants and some ended their lives in the Florentine domestic establishments that Christiane Klapisch-Zuber has analyzed. The merchant-class women that Katherine Reyerson studied in Montpellier, that Martha Howell observed in Leiden and Cologne, and that Maryanne Kowaleski documented for Exeter might control considerable capital as widows, but they never engaged in long-distance trade or went to the cloth fairs. Both the demands of family and household and the social attitudes that frowned on women traveling alone inhibited their personal participation in the larger market economy outside their cities and in the international markets.

Two other common threads running through these women's lives were that the domestic environment accommodated the vast majority of their work experience and that their primary mentor was likely to be their mother or another woman. A household, whether that of their own family or that of another, was the usual setting for their work. Peasant girls learned at their mothers' knees the care of chickens, milking, cooking, brewing, and other domestic occupations. They accompanied their mothers to the fields, weeding and making plaits to bind sheaves. The talents that they acquired in their home environment would serve them in good stead if they passed their late teenage years as servants in a neighbor's house or if they took these skills directly into marriage and their own domestic establishments. Among the artisanal workers in Lyon, as we find in Natalie Zemon Davis's study, girls learned from their mothers the rudiments of their fathers' crafts, helping with those tasks allotted to women.

If daughters could not learn their work from their mothers, a surrogate had to be found. In Ragusa noble and artisanal mistresses taught their slave girls how to serve and work. Orphaned girls in Lyon learned useful trades from skilled matrons in hospitals so that they could find employment in silk and cotton thread-making or as domestics. Apprenticeships in other people's homes were also possible for urban girls. They would learn a useful craft from the artisan's wife rather than learning from their own mothers.

Such apprenticeships, of course, had to be negotiated and paid for by the girl's parents or some other benefactor or benefactress. Sometimes a kinswoman or man would take in a relative and teach her a trade. In Nuremberg Merry Wiesner has found that midwives were so in demand that the city government tried to mandate that they take apprentices.

Residential arrangements were also primarily in household units. Although the Beguines established their own houses to accommodate young women working in urban areas, most women would live with their employers or their family. They slept in the house, took their meals with their employer's family, and submitted to familial discipline. Christiane Klapisch-Zuber has shown how the patriarchal discipline of Italian households extended to the regulation of servants and even control over their marriages.

We should not be surprised that the household and domestic production were such dominant features of women's work in preindustrial Europe. In urban centers the shop and the house were usually combined so that for men as well as women the house would be the center of production. In rural areas, the woman's sphere was the house, while the man's was primarily the field. Only a few of the medieval jobs employed women outside of the domestic framework. Some women did road work and thatching, the agricultural routine took women to the fields for weeding and harvest, and the specialized skills of silk manufacture could take women outside the home or family-run shop. Midwives, of course, took their skills to the home of their client.

Another reason that the domestic model was so common for organizing women's labor was that most women would eventually marry. Studies of permanent celibacy in early modern France and England show that only about 7 to 10 percent of women never married.[3] For most women, therefore, marriage would be the framework within which they would spend most of their adult, working lives. Skills learned as a teenager would eventually lead to a marriage in which the woman would continue to practice those occupations while adding to them the cares of family and the responsibility of training her daughters to become part of the new work force. For young women who were not fortunate enough to have parents who could provide a dowry toward marriage or pay for an apprenticeship that would make them an asset as a marriage partner, a period of employment would be necessary in order to accumulate sufficient money to make a marriage, as we can observe in Christiane Klapisch-Zuber's study of Florentine domestic servants. Young women in domestic service might have to work a number of years before accumulating sufficient savings to marry, and many waited until they were in their late twenties to marry. Employment, therefore, was a way station on the road to marriage for some young women.

Two observations may be made about the influence of marriage on women's work in preindustrial Europe. The first is that marriage itself was integral to the preindustrial economy for both men and women, and the second is that women had to accommodate their work pattern to the stages in their life cycle that marriage imposed. Work of unmarried, young, single women was somewhat different from that of wives, and widows made yet another adjustment in their work to accommodate their new status.

As I will discuss in my chapter on peasant women and the home econ-omy, modern economists have suggested a model for traditional marriages that is based on the complementarity of training and personal preferences for work of men and women. Women were trained by their mothers or some surrogate to become proficient in work related to domestic responsibilities. It was not simply homemaking and housework, but also included such production for the market as could be carried on at home. Spinning was the most typical activity for both urban and rural women to learn, but, as the essays indicate, a variety of other occupations could be practiced at home and contribute substantially to the household economy. Men as well re-ceived specialized training either from their fathers or from surrogates for them. Peasant lads learned the outdoor routines while their sisters were learning to take care of house, garden, domestic animals, and supplemental economic tasks. In the urban centers the youth learned a craft either as an apprentice or a laborer. For both men and women the spheres of activity were closely defined. In the country, women's space was the home and men's the fields. In the city, women worked in the home or shop along with their men, but they did not perform the same tasks and they did not take the finished product to the marketplace. Thus marriage was mutually ad-vantageous for men and women, for they were trained and socialized to different economic activities that complemented each other.

Marriage also influenced the rhythm of women's work over the course of their lifetimes. Men pursued a more or less steady course whether they were peasants or urban workers. They took up their occupation, acquired the necessary skills for it, and continued to work until old age or death either as employees or as independent artisans. Marriage and family might make their work more or less profitable but did not change what they did. Women's occupations, on the other hand, were very much influenced by changes in their life cycle. Judith Bennett has demonstrated that single women did not brew in rural England nor, according to Martha Howell, did they finish cloth in Leiden. In Exeter, Maryanne Kowaleski observes, they were unlikely to enter the retail trade. Unmarried women generally held lower-status jobs in cloth making or acted as domestic servants, although the wealthier ones would be apprenticed. In the countryside poor single girls would serve in another peasant's house or move to the town seeking unskilled employment.

Once married, women found that a range of new opportunities presented themselves within the context of household economy. Brewing was a common occupation for married women in both rural and market-town England. The retail trade, particularly that of victualer or tavern keeper, was also attractive. In all of the urban cases cooperation in the husband's craft or trade or taking in piecework such as leather finishing occupied wives when they were not involved with child rearing. As Leah Otis's essay informs us, some married women received stipends for nursing foundlings in their homes.

It was only in widowhood that a woman could have real opportunities as a *femme sole*. But one's capacity to carry on alone varied greatly with local custom and the pressures of the marriage market. In Exeter, for instance, local laws were generous to widows in property settlements, but because they were so well endowed they were in high demand as marriage partners. Only three widows remained single merchants. Widows in all contexts of the preindustrial European economy had more options than either married or single women. They could choose to remarry and, if they did, they were usually free to choose their marriage partner. They could remain single and invest in real estate, as Reyerson found many did in Montpellier, or continue with a husband's business, even one that involved considerable financial transactions. If they did carry on their husband's business, they had to hire men to do those parts of the labor or travel that only men were allowed to do. Thus a woman continuing a printing shop in Lyon could put her imprimatur on books but would have to hire men to work the press. Even wealthy merchant widows did not travel to foreign markets but had to hire men to do it for them.

A woman changed work patterns with her life cycle, but she might also alter her work within a particular phase of her cycle. Thus a dismissed servant girl or a laborer laid off because of an economic slump might turn to prostitution. During married life a woman might concentrate on thread production if that was paying well but switch to brewing or victualing if the market was more robust in those areas. Some of the shifts were responses not to market economy but to the amount of labor available to the house. If children were young and the mother had to spend most of her time with them, she would find thread making easier to accommodate to her limited time. When the children were growing up, they could be helpful in launching another supplemental economic activity, such as brewing or hawking pastries that their mothers made. Women could, therefore, change their work frequently over the course of their lifetimes.

It was not simply the domestic economy or the life cycle that influenced women's employment in the preindustrial era, however. Biology and social mores also determined their employment. Because childbirth was exclusively a woman's experience and ritual in the medieval and early modern period, women alone assisted with a birth. Male physicians did not yet have a role in this process, and as a consequence, midwives had a unique professional role. Merry Wiesner has shown that midwives were so highly valued in Nuremberg that they were paid as well as laborers, and both the government and the clergy gave them rather extensive responsibilities including distribution of some poor relief and baptism of endangered infants. The nurturing role also made wet nurses a respected and sought-after group in society. In Florence, the nurses were more highly paid than other female domestics and their moral qualities were as carefully guarded as those of the patrician's wife. In Montpellier the city willingly paid wet nurses to suckle its foundlings and orphans, and many women with milk must have nursed infants privately for a fee, using their biological capacities to supplement the family income. One of the obvious ways for an employer to use a woman's biological capacities was to take advantage of her sexuality, and the domestics and slaves of Florence and Ragusa were not alone in being sexually exploited by masters and their sons and friends.

Another factor that determined women's employment and their wages was demography and the social and economic reactions to population decline and expansion. Christiane Klapisch-Zuber notes that Florentines hired more female domestics in the middle years of the fifteenth century and paid them better than they did in the latter part of that century. Likewise in Montpellier, Leah Otis found that the real wages of the wet nurses decreased in the course of the late fifteenth and sixteenth centuries. Both attribute the decline in real wages to the increase of population, which forced women to face more competition for wages. Employers, since they had a larger pool to choose from, simply did not adjust wages to keep pace with inflation. When the nations of Europe were populous, therefore, women's employment and wages declined. In the northern European cities the population increase led to greater rigidification of social structure. Wiesner found that patrician women in the sixteenth century would no longer trouble themselves serving on a board to supervise midwives for the poor, and Howell found that the increased guild regulation in Leiden and Cologne excluded women from production, even the wives of cloth makers.

Olwen Hufton has aptly described the women's work pattern in preindustrial Europe as an economy of makeshift or expediency.[4] For the poor single women, spinsters or widows, a number of pieced together, temporary work arrangements would have to be their sole support. Married women in both town and country would supplement the family economy as best they could with the extra products or services that they could sell. Women always had to keep their eye on the main chance and to change according to economic opportunities. As Kowaleski and Howell have pointed out, because their socialization and training were primarily for the domestic sphere, they were unlikely to develop skills that would permit them to enter high-status positions. The magistrates of England recognized that women were dabblers, and when they reissued the Statute of Laborers in 1363, they required all men to choose a trade and confine themselves to it exclusively, but women could go on as they always had, brewing, baking, spinning, and doing other cloth work.[5]

Men were reluctant to admit women into their space and their mysteries. The plow was a man's implement: women might goad the ox, but rarely guide the plow. Only a part of this exclusion was based on the relative weakness of women compared to men. The plow was a carefully guarded prerogative having been part of the European male sexual metaphor since ancient Greece. With the development of male crafts, as well, women were allowed only a limited role. The wife and daughter, perhaps a female apprentice or laborer, might be taught part of the mystery, but they would not complete the whole product and would not be inducted as full members of the guild that regulated the craft. Eileen Power has suggested that part of the reason for keeping women out was the fear of competition. Many of the crafts did not require strength, but men believed that if women entered them they would take over because they were paid less.[6] Howell has shown that in Leiden the government organized the high-quality cloth workers into "crafts" and in doing so effectively eliminated women from this work. Depending on the rules of a particular guild, a widow may or may not have been allowed to continue as a guild member carrying on her husband's trade.

Men also effectively discouraged women from organizing their own crafts into guilds. In Cologne Howell found that, while the silk makers, gold spinners, and yarn makers were organized into a guild, the guild masters were males and the members were related to the chief merchants and traders of the city as daughters, wives, or widows. Two women sat on the guild board, but their only official capacity was investigating the quality of silk production. The existence of all-female guilds or of guilds permitting equal membership of both men and women performing a craft has a spotty record across Europe. While Paris had five female guilds, London had none. On the whole, all-female guilds tended to be rare both because such organization was discouraged and because most female labor took place within the context of family and the family craft.

The denial of any magisterial role for women was as effective as their socialization to the domestic sphere in limiting women to the economy of makeshift. Women could not hold urban or rural offices. Women might be the chief brewers, but they were never ale tasters. Women would never be mayors or aldermen; they would not be admitted as guild masters in their own right but only as wives of masters. Even the rare female guild was male run. Only occasionally were matrons called upon to determine a judicial matter, and these always dealt with such cases as the virginity of a suspected witch or the pregnancy of a condemned feloness. Matrons also supervised the specifically female service of midwives to poor women in Nuremberg.

The proscription of women from magisterial positions made it difficult for them to have any influence over regulations that would restrict their access to work or worsen their working conditions. Thus if journeymen dyers wished to restrict women of the dyer's household from taking the cloth from vats, they were most likely to succeed without opposition. As Howell points out, the greater the regulations over production, the more likely women were to lose employment. The situation meant that women tended to be limited to work requiring less skilled labor or marginal work that was not worth regulating. The only respectable alternative was to work within the home economy.

The restrictions on women in either organizing their own guilds or having any effective voice over rules that eliminated them from work opportunities brings us to Alice Clark's question: Were women better off in preindustrial economy? An overarching quest of women investigating their own history has been to discover some golden age when women had equal opportunity with men or at least more opportunity vis-à-vis male control. Victorian women authors became very polemical about the erosion of women's legal rights as they fought to pass the Married Women's Property Act. Dame Edith Stenton explains in her preface to *The English Woman in History* that she became fascinated with the topic because she perceived a decline in women's legal position from the Anglo-Saxon to the Norman period. JoAnn McNamara and Suzanne F. Wemple in "Sanctity and Power: The Dual Pursuit of Medieval Women" argued that in early Christianity and the early Christianization and political conquest of northern Europe, women were accorded a more equal position, but that their status deteriorated by the end of the Middle Ages and they were driven to retreat into mysticism.[7] In economic history scholars have had a tendency to look to the Middle Ages for examples of female iron mongers and widows taking over crafts of their former husbands and being allowed to continue guild membership. The essays in this volume suggest that the quest for an El Dorado in women's economic history is misleading. They show that women worked very hard both within and outside their families, but could not enter the magisterial ranks of guild, a government, or a court. They could accumulate capital and run a business, but the legal prohibitions would necessarily bar them from major entrepreneurial ventures or from building up a thriving manufacture or trade of their own. Most of the independent wealthy women were widows carrying on their husbands' trades or businesses.

While the authors have not found a golden age for women's work, those whose studies stretch up into the sixteenth century have found that medieval women had more access to high-status and independent employment than women did later. Women were less evident and were paid less as domestic servants in sixteenth-century Florence and wet nurses were more in demand but more poorly paid in Montpellier. Both Klapisch-Zuber and Otis attribute this deterioration of women's employment and wages to increased population and decreased standard of living. In Lyon even Protestantism could not give women the access to work they had enjoyed earlier, and in Leiden and Cologne legislation systematically set blocks in the way of women who might formerly have entered high-status employment. Davis and Howell see the growing power of city and state governments as encouraging an emphasis on patriarchy. The debate is not a new one.

Alice Clark argued that even when preindustrial women acted in the role of *femme couvert*, legally and economically dependent upon the domestic environment, their work was more valued than in the modern period. Her view of the plough and craft economy is in sharp contrast to that of social scientists such as the Lenskis, Ester Boserup, Jack Goody, and Ernestine Friedl. These authors argue that women were at a closer approximation to equality in the hunting and gathering societies and early horticulture societies. Although women could only gather in this early economic form because of their reproductive responsibilities, their contribution was as important as men's if not more so. Game was readily available and generally shared, but nuts, seeds, fish, and such food gleaned by women could only serve the needs of one family. The horticulture society employed men to clear the land and women with wooden hoes to provide the basic necessities for cultivation of domestic crops. The arrangement was a fairly equal one. But as metal became more common for both fighting and farming, men relied on conquest to give economic supplement to agriculture.

The most oppressive economic arrangement in this scheme, however, was precisely the one that we have been looking at, the agricultural society. Women were banished from the fields and men took over the agrarian output using plows, the male symbol. It was not only lack of physical strength that drove women from a major role in food production, but also the fact that cultivating large fields could not be accommodated to women's reproductive and nurturing roles. Because their productive capacity is lower, women are less valued in plow societies unless they can bring landed wealth with them, for land becomes the measure of wealth. The landed heiress or the woman dowried with land becomes highly valued, but her own contribution to the economy, outside of reproduction, is less valued.[8]

Close scrutiny of even peasant women in preindustrial Europe does not entirely bear out these conclusions. The women's contribution was highly valued because they provided the domestic skills that balanced and formed an economic complementarity with the agrarian skills of the husbandman in the fields. Here the dismal science of economics, with the complementarity of marriage discussed earlier, seems to provide a better model than the humane one of the anthropologist. In addition to the tasks of running the household the wife produced and trained the new work force, gathered berries and nuts, sent sons out to fish and daughters to get water, cared for the garden and domesticated animals, and engaged in a number of supplemental economic activities. A good part of the extra cash, in addition to the running of the domestic side of the economy, came from the woman's work. Hufton quotes the French peasant proverbs that a family can survive without the husbandman, but not without the goodwife.[9] One has no trouble arguing that the peasant woman's contribution to the home economy in preindustrial western Europe was indispensable, and that the economic unit of production was a household one with well-defined and mutually beneficial productive roles for man and wife. But the women's productivity did not lead to broad control over resources and expenditures.

The urban woman in preindustrial Europe functioned economically as a transplanted version of the rural woman, as Louise Tilly and Joan Scott have pointed out. Their economic contributions were essential, but within the familial context. They, too, were not the chief force in the market, but rather a supplemental part of the family economy. Indeed, the family economy of preindustrial rural and urban dwellers helped the population of Europe adapt to the industrial revolution, for in its initial phases women and children continued their supplemental activities in the industrial context and remained faithful to the idea of the family economy as the basic unit.[10]

Clark, to return to this early theorist on women's status in preindustrial Europe, labeled the rural and urban production types as "Domestic Industry," in which labor of all family members goes to the support of the domestic unit, and "Family Industry," in which the family was the unit for the production of goods to be proffered in the marketplace. The question finally to grapple with is whether women had more financial independence and respect in the domestic or family industry of preindustrial Europe or in the "Capitalistic Industry" of later Europe. Clark argued that in the capitalist economy women of all status groups lost their economic importance. Among the upper classes the ideal was to accord women leisure time, and among the wives of yeomen this pernicious ideal was emulated. Where in the past such women had organized home production and supplemental economic activities such as spinning and brewing, they now disdained such work. Those poor women who continued spinning could not make enough on it to support their children. The wives of journeymen did not have the same entrée into crafts as the wives of masters had in the Middle Ages. Not only did capitalism gradually undermine the viability of "Family Industry"; it destroyed "Domestic Industry" as well. Rather than the married woman being more economically viable than her daughters, single women who were free from child care were more valued in the market. Thus the house-wife was stagnant in a position that was less economically desirable than it formerly was. Cheaper industrial products and the move away from the home as the basic unit of production left her with a lower economic value. The old couple were left on marginally productive land holdings while their sons and daughters sought wage labor in agriculture or new industries.[11]

Clark's analysis is initially a very appealing one. Women's contribution to the home economy was both necessary and rewarded, but the domestic framework was restrictive as well as secure. The family-based economy gave more dignity to women's work, but only as long as women remained within their space and their sphere. A "good woman" managed her household well, contributed to its well-being, and took over in the event of an early widowhood. But what happened to the women who wished to step outside their allotted area? It does not stretch the imagination to regard the house-hold economy as a trap that kept women from having access to the market economy. No signs of an active rebellion against the division of work by sex appeared. Women rioted, but only in bread riots, which were considered the woman's prerogative because ultimately she had to feed the family. The first real rebellion against the domestic economy may be seen in the young women who, in spite of health and moral risks and possibly bad living conditions, flocked to the new job opportunities in the early years of the industrial revolution partly because they wanted to throw over the old domestic work environment.

Preindustrial women's work appeared to be an El Dorado only to reflec-tive women and men at the turn of this century who had the leisure to observe that the shop girls had exchanged the security and respect of work in the familial milieu for the hardships of work in the capitalistic environ-ment. The old options did not seem golden enough to many young women or men to keep them down on the farm in a traditional economy.

This volume of essays has at last permitted us to form an overview of women's work in preindustrial Europe, but it has hardly exhausted the subject. Whole areas, such as gentry and upper-class women who became estate managers, are missing. Also lacking is mention of those women, mostly nuns, whose work was in the charitable institutions of preindustrial Europe. The oldest profession, prostitution, also has received only slight mention. The authors in the volume do not claim to have made the final statement on women and work, but to have opened new doors only to see that more remain to be opened.

## Notes

The present volume grew out of a session on women and work in medieval Europe at the American Historical Association in 1982, for which I was the commentator. The three excellent papers by Judith Bennett, Maryanne Kowaleski, and Martha Howell inspired the idea of a collection of essays on the topic. The project was aided by a grant-in-aid of research from the Women's Studies Program at Indiana University. Both the volume and my contributions to it were furthered by a grant from the National Endowment for the Humanities Senior Research Fellowship at the Newberry Library (1979–80), a sabbatical grant from Indiana University, and a National Endowment for the Humanities Grant given by the Institute for Advanced Study at Princeton, where I had the honor of being a member of the School of Historical Studies for the year 1982–83. I am very grateful for the aid that these resources provided in furthering both my scholarship and the completion of this fine volume of essays.

1. Olwen Hufton, "Women in History: Early Modern Europe," *Past and Present*, no. 101 (1983): 131.

2. Alice Clark, *Working Life of Women in the Seventeenth Century* (London, 1919).

3. J. Dupaquier, E. Helin, P. Laslett, M. Livi-Bacci, S. Sogner, *Marriage and Remarriage in Populations of the Past* (London, 1981).

4. Olwen Hufton, "Women and the Family Economy in Eighteenth-Century France," *French Historical Studies* 9 (1975): 1–22.

5. Eileen Power, *Medieval Women*, ed. M. M. Postan (Cambridge, 1975), pp. 63–64.

6. Ibid., p. 60.

7. Georgiana Hill, author of *Women in English Life from Medieval to Modern Times* (London, 1896), is one of the most interesting of the Victorian polemical writers of women's history. Edith Stenton, *The English Woman in History* (London, 1957). JoAnn McNamara and Suzanne F. Wemple, "Sancity and Power: The Dual Pursuit of Medieval Women," in *Becoming Visible: Women in European History*, ed. Renate Bridenthal and Claudia Koonz (Boston, 1977), pp. 90–118.

8. Gerhard Lenski and Jean Lenski, *Human Societies* (New York, 1978). Ester Boserup, *Women's Role in Economic Development* (London, 1970). Ernestine Friedle, *Women and Men: An Anthropologist's View* (New York, 1975). Jack Goody, *Production and Reproduction* (Cambridge, 1976).

9. Hufton, "Women and the Family Economy," pp. 20–22.

10. Joan W. Scott and Louise A. Tilly, "Women's Work and the Family in Nineteenth-Century Europe," *Comparative Studies in Society and History*, 17 (1975): 36–64, has a summary of their thesis. Also see Louise Tilly and Joan Scott, *Women, Work, and Society* (New York, 1978).

11. See Clark, *Working Life of Women*, pp. 6–12, for a statement of her thesis.

# PART I

# Peasant Women's Work in the Context of Marriage

Since the bulk of the population of late medieval and early modern Europe were peasants living in rural areas, it is fitting to begin an investigation of women in the traditional society of the preindustrial period with the peasantry. It was the division of labor and patterns of work learned on the land and in the villages that peasants carried with them when they moved to urban centers seeking wages for their labor. The familial roles established in the country readily transferred to towns. For most women, these traditional roles would mean that the context of their work would center on their obligations to family, either their natal family or their family by marriage. The vast majority of women would marry, although the proportion remaining single in the urban environment was slightly higher than in rural areas.

In peasant society the woman's sphere and place were the house, close, and village; the man's were the fields, roads, and forests. The peasant woman rose at dawn and began her workday by starting a fire to warm the dwelling and cook a breakfast. A woman's daily round of work comprised the routine of housework, including laundry, cooking, brewing, and rudimentary housecleaning. In addition, she fed the farm animals such as chickens, geese, cows, and pigs. The kitchen garden and fruit trees in the close were her concern as well. Her daily chores took her to the village well, to an ale-wife's house and a bakery, to church, and perhaps to a tavern for a good gossip with other village women. Only seasonally did her work take her to the fields. When weeding needed to be done, a plow ox goaded, and harvests gotten in, her labor was necessary in the fields.

One of her major contributions, however, would be producing and training the new work force, her children. A girl learned the female tasks at her mother's knee from the moment she began to crawl, and under her mother's tutelage she eventually learned the more skilled work of the housewife, including brewing. Child rearing she readily learned as she took care of younger siblings or babysat for other village children. The learning process was centered on her mother and her natal home.

1

It would be a mistake, however, to equate these medieval rural women with pioneers or farm wives. The peasant economy was not a self-contained, family economy but rather one that relied upon purchasing a number of goods and services either from fellow villagers or from towns. While women, for instance, carried their spindles with them through most of the day so that their hands would not be idle in a free moment, they did not usually turn the thread that they produced into cloth for family consumption and they did not make the family clothing. The money that they could make selling their thread went to purchase goods and services for their family.

Women had a variety of supplemental economic activities that contributed to the home economy, but the most apparent one in reading village records was brewing, the subject of Judith Bennett's essay. Because ale was a staple of diet and because it did not keep well, it had to be produced frequently or some people had to supply it on a commercial basis. The ale-wife became a common village figure, although not in every village, for in some men dominated brewing.

The ale-wife's career demonstrates the way in which women fit their supplemental economic ventures into their life cycle. Only married women brewed and they did so periodically. The inconsistency of their brewing careers indicates much about women's work patterns in general; they embarked on extra work when time allowed or when family need dictated that they add further work to their daily routine.

The separate spheres of women's and men's work and the accommodation of women's contributions to family needs illustrate the basic characteristic of medieval marriages. From an economic standpoint, they were partnerships. With the contracting of the marriage, when the woman bought the dowry for establishing a household and the husband assured his wife of a dower, the basic economic unit was formed. Although the division of labor by sex was fairly rigid, it maximized the economic contributions of both partners. The work of each was equally important, but one suspects that the husband usually had the ultimate authority over the distribution of common profits. At least, only men had regular access to village courts and offices.

*Barbara A. Hanawalt* **1**

# Peasant Women's Contribution to the Home Economy in Late Medieval England

**A** woman's work is never done, we say, and yet we do not know what work rural women did in the late Middle Ages. The hours must have been very long and the work hard, for the only literary piece that speaks of the peasant woman's day with envy is that old saw of the tyrannical husband who taunts his wife into changing places for a day because he thinks her work is easier. He, of course, learns his lesson.[1] Since the basic unit of economic production and consumption was the peasant household, a woman's contribution normally was made within the context of her family. Contrary to the opinion of some historians of the early modern family, medieval English families were not normally extended with many female kin to lend a hand.[2] A household consisting of parents, children, and sometimes another kinsperson or servant relied heavily on the housewife's contribution to the home economy. But what was the nature of a wife's contribution? The tyrannical husband of the ballad argues: "And sene the good that we have is halfe dele thyn, / Thow shalt laber for thy part as I doo for myne." Two areas are traditionally assigned to the wife: the daily running of the household and the raising and training of the next generation. But there were a variety of other activities, including the classical occupation of spinning, that were supplemental to the routine management of the house and family and brought in extra earnings.

The problem for historians has been to find evidence on how married couples divided the economic responsibilities of the household. Men's share emerges more quickly because men frequently appeared in the manorial court rolls in cases related to their work and landholding or in the account rolls where their wages were recorded. Women's work was more often directed toward the private household economy than toward the

3

public one of the manor. One might take the excellent studies that have been done of early modern and modern peasant women[3] and cast their picture back into earlier centuries, but the early modern economy was different in many ways from the medieval one. Women in early modern Europe had many more opportunities to engage in cottage industry or to sell their labor in the rapidly expanding cities. The economy of the thirteenth through mid-fifteenth centuries in England was still largely centered on the exploitation of individual holdings on manors. Manorial records do contribute something to our knowledge of women's work. More information can be gleaned from wills, poll tax returns, and coroners' inquests. These last provide a vignette of people's activities in the last few hours of their lives before they died a sudden death by homicide or accident. They are rich in details about the daily routine of peasants and give the reader a sense of being at the scene.

Most rural women would eventually marry, because they had so few options for employment outside the household economy. Peasant women would not become nuns, and the position of servant was usually a temporary one limited to the teenage years of the life cycle. The other possibilities for unmarried peasant girls were not entirely attractive. They could stay at a brother's home and work for his family; they could hope to find work in an urban center or on a manor as a servant; or they could become prostitutes. J. C. Russell's work on the 1377 poll tax showed that in villages with a population of 1 to 800, 75 percent of the women were married. This percentage tended to decrease in boroughs. The figure represents all women over fourteen years of age (the taxable age) but does not indicate widows or those who would eventually be married.[4] Determining the number of men and women who remained single is particularly difficult, even with demographic models. Wrigley and Schofield, however, estimated that only about 7 percent of the population in the mid-sixteenth century never married. Thus the number of permanently celibate woman was very low.[5]

A woman's first contribution to the household economy, therefore, was the money, goods, animals, or land that she brought to the marriage in her dowry, dower from a former husband, or inheritance in her own right. These possessions came from a variety of sources, but wills give the most detailed information. One must remember, however, that they are a biased source since they tend to overrepresent the wealthier elements in the community. The vast majority of wills were left by men so that women appear as beneficiaries of husbands, fathers, grandfathers, godfathers, and masters.

A father dying without a son could provide in his will for his daughter or daughters to inherit his property. In the customary law of most manors and in common law, the inheritance would be divided equally among the surviving daughters. The will gave a man of property an opportunity to divide the inheritance himself so that he could favor one daughter, usually the eldest, and keep the family lands intact. Of the 319 married men leaving wills in Bedfordshire in the late fifteenth and early sixteenth centuries, 44 of them, or 14 percent, had only daughters as heirs.[6] Sometimes the daughter was already married and the will makes clear that the son-in-law would have control over the land, but the right to the land remained to the issue of the marriage. Heiresses of property would have been much sought after in marriage, and the father of an adult heiress would have carefully selected a congenial adult son-in-law. After all, the father might have to retire and live with them. Other fathers died young and left the lands in care of their widows until the daughters were of marriageable age.

Even if the daughter was not the chief heir, she could claim some part of the family wealth, usually payable in animals, grain, household goods, or money. These inheritances might have been in addition to an earlier dowry or they might be a provision for a future one. Only 9 percent of the wills specifically mention that the bequest to a woman was for her marriage. Henry Davy, a prosperous man, died with two daughters still unmarried. He left them both considerable grants of land, which they were to receive on their marriage.[7] Monetary bequests for dowries ranged from 13s. 4d. to £40. John Derlynge, who left his daughter 20s., was fairly typical of the humbler will makers.[8] Other relatives might also contribute toward a girl's marriage. An uncle on the father's side was the usual source, but one grandfather generously gave each of his granddaughters £10 toward her marriage. In the poem "How the Good Wife Taught Her Daughter," the mother meets her obligation to her daughter's dowry by collecting goods for her as soon as she is born.[9]

The dying men also raised the issue of their wives' remarriage and made provision for them accordingly. Of the 319 married men leaving wills, 85 percent were survived by widows. Common law allowed a widow a third of the husband's property for life and would permit her to take this land into a new marriage.[10] Wills, however, permitted husbands greater flexibility, and most chose the more generous provisions of customary law that gave the wife life interest in the tenement or control until the son reached the age of majority. Some other dower would be settled on her when she relinquished the land to their heir. The husband might stipulate that the dower was hers only if she did not remarry. Other husbands left their widows clear title to some property that they could take with them if they married, but they could not take the family land. Thus, John Heywood provided his widow with £20, a number of animals, grain, and the household goods she had brought with her as dowry. These were to be given her "wit owt eny grugge . . . of my children."[11]

The women of whom we have been speaking received sufficient property from fathers, husbands, or other kin to make them sought-after marriage partners. Society did not dictate a specific value for the dowry in order to marry; that was a matter of individual negotiations. But if family could not provide, how could a single woman hope to accumulate a dowry or supplement a meager one?

Servants received bequests from dying masters or mistresses in addition to wages. The typical bequests included items of clothing, sheep, a small sum of money, or malt.[12] Occasionally, a favored servant would inherit a substantial bequest; Elizabeth Lamkyn was given 26s. 8d. "to her profeccion."[13] Since servants were often the social equals of the masters, some of these gifts may have been part of a social network of village mutual support. Thus servants were rather like godchildren and received similar types of gifts in wills.

Female servants also converted wages into bits of land of an acre or two that they could add to their dowry, as the entrance fines they paid in manorial court indicate.[14] In the tight land market of pre-plague England, even a woman with only an acre or two of land would be an attractive marriage partner. The living that such a small dowry could provide was not much and would probably be matched by a groom with equally meager resources, but five acres could support a couple in good years. Undoubtedly some young people even married without the cushion of land or savings and would have to rely on their labor for survival. One such couple appeared with a small band of petty thieves who were trying to flog a pelt in Bedfordshire. They apparently met on the road, for he was from Berwick-upon-Tweed and she was from Stratford, outside London.[15]

Young women who worked for their dowries did not necessarily turn to their fathers to find them a husband on whom to bestow it. Thus these wage-earning women were making their own decisions about marriage independent from their families. Judith Bennett has shown that, of the 426 merchet payments appearing in the Ramsey Abbey *Liber Gersumarum,* 141 of the brides, or one-third, paid their own marriage fines. Furthermore, when they did pay for themselves, they usually paid less, probably because there was less property involved. They bought general licenses to marry whom they pleased more frequently than those whose father or bridegroom paid the marriage fine. Bennett suggests that the reason for this greater freedom was that these women were not part of their family's strategy for economic and social success in the village.[16]

The dowry having been contributed to the new household, the bride settled into her other roles of providing her labor, reproductive capacity, and child rearing to the economy. The literature and folklore of the Middle Ages are decisive in dividing the men's sphere from the women's, both in physical environment and in types of work. We all learn John Ball's revolu-

tionary jingle on class consciousness: "When Adam delved and Eve span /
Where then were all the gentlemen." It is instructive that Ball found
nothing wrong with the sexual division of labor, but noted only that in the
beginning there were not class distinctions. Men and women were also
distinguished by the symbols of their particular spheres of work, and these
are common identifying characteristics in art and literature. The poem
"The False Fox" provides a classic example:

> The good-wyfe came out in her smok,
> And at the fox she threw hir rok [spindle].
> The good-man came out with his flayle,
> And smote the fox upon the tayle.[17]

The accidental death patterns in the coroners' inquests and manorial
court evidence confirm the sex-specific division of labor in rural England.
Women's work and general round of daily activities were much less physically dangerous than men's; women constituted only 22 percent of the 2022
adults (over the age of fourteen) in the accidental death cases in the
coroners' inquests. Compared with the men, women spent much more of
their workday around the house and village: 21.2 percent of the women
compared with 8.3 percent of the men died of accidents in their houses or
closes. They also spent more time visiting and working with their neighbors: 5.8 percent of the women's accidents were in a neighbor's home or
close compared with 3.8 of the men. When women did venture from home,
it was often in connection with their domestic duties. Thus 5.9 percent of
the women drowned in a public well compared with 1.6 of the men, and
9.7 percent of the women died in a village ditch or pond compared with 4.9
percent of the men. Men were much more likely than women to die in
fields, forests, mills, construction sites, and marl pits. The place of death,
therefore, confirms women's chief work sphere as the home and men's as
the fields and forests.

Time was given very roughly in the inquests, but there was a definite
pattern of greater and lesser risks for men and women as they pursued their
daily routines. Both rose at dawn, but women had only 4.2 percent of their
accidents then compared with men, who had 9.8. The morning work was
more risky for women, with 15.6 percent of their accidents occurring at that
time compared with 9.8 percent of the men's. Noon was high for both,
probably as they tired of their labor and became hungry: 20.8 percent for
women and 17.7 percent for men. Women might have had a slightly higher
number of accidents because they were involved with cooking at noon.
Afternoon for both sexes represented a lull (4.2 and 7.5 respectively), and
may even indicate a postprandial nap. But evening saw another increase

(15.6 and 18.9 respectively). Night was the real killer for both at 39.6 percent for women and 33.9 percent for men.

When one looks at the causes of women's accidental deaths and the places they occurred at these hours, the round of daily work becomes apparent. The morning, noon, and some evening deaths were connected with fetching water from wells for washing and preparing meals. Working with large animals and brewing also took place in the morning and at noon. The afternoon deaths were from laundry or field work in season. The high number of deaths at night resulted from dangers in the home, usually house fires or walls falling on unsuspecting sleepers, or from wandering about at night in the pitch black without candles. There were many bodies of water and pits and wells that one could fall into after nightfall and drown.

The seasonal pattern of women's and men's deaths were closer. Women had a significantly higher percentage of accidents in May (12.9 percent compared with 7.7 percent for men), but there is no ready explanation for this difference. The cause of death indicates that women were more prone to falls and drowning during May, but their work does not seem to be particularly seasonal. It is possible that more women were pregnant or recovering from pregnancy. Wrigley and Schofield's sixteenth-century data, however, indicate that February and March were the highest months for births.[18] The two high months for men's accidents, June and August, can be readily explained by harvest and other heavy field work.

The division of labor by sex was set early in a child's life. By the age of two and three the accidental death patterns of children reflected that of their respective parents. Among the little girls, 27 percent of their deaths involved accidents while playing in the house with pots and cauldrons; these objects accounted for only 14 percent of the little boys' deaths. Accidents that occurred outside the home accounted for 64 percent of the boys' and only 44 percent of the girls' deaths.[19]

Women's work in peasant households has been largely misrepresented by modern historians who tend to equate peasant women with pioneer women. Medieval peasant women did not spend much of their time producing from scratch the basic necessities for their families. Medieval society had very specialized service occupations, even at the village level, and most households availed themselves of specialists in weaving, tailoring, and even brewing and baking. One has only to think of the many occupational surnames such as tailor, baker, cook, and weaver to appreciate the medieval roots of service trades. A second misconception that must not be allowed to stand is Boserup's suggestion that peasant women's work involved fewer hours than men's or that, because women had fewer accidents, their work was not as strenuous. Such a view overlooks the dual nature of women's economic contribution. One side was the maintenance of the household and rearing of children, the other was the supplemental economic activities that brought profits in addition to those gained through agriculture.[20]

Women's daily household routines are very well summed up in the "Ballad of the Tyrannical Husband." The goodwife of the poem had no servant and only small children, so that her day was a full one. She complained that her nights were not restful because she had to rise and nurse the babe in arms. She then milked the cows and took them to pasture and made butter and cheese while she watched the children and dried their tears. Next she fed the poultry and took the geese to the green. She baked and brewed every fortnight and worked on carding, spinning, and beating flax. She tells her husband that, through her economy of weaving a bit of linsey woolsey during the year for the family cloths, they were able to save money and not buy cloth from the market. Her husband insists that all this work is very easy and that she really spends her day with the neighbors gossiping. But she retorts:

> Soo I loke to our good withowt and withyn,
> That there be none awey noder mor nor myn,
> Glade to pleas yow to pay, lest any bate begyn,
> And for to chid thus with me, i-feyght yow be in synne.[21]

The housewife's first task in the morning was lighting the fire. She had to go into the close to get kindling or straw to light the embers and get the wood started. One woman, we are told in a coroners' inquest, went out early in the morning to get kindling and climbed onto a tree leaning over the common way and fell. A housewife who was over seventy went to her straw stack to get straw to start a fire, as she had for many years, but fell from her ladder on this occasion.[22] When the fire was started, the housewife heated the morning porridge and other food for breakfast.

Cleaning house would occupy very little of a woman's time. The houses were usually one story and had two or three rooms. Furniture was rudimentary. There would be a trestle table that was taken down at night to make room for sleeping on the floor. The household might have beds or only straw pallets on the floor. There were benches, but few chairs, and a chest or two for storage. The floors were covered with straw, and chickens, pigs, cats, and dogs wandered in and out at will. The peasants owned few pans and dishes. Wooden and clay implements were used when possible and a brass pot or pan or an iron trivet was a considerable investment. But the sparsity of furnishings and the straw on the floor should not lead one to conclude that the housewives were slovenly and cared nothing about cleanliness. Archaeological evidence has shown that the floors were swept frequently enough that the brooms left u-shaped depressions on the floors. But the standards for a well-kept house were hardly the same as ours, provided as we are with a multitude of "time-saving" products to keep our houses spotless, so that housecleaning was not a major consumer of women's work time.

Of the 237 women whose activity at the time of death is specified, 37 percent were doing work around the house. The most dangerous task was drawing water from wells and pits (17 percent of accidental deaths). The water was for cooking, washing, and drinking. Either the housewife or the children got water for the household. Doing the laundry was also a danger- ous activity, with 3 percent of the women either drowning or being scalded. The earth around wells, ponds, and ditches became treacherously slippery so that it was easy to fall in. Thus one woman sitting by a ditch washing linen cloth in December 1348 slid into the water and drowned. Other activities resulting in accidents included cutting wood, baking, cooking, taking grain to the mill, and general housework.[23]

Women's routine work for the household also included agricultural work. Women had the chief care of the domestic animals other than the plow oxen or horses. The work included feeding the animals, milking cows, and helping at calving time. They also kept the poultry: geese, hens, and maybe doves. The pig was in their charge, as was the garden in the close that produced vegetables and fruits. When their help was needed in the fields, they hoed, weeded, turned hay, tied sheaves, and even reaped. They gleaned when the harvest was over, a back-breaking task. One old woman was so tired after her day's gleaning that she fell asleep among her sheaves and failed to put her candle out. She died in the ensuing blaze.[24]

We tend to make our economic boundaries too rigid and assume that in a peasant economy people will not hunt and gather. But women picked nuts, wild fruits, herbs, and greens from the woods and roadways. If they lived near the shore they also gathered shellfish. Women also gathered firewood and occasionally dug for peat. One woman, over forty years of age, went to cut turves for the family fire and was killed when a piece fell on her.[25]

One of the most significant contributions a wife could make to the household economy was the production and training of children. Children were an asset in the peasant economy. By the age of seven they could already be a help to the housewife, taking geese to the green, collecting eggs, picking fruits and vegetables, fishing, babysitting, and going to the well for water. When they were older they took over more of their parents' work load. The early years were difficult, however, as the woman in the ballad of the tyrannical husband points out. During that time the housewife added the burden of caring for young children to her other chores. But the production and training of the new work force were essential for a successful peasant household; otherwise, one had to hire servants.[26]

Women could also diversify their labor to bring more cash into the family. In addition to the usual egg, butter, and cheese production, some women engaged in fairly large-scale beer and bread making. Both these occupations required investment in large vessels or ovens. Britton found that in Broughton the wealthier peasant families tended to be the chief producers of beer on a large scale.[27] Bennett has covered the matter fully in an essay in this book and so it need not detain us here. Brewing was an arduous and rather dangerous activity since it involved carrying 12-gallon vats of hot liquid and heating large tubs of water.

> About nones on 2 October 1270 Amice daughter of Robert Belamy of Staploe and Sibyl Bonchevaler were carrying a tub full of grout between them in the brewhouse of Lady Juliana de Bauchamp in the hamlet of Staploe in Eaton Socon, intending to empty it into a broiling leaden vat, when Amice slipped and fell into the vat and the tub on top of her.

Five percent of the women in the coroners' inquests lost their lives in brewing accidents.[28]

Spinning was the traditional supplemental economic activity for women. The spindle could be taken anywhere to occupy idle minutes. The women may or may not have turned the thread into cloth. Most likely, they sold it to a weaver unless they were making rough material for daily wear and sheets.

Women could also work as wage laborers to aid the family economy. In a poor household, which was supported by very little land, both the husband and wife would have to hire out their labor. In larger, more prosperous households, the growing children might also go to work for neighbors, if their labor was not needed on the family holdings. We do not know yet if women received equal pay for equal work. The matter will require considerably more study because of the problems of assessing the nature and difficulty of the tasks performed. For instance, a thatcher received 2d. a day in the thirteenth century but his female assistant received only 1d. Her work was gathering the stubble and handing it up to him while he did the more skilled labor. In general manors hired female laborers and boys for unskilled agrarian tasks with correspondingly low pay. The work of picking over seed grain, however, was a highly skilled occupation in which women, with their more nimble fingers, excelled and, therefore, tended to receive higher pay. When men and women did the same work, they received equal pay. Thus, although women did not normally work for the lord either hoeing or stacking hay, when they did so they received the same pay as men.[29]

Some historians have maintained that, with the decline of population after the Black Death, women's wages became competitive with those of men.[30] More systematic data will have to be accumulated to demonstrate this, however, for the statutory evidence indicates that women were supposed to be paid less than men. A statute of 1388 decreed that women laborers and dairymaids should earn a shilling less a year than the plowman. In a 1444 statute women servants would receive 10s. annually for their work compared to men's 15s., and in 1495 women's labor was to be reimbursed at still only 10s. annually, but men's had gone up to 16s. 8d.[31]

The village credit and land markets as well as fairs and regional markets attracted women.[32] A variety of sources show women actively engaged in market activities. For instance, Mabel the Merchant was charged in 1294 in Chalgrave court with taking ash trees. Women made loans to other villagers that are recorded in the court rolls. And there is even a case in the coroners' inquests of a woman who went out to negotiate a debt, leaving her nine-month-old baby alone in the house so that it died of a fire in its cradle.[33] Since women could inherit property and buy it as well, they played a fairly active role in the village land market even after marriage. Married women sometimes sold land they had brought with them to the marriage to help the family through a difficult time, or they might buy or inherit land that would eventually go to a child's marriage portion. Women were somewhat disadvantaged in the marketplace because, while they could bring suit on their own, they had no access to magisterial roles and seldom even used attorneys. Their pledges had to be men although one woman tried to use all women in her case.[34]

One can easily overlook the extralegal contributions of both women and men to household ease and even survival. Olwen Hufton has emphasized the economy of makeshift, which both peasant and urban women practiced in preindustrial France. The economy of expediencies included petty illegalities or tolerated transgressions that provided a source of additional food. In France the rioting for bread was the woman's provenance.[35] In medieval England illegal gleaning was the most common way for a woman to get extra grain for her family. Gleaning after the main harvest was regulated on most manors, usually with the provision that only the poor or decrepit could glean, and the community always established the day and hours. But gleaning could be so profitable that wives of even prominent villagers engaged in illegal gleaning. Reaping could pay only 1d. a day for women but gleaning would bring in considerably more. Even being caught and fined was worth the risk because the fines were so low. The illegal gleaners appear in the coroners' inquest when they are caught in the act. Amicia, daughter of Hugh of Wygenale, died warding off an illegal gleaner. She had been hired by Agatha Gylemyn to guard her grain. During the night Cecilia, wife of Richard le Gardyner, came to steal the grain and threw Amicia to the ground when she tried to stop her. Three illegal gleaners got their punishment through an act of God. They became frightened during a bad storm as they were gleaning illegally and hid in a haystack. Lightning struck them.[36]

The only limit to these illegal petty economic gains was the imagination. It was common to graze animals on other people's crops, to reap grass illegally, to dig turves and collect nuts and wood in prohibited areas. In Yorkshire, Alice, daughter of Adam son of William, dug a pit for iron and another woman dug up the high road for coal. Women were even occasionally accused of bleeding a cow for blood sausage or clipping sheep in the pasture for their wool. Isabel of Abyndam came to the fields of the Abbess and took three pounds of wool from four sheep there. When the shepherd found her she fought him off so that he was forced to hit her in the legs with his staff in self-defense. She was taken into custody but was so frightened that she refused food and drink and died of hunger.[37] Poultry theft and other petty thefts appear frequently in the records of manor courts.

In clearly felonious activities women also showed their concern for provisioning the family. They stole sheep and poultry rather than larger animals and stole proportionately more household goods and foodstuffs than did men. In the period of famine in the early fourteenth century, female crime increased to 12 percent and then dropped to 9 percent after the period of dearth.[38]

When the day was done, it was the woman of the house who tucked in the family and turned out the light. We know about this sex-specific role because of the times that she forgot to blow out the candle and it fell to the straw on the floor, setting the house afire. Five percent of women's accidental deaths are attributed to this cause, while among men only aged priests failed to blow out the candle. For instance,

> On Tuesday [24 April 1322] a little before midnight the said Robert and Matilda, his wife, and William and John their sons lay asleep in the said solar, a lighted candle fixed on the wall by the said Matilda fell by accident on the bed of the said Robert and Matilda and set the whole house on fire; that the said Robert and William were immediately caught in the flames and burnt and Matilda and John with difficulty escaped with their lives.[39]

We have argued that the woman's sphere of activity centered largely on production for the home, providing both food and supplementary earnings for the household economy. She also reared the children and put them to work in the house and close at an early age. We have yet to investigate the value that her husband and society placed on this contribution. Joan Scott and Louise Tilly have argued that "the separate spheres and separate roles did not . . . imply discrimination or hierarchy. It appears, on the contrary, that neither sphere was subordinate to the other."[40]

Literary sources are not neutral in their opinion of women. The clergy did not have a monopoly on the antifemale traditions, and popular lyrics fault women who gossip, cheat, and scold.

> Sum be mery and sum be sade,
> And sum be besy, and sum be bade;
> Sum be wilde, by Seynt Chade;
> Yet all be not so,
> For sum be lewed,
> And sum be shrewed;
> Go, Shrew, whersoeuer ye go.[41]

Others praise women for their constancy and counsel and advise men to place their trust in their wives.

> ffor by women men be reconsiled,
> ffor by women was neyer man begiled,
> ffor they be of the condicion of curtes grysell (Griselda)
> ffor they be so meke and myled.[42]

But even the tyrannical husband indicated that the wife's work was half the productivity of the household and whatever the personal attributes of a wife, laziness would have been the most disastrous.

Other sources are better for assessing appreciation of the wife's contribution than literary ones, because the latter are so steeped in tradition that they are difficult to use. Wills are, perhaps, the best. As a man lay on his deathbed he considered how he could insure his family's well-being and reward all for their contribution to the household economy. The wills show that the men entrusted their wives with considerable responsibilities and rewarded them generously for their contributions during their lifetime. Most men (65 percent) made their wives executors. Others indicated through specific phrases the reliance they placed on their wives. One man left his son a bequest if he would obey his mother, others left the wife responsible for choosing in profession for a son, and one Yorkshire father went to great lengths in his charge to his wife: "that my wiffe have a tendire and faithfull luffe and favour in brynging uppe of hir childir and myne, and she will answer to God and me." He went on to direct her to "reward them after her power for us both."[43]

The amount of property and responsibility a husband left to his wife depended upon the stage in the life cycle in which a man died. In Howell's study of 193 wills from Kibworth, she found that in the 33 cases in which a

the town or get drunk on the money they made from selling cloth, thereby implying that they had control over their butter and eggs money.[47] The law protected women's rights to their dowry and a husband could not demise it without the wife's permission. But more than one woman came into court complaining that she had not been consulted about the sale of land or that she feared to cross her husband. Joan, wife of Hugh Forester, is a typical case. She demanded and won the rights to one and a half acres that her husband demised without her permission because she was "not able to gainsay it in his lifetime."[48]

The argument for a partnership in the peasant marital economy, how-ever, is a persuasive one, even if some husbands were tyrants. Many of the decisions that would have to be made during the course of the marriage would be ones in which mutual expectations or needs would determine the course of action. Both partners shared the common assumption that chil-dren should receive a settlement from the accumulated family wealth. If the parents could afford it, girls would receive a dowry and boys would be established with land or an education. The couple would also share assump-tions about investment in seed, tools, and household equipment. The needs of the economic unit were common to both. If the couple survived to retirement age, they would have a mutual interest in making arrangements for their support. Land transactions in manorial courts indicate a strong practice of mutual responsibility and decision making. When a villein couple married it was common for the man to come and turn the land back to the lord, taking it again in both his name and that of his wife. Husband and wife also appear in purchasing or leasing pieces of land either for themselves or for their children. They also frequently appear acting in concert in other business matters. While men appeared more frequently in economic transactions, they were not necessarily acting unilaterally, but more likely with some consensus if not consultation. After all, a man would not leave his wife executor after death if he did not have some respect for her economic judgments during life.

The separate spheres of activity probably decreased economic tensions between husband and wife. Even the tyrannical husband of the ballad recognized that there was a basic equation to marital economics. Econo-mists have devised a model for the complementarity of economic roles in traditional marriages that adapts well to peasant marriages.[49] Since the husband, by virtue of his training and his and society's social values, can function more effectively in the fields and marketplace than the wife and since he has no expertise or inclination for domestic work, he will find it profitable to rely upon his wife for these skills and to share with her the proceeds from his agricultural endeavors. The wife, by virtue of her training and values, functions most efficiently doing tasks related to homemaking and, therefore, finds it to her economic benefit to supply these in exchange for her husband's farming expertise. Since neither could easily purchase the skills of the other in hired help, marriage is the most efficient way to pool skills. It is for this reason that remarriage is so common in peasant society when one of the partners dies. Medieval peasant marriages are a classic partnership in which each person contributes a specialized skill that complements the other. One enters such a partnership with the hope that the other person is truly proficient and diligent about providing his or her side of the services.

The peasant family economy, therefore, was based firmly on the partnership of husband and wife, each contributing their separate skills and their separate domains of labor. The initial goods and capital of the woman's dowry helped to set up the household, and her labor and supplemental economic activities kept it going. In the marriage partnership gender ordinarily determined the division of labor, but the goal of both partners was the survival and prosperity of the household unit.

## Notes

1. *Reliquiae Antiquae*, II, ed. Thomas Wright and James Halliwell (London, 1843), pp. 196–99.

2. Philippe Ariès, *Centuries of Childhood*, trans. Robert Baldick (New York, 1962), pp. 365–69. Lawrence Stone, *The Family, Sex, and Marriage in England 1500–1800* (New York, 1977), pp. 23–26.

3. See for instance, Louise A. Tilly and Joan W. Scott, *Women, Work, and Family* (New York, 1978), and Olwen Hufton, "Women and the Family Economy in Eighteenth Century France," *French Historical Studies* 9 (1975): 1–22, and "Women in the Revolution, 1789–1796," *Past and Present*, no. 53 (1971): 90–108.

4. Josiah Cox Russell, *British Medieval Population* (Albuquerque, 1948), pp. 154–56.

5. E. A. Wrigley and R. S. Schofield, *The Population History of England, 1541–1871; A Reconstruction* (Cambridge, Mass., 1981), pp. 257–65.

6. The wills are taken from the full collection for Bedfordshire: Patricia Bell, trans., *Bedfordshire Wills, 1480–1515*, Bedfordshire Historical Record Society, XLV (1966), and A. F. Cirket, ed., *English Wills, 1498–1526*, Bedfordshire Historical Record Society, XXXVIII (1956). In using the wills for these figures I have omitted all clerics' wills and those of the few men who were bachelors.

7. *Bedfordshire Wills*, p. 87.

8. *English Wills*, p. 33.

9. Ibid., pp. 9, 76; Frederick J. Furnivall, ed., *Manners and Meals in Olden Times* (London, 1868), p. 46.

10. F. Pollock and F. W. Maitland, *History of English Law before Edward I*, new ed., II, (Cambridge, 1968), pp. 404–407.

11. *English Wills*, p. 80.

12. Ibid., pp. 17–18, 22.

13. Ibid., p. 70.

14. The poll tax returns of 1379–81 show that children over fourteen from established agricultural families and other village youths were listed as servants in the assessments. About a quarter of the villagers were recorded as unmarried servants and single women constituted half or more of these. The position of servant appeared to be a phase in the life cycle of a woman that ended upon marriage. Almost all of the husbandmen and artisans were listed as married. "The Poll Tax of 2–4 R. II, A. D. 1379–81," *Collections for a History of Staffordshire*, The William Salt Archaeological Society, XVII (1896), 159, 169, 172–73, and *passim*. A. Raistrick, "A Fourteenth-Century Regional Survey," *Sociological Review* 21 (1929): 242–46. Edgar Powell, *The Rising in East Anglia in 1381* (Cambridge, 1896). For women using such wages for the purchase of bits of land, see: Marian K. Dale, ed., *Court Roll of Chalgrave Manor, 1278–1313*, Bedfordshire Record Society, XXVIII (1950), 22; Sue Sheridan Walker, trans., *The Court Rolls of the Manor of Wakefield from October 1331 to September 1333*, Yorkshire Archaeological Society, 2nd ser., II (forthcoming), ms. pp. 152, 153, 162, 170; W. P. Baidon, ed., *Court Rolls of the Manor of Wakefield*, I, Yorkshire Archaeological Society Record Series, XXIX (1901), 81, 96, 106, 115, 122, 124, 174.

15. R. F. Hunnisett, trans., *Bedfordshire Coroners' Rolls*, The Publications of the Bedfordshire Historical Record Society, XLI (1961), 48–49.

16. Judith M. Bennett, "Medieval Peasant Marriage: An Examination of Marriage License Fines in *Liber Gersumarum*," in *Pathways to Medieval Peasants*, ed. J. A. Raftis (Toronto, 1981), pp. 208–11.

17. Rossell Hope Robbins, *Secular Lyrics of the Fourteenth and Fifteenth Centuries* (Oxford, 1952), p. 44. Ester Boserup, *Women's Role in Economic Development* (London, 1970), pp. 24–30, maintains that in all plow cultures, plowing is a male role and women seldom do it. There is in the folklore of plow cultures a male sexual connotation to the act of plowing.

18. Wrigley and Schofield, *The Population History of England*, pp. 503–504.

19. Barbara A. Hanawalt, "Childrearing Among the Lower Classes of Late Medieval England," *Journal of Interdisciplinary History* VIII (1977): 1–22.

20. Boserup, *Women's Role*, pp. 27–29. Carlo Poni, "Family and 'Podere' in Emilia Romagna," *The Journal of Italian History* I (1978): 201–34, has shown that nineteenth-century Italian peasant women spent more time in the house from November to March, working largely on linen; from April to October their field work surpassed their housework. Their day was often longer than the man's.

21. *Reliquiae Antiquae*, pp. 197–98.

22. Just. 2/78 m. 2. All Justice 2 manuscript citations are taken from the Coroners' Rolls in the Public Record Office, London.

23. Just. 2/18 m. 19, 2/69 m. 7d.

24. Two percent of women's accidents came from dealing with animals. See, for instance, Just. 2/67 m. 40d., 2/70 m. 10, 2/86 m.2. In the latter case a woman had put a ladder against the post of a barn to get straw down for her cows when the ladder broke.

25. Twenty-three percent of the women died in accidents related to supplementary activities such as wood gathering, fishing, and begging. See, for instance, Just. 2/18 m. 11, 2/104 m. 3.

26. Hanawalt, "Childrearing," pp. 14–18.

27. Edward Britton, *The Community of the Vill* (Toronto, 1977), p. 88.

28. *Bedfordshire Coroners' Rolls*, p. 13. See in addition, Just. 2/67 m. 23, 2/91 m. 4, 2/81 m. 8, 2/106 m. 3.

29. William Beveridge, "Wages in the Winchester Manors," *Economic History Review* VIII (1936): 33–34.

30. Ibid., p. 34. R. H. Hilton, *The English Peasantry in the Later Middle Ages: The Ford Lectures of 1973 and Related Studies* (Oxford, 1975), pp. 101–102.

31. F. W. Tickner, *Women in English Economic History* (London, 1923), p. 23.

32. Walker, *Wakefield*, p. 22. Hilton, *The English Peasantry*, pp. 103–105. R. H. Britnell, "Production for the Market on a Small Fourteenth-Century Estate," *Economic History Review*, 2nd ser. XIX (1966): 383. Elaine Clark, "Debt Litigation in a Late Medieval English Vill," in *Pathways to Medieval Peasants*, ed. J. A. Raftis (Toronto, 1981), p. 252, found that 7 percent of the creditors were women. Just. 2/17 m. 4d., woman taking reeds to market and Just. 2/200 m. 7, woman taking cheese to market. Dale, *Chalgrave*, p. 33.

33. Just. 2/18 m. 44.

34. Hilton, *English Peasantry*, p. 105. *Wakefield*, I, p. 194: "Sara, widow of Henry son of Robert de Hertesheved, came and waged her law with women, and the said John de Dychton sought judgement because she waged her law with women." She lost. A. E. Levett, *Studies in Manorial History* (Oxford, 1938), pp. 242–43.

35. Hufton, "Women in Revolution," pp. 92–95.

36. W. O. Ault, "By-Laws of Gleaning and the Problems of Harvest," *Economic History Review*, 2nd ser., XIV (1961): 212–14. Just. 2/17 m. 3d, 2/77 m. 2.

37. Walker, *Wakefield*, pp. 28, 164, 169, 175. *Wakefield*, I, 91, 117, 149. Just. 2/195 m. 11.

38. Barbara A. Hanawalt, *Crime and Conflict in English Communities, 1300–1348* (Cambridge, Mass., 1979), pp. 120–22, 158–68.

39. Just. 2/106 m. 1. See also Just. 2/114 ms. 3, 7, 8, 17.

40. Joan W. Scott and Louise A. Tilly, "Women's Work and the Family in Nineteenth-Century Europe," *Comparative Studies in Society and History*, 17 (1975): pp. 44–45.

41. Richard Leighton Green, *The Early English Carols*, 2d ed. (Oxford, 1977), no. 401. See also nos. 400, 402, 403.

42. Robbins, *Lyrics*, pp. 35–36. Green, *Carols*, no. 399.

43. *Testamenta Eboracensia*, III, Surtees Society, XLV (1865), 203.

44. C. Howell, "Peasant Inheritance Customs in the Midlands, 1280–1700," in *Family and Inheritance: Rural Society in Western Europe*, ed. J. Goody, J. Thirsk, E. P. Thompson (Cambridge, 1976), pp. 141–43.

45. *English Wills*, pp. 17–18. Michael Sheehan, "The Influence of Canon Law on the Property Rights of Married Women in England," *Mediaeval Studies* XXV (1963): 109–24.

46. Just. 2/111 m. 15.

47. Furnivall, *Manners and Meals*, p. 39.

48. Walker, *Wakefield*, p. 264.

49. Fredricka Pickford Santos, "The Economics of Marital Status," in *Sex Discrimination and the Division of Labor*, ed. Cynthia Lloyd (New York, 1975), pp. 249–50. She further explored a model of Gary Becker, "A Theory of Marriage, Part I," *Journal of Political Economy* 81 (1973): 813–46, and "A Theory of Marriage: Part II," 82 (1974): S11–S26.

Judith M. Bennett  2

# The Village Ale-Wife: Women and Brewing in Fourteenth-Century England

The medieval peasant diet was plain and basic; most peasant meals consisted only of bread, ale, and soup with some variation provided by seasonal fruits, legumes, and vegetables. But the simplicity of the fare did not guarantee that most families could fill their daily needs by domestic production alone. Because the manufacture of bread and ale necessitated expensive equipment and required considerable labor, medieval households were seldom able to stock these products without recourse to commercial markets. In the towns and villages of medieval England, most families depended heavily upon commercial bakers and brewers to provide the basic foodstuffs that were consumed daily. Even in the countryside, where so many of the everyday needs of the family economy were met through direct production, dependence upon the purchase of bread and ale was common. The tension created by the absolute need for these products and the inability of most households to produce them directly was reflected in the animosity directed against food purveyors in medieval literature. The author of *Piers Plowman* bitterly urged officials:

> To punish on pillories     and punishment stools
> Brewers and bakers     and butchers and cooks
> For these are this world's men     that work the most harm
> For the poor people that     must buy piece-meal.[1]

In the thirteenth century, the English government began to regulate the sale of these two basic foodstuffs through the Assize of Bread and Ale, which created national standards of measurement, quality, and pricing. Weights and measures were to be checked for accuracy, quality was to be carefully

20

monitored, and prices were to be determined by a sliding scale based upon fluctuations in the cost of grains.[2] The right to enforce the regulations of the Assize of Bread and Ale quickly devolved upon local authorities. In the countryside, jurisdiction fell to manorial lords, who supervised sales of bread and ale through frequent meetings of the manorial court. As actually administered in these rural tribunals, the Assize became a licensing system; all commercial brewers and bakers paid regular fines for the right to practice their trades. Persons who sold bread or ale illegally—with improper measures, at exorbitant prices, without adequate quality control—paid especially heavy, punitive fines, but all vendors of these products were liable for some payment.[3] Bakers commonly paid one large annual fine (usually rendered at the yearly Great Court or View of Frankpledge). Brewers, however, were often assessed at regular intervals throughout the year. At every triweekly meeting of the manorial court, the ale-tasters (officers responsible for the onerous task of tasting and certifying all batches of ale prior to sale) identified and fined all persons who had sold ale in the interval since the last court meeting.

The different tactics adopted by most manorial courts to supervise the bread and ale industries reflect differences in the crafts. Baking could be adequately regulated by yearly presentments because it was a more stable industry. Requiring ovens that were comparatively expensive to obtain and to operate, baking quickly professionalized, with most villages serviced by a handful of bakers strongly committed to the business.[4] The skills and equipment required for brewing, in contrast, were readily available in many households, and commercial brewing was much more widely dispersed through most rural communities. The necessary supplies were extensive, but available in most households; large pots, vats, ladles, and straining cloths were found in the *principalia* of even the poorest households.[5] But although the capacity to produce ale was present in many households, the process was so time-consuming and the final product soured so quickly that most families simply could not meet their needs by domestic production alone. The grain, usually barley, had to be soaked for several days, then drained of excess water and carefully germinated to create malt. After the malt was dried and ground, it was added to hot water for fermentation. From this mixture was drained off the wort, to which herbs or yeast could be added as a final touch.[6] Ale production took many days and much labor, but until hops were introduced from the Continent in the late fourteenth century (producing a new beverage called beer), English ale soured within only a few days. And since ale was virtually the sole liquid consumed by medieval peasants (water was considered to be unhealthy), each household required a large and steady supply of this perishable item.[7] The solution for many households was to alternate buying ale and producing ale for domestic consumption, selling to neighbors any excess ale from such brewings. As a result, a large number of people sold ale unpredictably and intermittently, and triweekly presentments by ale-tasters were necessary to ensure proper regulation of the industry.

The abundant records generated by official supervision of the ale industry offer unusual insights into the rural family economy of the late thirteenth, fourteenth, and fifteenth centuries. In several respects, the brewing industry of the later Middle Ages foreshadowed the domestic industries that would flourish in the villages of later centuries. Commercial brewing in the medieval countryside lacked, to be sure, the entrepreneurial element so crucial to the putting-out of textile production in the cottages of early modern England; no merchant-entrepreneurs organized or profited from rural ale sales in the fourteenth century. But brewing was, like domestic industries, an economic activity particularly attractive to women seeking ways of supplementing their household economies.[8] Commercial brewing was seldom the primary support of a peasant household; most brewing households possessed lands that provided the mainstay of the domestic economy, and most brewers sold ale so intermittently that their households could not have relied upon ale profits for basic support. As a supplementary source of income, brewing was often relegated to women, who found that its amenability to home production matched well with their other domestic responsibilities.[9] In preindustrial Europe, women characteristically sought out market activities associated with other home work that could bring income into their households. They sold surplus produce, they worked as carders or spinners, they hired themselves out as wet nurses, and, before the ale industry centralized and capitalized in the early modern centuries, they sold ale to their neighbors. Women's commercial ale production is distinguished from other market activities only by its rich documentation from a very early period.

In this essay, the ale fines recorded in the manorial court of Brigstock (Northamptonshire) during the six decades prior to the arrival of the Black Death in 1348 will be used to explore the part that brewing for commercial profit played in women's lives. Looking at which women brewed for profit, under what circumstances they entered the ale business, and what advantages they did (or did not) obtain from their commercial activities, we will use the Brigstock data to assess the importance of commercial work in the lives of preindustrial women. We have heard much in the recent past about the weak work-identity of women in both preindustrial and industrial economies. Women were/are dabblers; they fail to attain high skill levels; they abandon work when it conflicts with marital or familial obligations.[10] For a medieval ale-wife, as we shall see, such behavior was both practical and rational.

Brigstock, with its daughter settlement Stanion, lay in the heart of Rock-
ingham Forest surrounded on all sides by royal preserves, and its economy
was roughly typical of other forest manors. Cultivating the open fields of
their community, the constituents of Brigstock manor also supplemented
their incomes by exploiting (both legally and illegally) the many resources
of the adjacent parks and woodlands—using these areas for pasturing pigs,
for hunting, for making charcoal, and for assarting (converting wasteland or
woodland into arable). As in many other contemporary manors, the first
half of the fourteenth century was not a boom period in Brigstock; its
economy was faltering, and its population (of roughly 300 to 500 male
adults) was stagnant, if not declining.[11]

Because at least one-fourth of the women identified in pre-plague Brigstock paid ale fines, selling ale must have been characteristic of many
households on the manor. Indeed, the high proportion of women known to
have sold ale suggests that all adult women were skilled at brewing ale, even
if only some brewed ale for profit.[12] Although female participation in the ale
trade was widespread, it varied greatly (see Table 1). Selling ale only infrequently and sporadically, most of Brigstock's female brewers were simply
making an occasional profit from a household task; when these women
sometimes brewed for domestic consumption, they brewed larger amounts
than necessary and sold the excess to their neighbors. Although minor
brewers collectively accounted for over one-third of the manor's ale trade,
their market activity, on an individual level, was fairly insignificant. On
the average, each paid only about five ale fines during her career. And most
minor brewers paid their few ale fines over the course of many years; Emma
Pote, for example, accumulated twenty-two ale fines over a period of

TABLE 1

**Distribution of Ale Fines in Brigstock**

| CATEGORY | INDIVIDUALS | | FINES | |
|---|---|---|---|---|
| | Number | Percent | Number | Percent |
| ALE-WIVES | | | | |
| (30 or more fines each) | 38 | 11.5 | 2265 | 61 |
| MINOR FEMALE BREWERS | | | | |
| (1–27 fines each) | 273 | 82.5 | 1412 | 38 |
| MINOR MALE BREWERS | | | | |
| (1–16 fines each) | 20 | 6.0 | 47 | 1 |
| ALL BREWERS | 331 | 100.0 | 3724 | 100 |

Note: This table excludes 120 fines paid by women who were incompletely identified.

TABLE 2

**The Social Backgrounds of Brigstock's Ale-Wives**

| CATEGORY | Number | Percent |
|---|---|---|
| SOCIOECONOMIC STATUS | | |
| Husband held local office | 13 | 34 |
| Husband never held local office | 22 | 58 |
| Unknown | 3 | 8 |
| LONGEVITY OF RESIDENCE | | |
| Identified by permanent surname | 23 | 61 |
| Identified by impermanent surname | 13 | 34 |
| Unknown | 2 | 5 |

twenty-two years. This informal and unpredictable source of commercial ale was underpinned in Brigstock by a small elite group of thirty-eight brewers, who steadily met the basic needs of the manor's ale market. Dominating the ale trade of their community, these few dozen women were not making a casual and occasional profit from a household chore; they were ale-wives— women who frequently supplemented their household economies by selling ale on the commercial market.[13]

Who were these ale-wives? Commercial brewing was not a preserve of the privileged, nor was it abandoned to the poor (see Table 2). Since households headed by officeholders were usually wealthier and more powerful than other households, socioeconomic position has been estimated by tracing each ale-wife's place in the official structure of the community.[14] The households of some ale-wives were headed by males who wielded considerable political and economic influence in Brigstock, but many other ale-wives were less fortunate and came from households headed by men of more modest influence. The distribution of ale-wives between officeholding and non-officeholding households roughly paralleled the overall pattern in the community. Of the 277 surnames identified in Brigstock, 35 percent were associated with officeholding; 34 percent of ale-wives came from such officeholding households. Although socioeconomic position was relatively unimportant to the trade, long residence on the manor was vital. Only 32 percent of Brigstock's surnames betrayed permanency of residence (appearing in the records throughout the period surveyed), but almost two-thirds of Brigstock's ale-wives were identified by such enduring surnames.[15] Neither itinerants nor newcomers (of whom there were many in Brigstock) could hope to turn a tidy profit in the ale business. The most distinctive characteristic of ale-wives, however, is that they were, just as their title implies, not daughters, not widows, but wives. Although Brigstock's professional brewers included a few widows, these women had begun selling ale before their husbands died, and several withdrew from the ale market within a few years of widowhood. Similarly, no single women or dependent daughters have been identified among Brigstock's major commercial brewers.[16]

As suggested by the preponderance of wives, brewing seems to have been too complex and costly a business to be pursued by women who lacked the support of a full household. Instead, it was usually a family affair that wives organized and supervised. The ale-wife's position as overseer of a household activity is best seen in the brewing histories of single households that often included not only the wife but also occasionally the husband and/or daughter. Alice, the wife of Richard Coleman, for example, accumulated seventy ale fines between 1299 and 1325. On one occasion, in November 1313 (when Alice was perhaps ill or otherwise incapacitated), her husband Richard paid the ale fine. When Alice stopped commercial brewing a little over a decade later, her daughter Emma took over the business for several years. During these decades, the entire Coleman household was clearly committed to commercial brewing; the family's female head usually paid the ale fine, but other family members replaced her whenever necessary. Alice Coleman did not work independently at a lucrative trade, but rather super-vised an activity that involved her entire household.

The brewing history of Richard and Alice Coleman's household was also typical in its relationship to other brewing households in the community. As a rule, most ale-wives were related to other women active in the ale trade. At the same time that Alice Coleman and her household were producing and selling ale, the wives of Richard Coleman's two brothers were also active in the ale market. Alice Coleman might have exchanged supplies, tools, and techniques with her sisters-in-law, but these women did not sell ale in common. Instead, they competed in the ale market, offering their products for sale simultaneously. In Brigstock, the nuclear family house-hold was the basic unit of the brewing business.[17]

Although ale-wives spent many active years in the industry, their market activity was neither steady nor predictable. Most ale-wives worked in com-mercial brewing for about two decades (average length of career: 20.6 years), but during that period they brewed irregularly and often stopped brewing for considerable lengths of time. Usually an ale-wife sold ale on only about one-third of the occasions available to her; the surviving courts contain about nine presentments by the ale-tasters for each year, but ale-wives averaged only three or four ale fines annually during the course of their careers. The wife of Richard Gilbert, for example, accumulated fifty-eight ale citations between 1328 and 1345. In some years, her market activity approached saturation, but in other years, her participation dropped to negligible levels, and for five years in the midst of her brewing career, she totally ceased brewing.[18] Her career was typical; the average ale-wife accumulated a large number of fines not because she brewed regularly but because she brewed intermittently over long periods.

The Brigstock ale-wife was, insofar as information is available, fairly typical.[19] But she did differ from other rural brewers in one important respect: she faced almost no significant male competition. Only a few dozen ale fines were assessed against Brigstock males, and all such men were married to women already active in the ale market. Brigstock was rather unusual in this respect. For comparison, consider (1) the Midlands manor of Houghton-cum-Wyton, where—during the same decades—11 percent of all brewing fines were levied against men, and (2) the pastoral manor of Iver in Buckinghamshire, where males accounted for 71 percent of all brewing fines.[20]

These vastly different levels of male/female brewing are not reflections of broad variations in the organization of the ale industry on these three manors. As in Brigstock, brewing activity in both Houghton and Iver was dispersed among households of diverse socioeconomic status, but was especially pursued by long resident families. Similarly, the distribution of casual and committed brewers did not vary significantly; on all three manors, a large proportion of fines were paid by very occasional brewers. Insofar as the economic viability of the ale industry can be judged by patterns in ale fines (both total number levied and average amount assessed), it also does not correlate with shifts in the numbers of men and women involved in the trade. Except for their widely divergent sex ratios, the ale industries of Brigstock, Houghton, and Iver were remarkably similar.[21]

The explanation for these different levels of male/female brewing lies less with industrial organization than with the internal dynamics of the family economy. Every rural household had to decide how best, in view of local economic opportunities, to distribute its labor resources. The decision about whether the male or female head of household would supervise brewing probably reflects regional variations in the rural economy. In some environments, it made sense to leave the brewing to women, but in other areas men had both the time and the inclination to get involved in commercial ale production. Iver's villagers supported themselves primarily through stock-raising and fishing. Because these activities were not particularly labor-intensive, Iver's males got involved in brewing and dominated this industry in their village. Houghton was a classic open-field farming community, and the yearly cycle of plowing, sowing, and harvesting left considerably fewer males free to engage in commercial brewing. In the forest manor of Brigstock, males not only worked in the village's open field but also were diverted from brewing by their activities in the surrounding woodlands (hunting, assarting, etc.).[22] Women were, it seems, most likely to supervise their families' brewing businesses when their husbands' primary work responsibilities were arduous and time-consuming. Historians have long recognized that certain rural economies were especially suited for the introduction of domestic industries in the sixteenth and seventeenth centuries; regions with many small holdings or much pastoralism boasted populations both willing and able to take industrial work into their homes.[23] The data on the sex ratios of the medieval brewing industry suggest that this same regional dynamic also influenced the sexual division of labor within families involved in industrial activities.

The hypothesis that different levels of male/female brewing are related to variations in the allocation of labor within the peasant household is confirmed by a characteristic common to the food markets of all three villages. Despite the widely different ratios of female brewing in Iver, Houghton, and Brigstock, the relative number of women involved in food trades in all three communities steadily increased through the early decades of the fourteenth century. In other words, proportionally more females were selling foodstuffs in the 1340s than in earlier decades.[24] The best explanation for this common trend lies in changing economic opportunities that, in turn, altered the distribution of work within the rural family economy. It seems highly probable that the economic problems of the decades that preceded the plague drew male attention away from secondary pursuits like commercial brewing. Brewing was an almost universal female skill that confined workers to the household area; as a result, families faced with economic hardship could most easily relegate commercial brewing to their female members and hence, release males to seek economic relief in other sectors. In short, the internal dynamics of the rural household economy best explain fluctuations—both regionally and chronologically—in levels of female commercial brewing.[25] Women only dominated the brewing industries of their communities when the economic energies of the men in their households were diverted elsewhere.

What did their commercial activities mean to the women who worked in these rather tenuous circumstances? The records are largely silent on this issue—we have no personal diaries, no observers' reports, no letters that can illuminate the private satisfactions of rural ale-wives or the subtle ways in which commercial brewing might have enhanced a woman's stature in the eyes of relatives, friends and neighbors. Because an ale-wife brought cash into the peasant household, her efforts might have somewhat equalized her relationship with her husband. Because her sales of ale helped to maintain or even to enhance her family's socioeconomic status, she might have gained personal prestige as a clever household manager among her friends and neighbors. Because her market work brought her into contact with many other villagers, she might have enjoyed a breadth of social acquaintance that distinguished her from other women. Such benefits, however probable, cannot be verified.[26]

Instead, the extant records demonstrate quite clearly that ale-wives— despite their public activity in the ale market—did not derive any special public benefits from their work. As a general rule, women in all medieval villages lacked basic political, legal, and economic rights. Manorial courts refused to accept women as personal pledges or tithing members (excluding them from the systems of mutual dependence and reciprocity that bound males together), denied women the right to serve in the numerous offices of rural communities (excluding them from political power and prestige), and guaranteed the rather extensive rights of husbands over their wives' real properties (denying economic autonomy to married women). Women appeared before these tribunals much less frequently than men and were usually accompanied or assisted by male relatives.[27] The records of any manor court show most men acting comfortably as individuals in a male forum, and many women acting as household dependents when they hesitatingly ventured into this male world.

Work in the commercial ale market did not give women access to these male privileges and obligations. On a broad comparative level, one might have anticipated that strong contrasts in female rights and public visibility would have distinguished manors where women were commercially active from manors in which most commerce was controlled by men. Such contrasts have not been found; Brigstock women, who thoroughly controlled their community's major commercial product, enjoyed no special rights or legal perquisites that were denied the women of manors like Iver, where men dominated the brewing industry. A similar inertia is found in comparisons of brewing and nonbrewing women within a single community; Brigstock ale-wives—despite their very public activities in the ale market of the manor—were just as disabled in the manorial court as other women. Consider Brigstock's ten most active ale-wives (who each accrued 70 or more citations for ale sales). These women seldom came to court except to pay ale fines, and they were almost invariably accompanied or assisted by their husbands.[28] Margery, the wife of William Golle, is the exception who proves the rule. She was unusually active (for a woman) in the Brigstock court, paying 119 ale fines and appearing on numerous other occasions (including 11 court cases against other villagers). She was sued several times by persons who claimed that she had unjustly slandered them in the community. But in every litigious appearance, Margery Golle pleaded jointly with her husband (even when the dispute arose from Margery's misconduct

alone).[29] Margery Golle's market activities doubtless brought her into contact with numerous persons in the Brigstock community, but she came to
the court shadowed and protected by her husband. Needless to say, Brigstock's ale-wives, despite their proven public reliability as ale sellers, could
not serve as personal pledges, and they were not, despite their obvious
qualifications, elected to serve as ale-tasters. In the eyes of one of the most
important institutions in medieval rural life—the triweekly gathering of the
community at the manorial court—an ale-wife was, quite simply, just
another dependent wife.

The failure of an ale-wife's public activity in the ale market to translate
into changed behavior in the manorial court is not necessarily remarkable.
But its full implications can best be seen by adding two contrasting perspectives to this picture of public immobility. First, commercial activity and
court responsibilities were not invariably separate but could be closely tied *if*
the brewer was male. Because women's court roles were so severely limited,
one cannot straightforwardly compare the public benefits acquired (or not
acquired) by males and females through commercial brewing. Since women
started from a position of legal disability, any advancement—women pledging, women pleading more cases alone, women controlling their own
lands—would have indicated a growth in public authority. But since men
were not so legally restricted, their public advancement can best be analyzed through tracing public behavior that was relatively unusual for
males—the holding of public office. If Iver was typical of other manors
whose ale markets were dominated by males, brewing could be a major
route to public advancement and authority for males. Male brewers in Iver
were twice as likely as nonbrewing males to wield political power through
public office. Indeed, most officers were also brewers.[30] Unlike female
brewers, whose court careers were undifferentiated from those of nonbrewing women, male brewers distinguished themselves from other men in the
political life of the manor. For men, commercial brewing and public power
were closely linked; the wall that separated commercial success and public
authority obstructed only women.

The second perspective complements the first. Although ale-wives failed
to penetrate the legal and political institutions of their society, some
women did break through and attain a public stature that was denied most
members of their sex. Women achieved this feat not by actively participating in commercial markets, but instead by passively outliving their husbands. On a few infrequent occasions, the Brigstock court accepted a
woman as a personal pledge, accepted a female guarantor for another's
conduct. The unusual women granted this privilege were not highly successful ale-wives, but widows pledging for the misdemeanors of their household
dependents. Widows also distinguished themselves from other women by

their greater independence of court action and more secure property tenure.[31] A woman most closely approximated the legal and political status of males not through her work, but through her household status.

The commercial work of the medieval ale-wife, then, was a very limited form of public activity constantly bounded by private requirements. Her experiences say much about the lives of all women in rural England during these centuries. The basic factor that distinguished the public lives of adult women and adult men was household position. Men, as heads of households, possessed legal, political, and economic authority. They acted freely in the manor court, they held village offices, they controlled landed properties, and they derived direct public benefits from commercial work. To be sure, men accepted familial responsibilities and limitations, but they represented (indeed, personified) the familial household whose other members were submerged into that corporate identity. Women, as dependents in these male-headed households, lacked the public rights and authority accorded their fathers and husbands. They required assistance in court actions, they never wielded official authority, they forfeited control of their landed properties to their husbands, and they obtained no direct public authority from their market activities. In early fourteenth-century Brigstock, a woman's life changed most dramatically not through her work but through changes in her status within her household (changes over which, in the case of widowhood, she had little control). Her public status waxed and waned as her familial status shifted (from daughter to wife to widow) and with the economic fortunes of her family. Hence, all of a woman's activities—including her commercial efforts—were merged into her more important familial role.

Given the familial context of these women's lives, the medieval ale industry well suited their needs.[32] Because ale transported poorly, it was unsuitable for large-scale, centralized businesses. Because ale soured quickly, most households had to purchase at least some of their drink. Because ale production involved widely known female skills, tools available in many households, and intermittent attention over long periods of time, it appealed to women who sought simple ways of supplementing their family economies. As a result, many rural women occasionally sold ale, but even long-term participants in the ale market betrayed the familial underpinnings of their work. Ale-wives were classic female workers: their work changed with shifts in marital status, their work was relatively low-skilled, their work was unpredictable and unsteady, and their work was highly sensitive to male economic priorities (and susceptible to male incursions).[33] These work habits made perfect sense in the rural family economy of a society that embedded female lives into the fortunes of their families. An ale-wife was a wife first and only secondarily an ale seller.

This chapter is largely based upon an analysis of the brewing industry of Brigstock found in my doctoral dissertation, "Gender, Family and Community: A Comparative Study of the English Peasantry, 1287–1349," University of Toronto, 1981, pp. 143–91. An earlier version of this paper was presented at the annual meeting of the American Historical Association in Washington, D.C., December 1982. This study was completed before the publication of Christopher Dyer's discussion of medieval diet (using maintenance agreements), but our findings are generally complementary. See "English Diet in the Later Middle Ages," in *Social Relations and Ideas: Essays in Honour of R. H. Hilton*, ed. T. H. Aston et al. (Cambridge, 1983), pp. 191–216.

1. William Langland, *The Book Concerning Piers the Plowman*, trans. and ed. Donald and Rachel Attwater (1907; rpt. London, 1959), p. 21. For the text in Middle English, see the edition by George Kane, *Piers Plowman: The A Version* (London, 1960), p. 232 (Passus III).

2. *Statutes of the Realm*, vol. 1 (London, 1810), pp. 199–204.

3. Helen Cam, *The Hundred and the Hundred Rolls* (London, 1930), p. 211; Rodney H. Hilton, "Women in the Village," in *The English Peasantry in the Later Middle Ages* (Oxford, 1975), p. 104; Edward Britton, *The Community of the Vill* (Toronto, 1977), p. 25. In Brigstock, some brewers purchased long-term licenses (*licencia braciandi*) to cover several months of brewing activity.

4. A full analysis of the baking industry is beyond the scope of this essay, but the Brigstock evidence suggests that baking was generally more professionalized than brewing. Commercial baking involved a considerably smaller number of people; 105 bakers were cited in Brigstock (of whom 15 people accounted for nearly one-half of all fines) as opposed to 331 cited brewers. Moreover, many more males were cited for bread sales; 42 percent of bread fines were paid by males against about 1 percent of ale fines. Because baking must have exceeded the production capacities of most households, bread was probably more frequently purchased than ale, making baking a more lucrative and concentrated business. See Bennett, "Gender," pp. 171–82.

5. R. K. Field, "Worcestershire Peasant Buildings, Household Goods and Farming Equipment in the Later Middle Ages," *Medieval Archaeology* 9 (1965): 105–45. Many of the households listed in Field's appendix boasted equipment used in brewing. For example, the goods belonging to the cottager Thomas atte Frythe of early fifteenth-century Stoke Prior included a brass pot, a mashing vat, and barrels for storing both ale and liquor (p. 138).

6. For a comprehensive survey of the processes involved in ale and beer production in preindustrial England, see H. A. Monckton, *A History of English Ale and Beer* (London, 1966), pp. 11–82.

7. The average daily consumption of ale by the English peasantry is unknown, but the normal monastic allowance was one gallon of good ale per day, often supplemented with a second gallon of weak ale. L. F. Salzman, *English Industries of the Middle Ages* (Oxford, 1923), p. 286.

8. For a general survey and introduction to domestic industries, see Hermann Kellenbenz, "Rural Industries in the West from the end of the Middle Ages to the Eighteenth Century," in *Essays in European Economic History, 1500–1800*, ed. Peter Earle (Oxford, 1974), pp. 45–88. For the participation of women in domestic industry, see Louise A. Tilly and Joan W. Scott, *Women, Work, and Family* (New York, 1978), esp. pp. 43–60, and Olwen Hufton, "Women and the Family Economy in Eighteenth-Century France," *French Historical Studies* 9 (1975): 1–22.

9. The assumption that women were prominent in commercial brewing because it merged well with their other domestic tasks has been challenged by Christopher Middleton, "The Sexual Division of Labour in Feudal England," *New Left Review* 113–14 (1979): 154–55. Middleton argued that we cannot assume that women's work, simply because of a biological imperative, centered around the home. But Barbara Hanawalt's analysis of coroner's rolls has established that women did generally spend their days in the vicinity of the home; see "Childrearing Among the Lower Classes of Late Medieval England," *Journal of Interdisciplinary History* 8 (1977): 1–22.

10. This was a recurring theme in a workshop entitled "Working Women in Early Modern Europe: A Cross-Cultural Approach," at the Fifth Berkshire Conference on the History of Women (Vassar College, 1981). See also Natalie Zemon Davis, "Women in the Crafts in Sixteenth-Century Lyon," chap. 9, this volume.

11. Some of the inhabitants of Stanion were subject to the Brigstock court, which recorded the presentments of a separate ale-taster for Stanion. As a result, the Brigstock ale industry described in this chapter incorporates the activities of all brewers on the manor—whether in Stanion or in Brigstock proper. The records for Brigstock cover the years from 1287 through 1348 and are found in the Northhamptonshire Record Office (Montagu Collection, Boxes X364A through X365) and the Public Record Office, Series SC-2: 194/65. For details on the economy and demography of Brigstock during these decades, see Bennett, "Gender," pp. 43–57.

12. Estimates of how many women in Brigstock actually brewed commercially can be only tentative. It is extremely difficult to trace female individuals in manor courts because women usually changed their names upon marriage. Hence, one woman could be counted twice: first under her natal surname and second under her marital name. This bias is partially offset by the fact that counts of individual women and counts of individual female brewers suffer from the same handicap. Of the 843 individual females counted in the surname groups of Brigstock, 309 (37 percent) were cited for brewing activities. This count excludes brewing by isolated individuals outside of the main 277 surnames on the manor (2 ale-wives were isolated individuals). A second method of measuring the proportion of women in Brigstock who brewed commercially also yields high levels. One can offset the chronic underrepresentation of women in the Brigstock court by assuming that the number of women on the manor was roughly equal to the known number of males (1,149 males). In such a case, 309 women brewed out of a possible 1,149 women on the manor (27 percent). These figures differ slightly from those discussed in my dissertation because of reanalyses undertaken in preparation for my book, *Women in the Medieval Countryside: Gender and Household in Brigstock before the Plague* (forthcoming from Oxford University Press).

13. The term "ale-wife" does not appear in the manorial records of Brigstock because the clerks wrote in Latin. In this essay, ale-wife applies only to major brewers (30 or more citations), on the assumption that contemporaries would have used this term only to designate women who frequently brewed or sold ale. *The Oxford English Dictionary* cites the first use of "ale-wife" in some versions of *Piers Plowman* as synonymous with brewster. It also notes that the term need not indicate marital status because wife in Middle English often simply signified woman. *The Middle English Dictionary* (Ann Arbor, 1956) defines ale-wife as barmaid, but presents no contemporary usages to support this curious definition.

14. The correlation between socioeconomic status and officeholding has been much discussed in the historical literature. For the most comprehensive analysis, see

Anne DeWindt, "Peasant Power Structures in Fourteenth-Century King's Ripton," *Mediaeval Studies* 38 (1976): 236–67. For specific data on this correlation in Brigstock, see Bennett, "Gender," pp. 59–76.

15. These proportions of officeholding and permanent surnames in Brigstock reflect recalculations undertaken since the dissertation.

16. Of Brigstock's thirty-eight ale-wives, twenty-eight (74 percent) were identified as wives throughout their brewing careers. Five additional ale-wives (13 percent) brewed both when married and during widowhood. The marital status of the five remaining ale-wives (13 percent) was unstated.

17. Of Brigstock's thirty-six traceable ale-wives (two ale-wives were isolated individuals who cannot be linked to any households in the community), thirty (83 percent) had presumed kin (shared surname) who were also brewers. Wives, husbands, and daughters were assessed for ale sales sequentially (with different persons in the household accepting legal responsibility at various times); non-household kin were frequently assessed in the same court sessions (indicating that they were both selling ale within the same time period—in probable competition with one another).

18. The wife of Richard Gilbert was chosen for detailed analysis because her career most exemplified the average pattern. She received fifty-eight citations (average for all ale-wives was fifty-nine). She brewed for seventeen years (1328–1345), and she averaged 3.4 fines per year. Between 1328 and 1334, she received fines in about half of the surviving ale presentments. In 1335, 1336, and 1338, she was fined in fewer than one of every five ale-tasters' reports. In 1337, however, she was fined on nine out of ten possible occasions. In 1339, 1340, 1341, 1342, and 1344, she received no ale fines. In 1343, she was fined once, and she received three fines in 1345 (a year with thirteen ale presentments). Although her career history might indicate that ale-wives brewed less regularly toward the end of their careers, the histories of other ale-wives do not support this notion. Margery Golle, for example, brewed between 1306 and 1345. Although she was fairly active between 1311 and 1322, she brewed irregularly from 1323 to 1331 (in many years she received no citations), but then resumed an active career in the 1330s.

19. Although specific points of comparison showed some variation, my analyses of brewing in both Iver and Houghton also indicated that ale-wives on those manors were usually married women from the more settled families in the community. Data from both manors also reinforce the conclusion that brewing for commercial profit was a household business that involved all members of a nuclear unit. Bennett, "Gender," pp. 262–72, pp. 320–28. The studies of Edwin DeWindt (*Land and People in Holywell-cum-Needingworth* [Toronto, 1972], pp. 237–38) and Edward Britton (*Community*, pp. 87–88) also demonstrated that producers of ale were neither poor nor itinerant. The only contrary evidence has been found by Richard Smith in his analyses of Redgrave and Rickinghall, where ale sellers were not only economically underprivileged but also often unmarried (either single or widowed women). See his dissertation, "English Peasant Life-Cycles and Socio-Economic Networks: A Quantitative Geographical Case Study," Cambridge University, 1974, pp. 150–78. Perhaps these differences were caused by different methods of ale production (manorial brewhouse versus home brewing?), but the matter is, at this point, only speculative. Clearly the subject merits more thorough enquiry.

20. Bennett, "Gender," pp. 262–72, 320–28.

21. It is exceedingly difficult to compare accumulations of ale fines in the courts of different manors because evidentiary factors—how frequently the courts were

held, how many courts have survived—make each manor's data unique. For example, the criterion used to distinguish major brewers in Brigstock (30 or more citations) is too rigorous for either the Iver data (1,654 citations for ale sales) or the Houghton data (188 ale fines). The best comparison (average fines paid per cited brewer) reveals figures that vary not according to the male/female composition of the industry, but rather according to the number of recorded fines: Brigstock average, 11.4 (3,844 extant fines); Iver average, 4.7 (1,654 extant fines); Houghton average, 1.9 (188 extant fines). Moreover, both Iver and Houghton generally parallel Brigstock in boasting many individuals who received only a few ale fines. Of Iver's 354 brewers, 190 received only one or two fines. In Houghton, 80 of the 99 cited brewers paid only one or two fines.

Both the amount of the standard ale fine and the number of fines levied varied tremendously in Brigstock. In the late thirteenth century, the standard ale fine was 6 pence, but it fell fairly steadily until the late 1340s, when most brewers paid fines of only 1 pence. The average number of brewers cited (calculated in five-year periods) also varied widely—from an average of fewer than 1 fine per extant court in the early fourteenth century to a peak of more than 11 fines per extant session in 1340–45. Despite these dramatic swings, women always dominated the Brigstock ale industry. The data for Iver are even more persuasive because fluctuations in number of fines levied failed to correlate with fluctuations in number of women active in the industry. Between 1332 and 1349, women steadily gained a larger piece of the Iver ale market (from 23 percent of the business in 1332–35 to 33 percent in 1345–49). During this period, the average number of ale fines assessed per court fluctuated widely but did not match the steady gain in female brewing (average number of fines in 1332–35, 23; 1336–38, 35; 1341–45, 28; 1345–49, 11).

22. See Bennett, "Gender," pp. 43–57, 240–46, 298–305, for the economic histories of these three manors in the early fourteenth century. For a discussion of the many opportunities offered by a forest economy, see Jean R. Birrell, "The Forest Economy of the Honour of Tutbury in the Fourteenth and Fifteenth Centuries," *University of Birmingham Historical Journal* 8 (1962): 114–34.

23. Joan Thirsk, "Industries in the Countryside," in *Essays in the Economic and Social History of Tudor and Stuart England*, ed. F. J. Fisher (Cambridge, 1961), pp. 70–88.

24. In Brigstock, male brewing was too insignificant to merit the tracing of change over time. In bread sales, however, female participation rose steadily from 21 percent of the market in the late thirteenth century to 83 percent of the market in the 1340s (Bennett, "Gender," p. 174). In Iver, female brewers, who controlled 23 percent of the market in the early 1330s held 33 percent of all ale sales by the late 1340s (p. 264). In Houghton, men controlled almost one-fifth of the ale market in the early fourteenth century but were much less active in the industry (7 percent) by the 1340s (p. 323).

25. The hypothesis that women's participation in commercial brewing was dependent upon household economic priorities accords well with the general rule that women's work in the rural family economy was more flexible and variable than men's work. See Tilly and Scott, *Women*, pp. 43–60. If this theoretical relationship between primary economic activities and involvement in commercial pursuits can be verified by further study, the easily retrievable data in medieval court rolls on commercial activities can provide basic indicators of rural economic structures. In other words, researchers could infer the labor intensity of a local economy by

examining the extent of male participation in commercial sales of bread and ale. Similarly, changes in the economic health of a single community could be traced through temporal shifts in male commercial activities. Clearly, then, the relationship between economic well-being, labor intensity of local economies, and gender differentiation in commercial activities has methodological implications that extend far beyond the confines of the history of the medieval ale-wife.

26. Many studies have shown that women who make significant economic contributions to their family economies gain considerable domestic power and prestige. See Ernestine Friedl, "The Position of Women: Appearance and Reality," *Anthropological Quarterly* 40 (1967): 97–108, and Stanley Chojnacki, "Dowries and Kinsmen in Early Renaissance Venice," *Journal of Interdisciplinary History* 5 (1975): 571–600. Because such benefits can clearly be significant and highly valued by women, they should not be neglected or belittled. But power associated with the private sphere commonly lacks the authority and breadth of public power. See Rayna R. Reiter, "Men and Women in the South of France: Public and Private Domains," in *Toward an Anthropology of Women,* ed. Rayna R. Reiter (New York, 1975), pp. 252–82.

27. See Bennett, "Gender," pp. 191–97. All adult males in medieval England were obliged to join tithing groups, whose members were mutually responsible in court for each others' behavior. As we shall see, some exceptions to the legal disabilities of women did occur; women in Brigstock were sometimes accepted as personal pledges. Some scholars have found occasional references to women serving in official positions (as ale-tasters); see Rodney H. Hilton, "Women," p. 105. As a rule, women accounted for only about 10 percent of all nonbrewing entries in these manorial courts. See Bennett, "Gender," p. 330.

28. Of these ten major ale-wives, six only appeared in court on one or two occasions not related to brewing; they always appeared with their husbands.

29. For examples of such cases, see the Montagu Collection in the Northamptonshire Record Office, Box 365, file 31, courts for 21 September 1318 and 12 October 1318 (Margery accused of slandering Richard Boys; she initially refused to answer the accusation without her husband, who was impleaded jointly with her); file 35, court for 28 November 1325 (Margery accused of slandering Galfridus Solar by calling him a thief; she refused to respond without her husband, who again was sued jointly with her).

30. Only 9 percent of Iver's males held public office, but 20 percent of the men involved in commercial brewing achieved official power. Of Iver's 72 officeholders, 44 (61 percent) sold ale. As a rule, officeholders were especially committed brewers; they averaged 8.6 fines (against a 5.4 average for all male brewers).

31. Bennett, "Gender," pp. 192–227.

32. As techniques of ale production changed in subsequent centuries, women would be slowly excluded from the industry. The most notable development was the inclusion of hops into the brewing process in the late fourteenth century. The new drink (called beer) lasted longer without souring. Christopher Dyer has traced a slow professionalization of the ale-beer industry on the estates of the bishopric of Worcester that coincides with the hops additive. In his brief survey, he fails to link professionalization with changing techniques, but the connection probably existed. Dyer, unfortunately, presents no information on the male/female composition of the ale-beer industry on the Worcester estates. Christopher Dyer, *Lords and Peasants in a Changing Society* (Cambridge, 1980), pp. 346–49. Alice Clark, however, has shown how women in the seventeenth century were slowly excluded from the beer industry

as it capitalized and centralized (*Working Life of Women in the Seventeenth Century* [1919; rpt. London, 1982], pp. 221–33).

33. It is worth noting in this context that the Iver data indicate that male brewers were more committed to the industry than were female brewers. Males were twice as likely as females to become major brewers (defined in Iver as those receiving five or more citations).

# PART II

## Slaves and Domestic Servants

Some women in preindustrial Europe spent all or part of their lives not with their own families but with those of their employers. They were slaves or domestic servants whose labor supplemented or substituted for that of their mistresses. They helped with crafts in artisanal homes, nursed the legitimate offspring of their master in noble establishments, and in all households they did the cleaning, cooking, and other domestic work. Rather than acquiring their skills from their mothers at their natal hearth, they learned their trade from other domestics or the mistress in the homes where they worked. These women would perhaps never marry, but they did bear children. Their subordinate position made them easy prey for sexual exploitation by their employers, their sons, and their masters' male friends.

Although slaves were not numerous in medieval or early modern Europe, they were a constant presence, particularly in the Mediterranean areas. They were valued for a number of reasons: they were more docile than regular servants, they could have a high resale value, and they could supplement household help when it was scarce in the towns. Furthermore, the ownership of a slave or two conferred a certain prestige on the master.

One of the chief sources of slaves was the mountainous Karst, above the eastern shore of the Adriatic. As Susan Mosher Stuard has shown, the inhabitants of Ragusa were dependent on slaves both for their own artisanal and domestic help and for the profits from slave trade. The Ragusan mistresses purchased the strong, primitive mountain girls and trained them for service in refined households. Italian traders were willing to pay high prices for these trained slaves and bought them to work in their houses in Venice, Florence, and other Italian cities.

Slavery could be and was disagreeable for many of these girls, but for others the opportunity to leave the mountains was sufficiently attractive that some voluntarily entered into contracts that would limit the term of their service and leave them with skills and some money put by to make a life of their own in Ragusa.

Those slaves sold abroad moved into the type of domestic environment described in Christiane Klapisch-Zuber's essay. These patriarchal, noble and bourgeois households employed servants and slaves to free the mistress of the house from the drudgery of domestic work and, incidentally, to provide sexual diversion for the men of the house. Contrary to popular assumptions about the number of servants in preindustrial Europe, Florentine households, even the wealthiest, did not employ a large number of domestic servants. The wealthiest had a nurse for the children, and her position was one that carried both greater dignity and higher pay than those of the other servants. Because her milk nourished the legitimate offspring of the house, her virtue was closely guarded. So too was that of young girls whose parents placed them in service in a household and who worked until they accumulated a dowry.

The demand for female domestics was tied to the economic and demographic configuration of Florence. The Black Death and the continued high mortality of the fifteenth century led to a labor shortage that encouraged employers to hire women rather than men for domestic labor. By the end of the fifteenth century 78 percent of the domestic labor force was female, but in the sixteenth century, men again came to predominate in this type of employment. Women's wages also reflected the economic and demographic trends, with wages higher in the period of labor shortage and gradually declining after 1470. Even nurses earned less in the sixteenth century than in the fifteenth century because there was a new abundance of young women in the population and hence considerable competition for nursing positions. This connection between women's employment and wages will reappear in other essays in the volume.

Susan Mosher Stuard 3

# To Town to Serve:
# Urban Domestic Slavery
# in Medieval Ragusa

In the Middle Ages towns were powerful magnets for rural people. In return for an opportunity to pursue a promising urban future, rural folk were known to settle for clearly disadvantageous terms for entry and initial employment. Among the least favorable terms were those available to the poor rural inhabitants of the mountainous Karst above the eastern shore of the Adriatic (primarily Bosnia and the Herzegovina). The nearest Dalmatian towns were ancient in origin, sometimes prosperous but small by force of necessity. Such towns needed unskilled labor, but that need was restricted and considerably below the supply of rural folk who would willingly fill it.

As a consequence citizens of a town such as Ragusa (modern Dubrovnik) might command labor on their own terms. They preferred women for most unskilled tasks. The earliest evidence, from the thirteenth century, indicates that they obtained mountain people for these tasks through capture and chattel slavery. Later, in the fourteenth century, women and a few men workers were obtained by contract labor charters. For those involved, conditions were scarcely altered despite the improved negotiating position implied by the introduction of contractual labor agreements. This study attempts to understand the women working in town under these disadvantageous terms, the households in which they served as cheap and frequently acquiescent laborers, and the advantages accruing to the town's citizenry from their work.

As practiced in Ragusa, slavery had as great a utility as the slavery practiced in classical Greece, and, again in parallel to classic times, it existed sympatrically with republican government.[1] Slavery as an institution remained an acceptable alternative for the organization of unskilled labor through the medieval era. It was particularly valuable to developing commer-

cial centers such as Ragusa; Yugoslav scholars have researched and reported
on it exhaustively for that reason.[2] Recently Charles Verlinden has re-
emphasized slavery's consequential role in Mediterranean life and trade well
into late medieval and early modern times.[3] In Ragusa an unbroken tradition
from the late Antique era allowed the institution to remain an acceptable and
viable alternative for solving urban labor problems. Statute law, codified in
1272, afforded slave owners protection and legal solutions for a broad spectrum of problems pertaining to slave owning and management.[4] By this date
slaves were registered through orderly procedures at the town chancellory
office.[5] They numbered proportionately high in comparison to the size of the
community and they attracted the attention of foreign merchants who visited
the port to do business.

Slavery may have been even more significant earlier in the century, when
the mouth of the Narenta (Neretva), north of Ragusa, served as a slave-
trading center.[6] In 1253 Prince Crnomir of Bosnia deplored the conditions
that prevailed in rural Bosnia, where people had no defense against foreign
traders capturing and enslaving them.[7] He addressed his complaint to the
Ragusans, so there is little doubt about whom he held responsible. Nor can
slave traders be exonerated on the grounds that they merely fulfilled papal
directives in enslaving known heretics.[8] There is no evidence that Ragusans
bothered to baptise their newly imported slaves as did Florentines and some
Venetians. This is a telling sign that they, devout Catholics, found slaves'
religious practices orthodox. It seems clear that the entire region condoned
the institution of slavery; a late thirteenth-century ban of Bosnia kept at
least a few slaves in his own court.[9]

The neighboring Serbs did a more effective job of protecting their rural
populations. The Code of Dušan, composed in the fourteenth century,
warned that any person selling a Christian into another and false faith
would have his hands cut off and his tongue cut out upon being caught.
The true faith was Orthodoxy, and the feared slave vendor a Catholic from
the coast.[10] The Code articulated what had long been practice for the
Nemanjić dynasty: the princes protected their subjects and regulated trade
with the foreigners from the Dalmatian ports in regard to both the manner
of trade and articles traded.[11]

Domestic slavery, as it was practiced in Ragusa, intersected at a number
of junctures with the Adriatic trade in slaves, yet remained a distinct, even
a unique, system. The documents allow a glimpse of how it functioned in
the late thirteenth century and permit a more thorough analysis of the
reasons for dismantling the system very soon after.

The most striking element of the local practice was its clear relationship
to Ragusa's strict immigration policies. Those policies, discernible in the
Deliberations of the town's councils (*Reformationes*), preserved from 1301

onward, remained loyal to the principle of restricted right to residence in the town. A person obtained the right to remain in Ragusa only if granted citizenship by the town's Small Council or if he gained the lesser, unenfranchised, status of resident (*habitator*). Between 1301 and 1350, eighty-three persons, six with their families or male heirs carefully enumerated, were admitted into the town as citizens or as residents.[12] Of those persons, 18 percent were described as skilled artisans or professionals. There is no question of the services they offered the community. Among those admitted, 55.4 percent were foreign by birth, that is, they had emigrated from overseas. Only 24 percent were identified specifically as immigrants to the town from the nearby islands, the coastal lands, or the Balkan hinterland. Another 14.5 percent bore Slavic names, which suggests origins from nearby territories. These latter groups contained some skilled individuals. Almost the entire local Slavic migration occurred between 1348 and 1350—in other words, in response to urban population losses resulting from the first visit of the Plague. Overall, rural-urban migration, which commonly stemmed from the lands lying nearest medieval towns, was severely restricted, and this impediment placed in the path of free wage laborers coming into the town created the context in which slavery existed.

Ragusa expanded and prospered nevertheless. Certain new industries were introduced that required an expanded pool of skilled laborers. Silver and gold smithery stood out among these. Cvito Fisković counted sixty-six goldsmiths active in the community in the first half of the fourteenth century; many of them were recent immigrants to the town. Josip Lučić counted thirty-five active in the trade between 1281 and 1301 (there is some duplication in the two lists).[13] Evidently, when a critical industry was being developed, the council loosened its enforcement preferentially. Yet each planned expansion into skilled manufacture placed further demands upon service from unskilled laborers. A closely monitored increase in nonspecialized labor was needed to keep pace with commercial development and even modest forays into manufacture.

Thus the town grew, but slowly, and in pace with improving access to scarce supplies of essentials such as sweet water and grain. Cisterns supplied water; by the early fourteenth century it became necessary to hire boats to round the Peninsula of Lapad to collect sweet water at Breno (the point where fresh water gushes out of the mountainous Balkan Karst just a few miles north and west of Ragusa).[14] Grain supplies represented a similar problem. As far back as there was documentation, urban inhabitants had relied upon grain imported from overseas to maintain themselves.[15] A strict immigration policy represented accommodation to these facts of life. A householder might stress the fragile ratio between commercial gain and limited resources by increasing the number of domestic nonskilled laborers

*Susan Mosher Stuard*

TABLE 1

**Slave Charters 1280–1301**

| | Sales | | | Registrations | | |
|---|---|---|---|---|---|---|
| Year | Male | Female | Subtotal | Male | Female | Subtotal |
| 1280 | 1 | 21 | 22 | | 1 | 1 |
| 1281 | 8 | 81 | 89 | 3 | | 3 |
| 1282 | 9 | 72 | 81 | | | |
| 1283 | 7 | 35 | 42 | | | |
| 1284 | | 2 | 2 | | | |
| 1299 | | 5 | 5 | | 5 | 5 |
| 1300 | 2 | 18 | 20 | 2 | 10 | 12 |
| 1301 | 1 | 9 | 10 | | | |
| Totals | 28 | 243 | 271 | 5 | 16 | 21 |
| | | Males 12.1% | | | Females 87.9% | |

within his establishment, but only to a point. Civil government lacked the capacity and the mandate to assume responsibility for extra, nonproductive mouths to feed in the town. In that sense civil policy, the established slave trade, and the economic functions assumed by the Ragusan merchant household in the community's commercial life, conspired to make of slavery a highly appropriate method for delivering nonspecialized labor to the urban community.

The number of slave sales and contracts from the late thirteenth century is impressive, particularly in the light of the community's scale. In the sixteenth century, at the height of its expansion, Ragusa housed only 7000 or so persons within the town's walls.[16] In the late thirteenth century the town's population was, possibly, half that great.[17] Between November 1280 and January 1284, 236 slaves changed hands, and most of them were women. Another series of contracts beginning in August 1299 and ending in May 1301 included thirty-five records of slave sales, augmented by twenty-one charters that registered a slave at the chancellory. In the last two decades of the century, almost 300 slaves entered, lived in, or passed through Ragusa during the eight years for which we have records.[18] If these eight years reflect normal conditions, then an average of 37 slaves were registered or sold a year, yielding a total of 740 slaves for those two decades. By year and sex the charters present the picture in Table 1.[19]

The first series, November 1280 to January 1284, is most useful for analysis. In that period, comprising 39 months, 154 or 64.7 percent of the sales were between Ragusans, to Ragusans, or by Ragusans. In the other 35.3 percent of the sales Bosnian traders or other slave vendors sold slaves man died leaving children who were all minors, the preference was to give the wife the tenement and residue to raise the family (42 percent), although 39 percent jointly endowed the wife and a son, and 18 percent bequeathed everything to the son even though the wife was still alive. When at least some of the children had reached the age of majority, the inheritance strategy changed. The mature sons were favored in 41 percent of the wills while in 29 percent of the cases the wife alone was left the estate and in another 29 percent the wife with a son inherited it. In the 18 cases in which the testator died childless, he left his estate to his wife (81 percent) or the wife and another kinsman (17 percent).[44] In almost all of the wills the husband preferred to make individual and often more generous arrangements for his wife than simply that of the dower. One man specified that his wife was to have a place with the second son and receive 20s. annually from each of the three younger sons when they reached the age of majority, but if she were not satisfied she could have her dower as provided by law.[45]

The men leaving wills, therefore, both rewarded a wife's services and placed upon her the responsibility of raising a family of young children and running both the house and lands. The widow with young children thus had an increased burden for maintaining the household. She would either have to hire labor in the fields, rely on other family members for aid, or remarry. It was not tradition alone that kept women from doing the plowing themselves, but rather their already full work load. Although women tended to outlive men and were more likely to be widowed, widowers were also left in dire straits in managing the household economy. They too would have to hire servants or rely on kin to rear young children and take care of routine household chores. In the poll tax the great majority of cultivators were married couples. It is rare to find households of father/daughter or mother/son.

Although wills clearly establish the value and trust a man placed in his wife on his death bed, they do not indicate how or if he expressed these sentiments during his lifetime. Battered wives were not common in the coroners' inquests or even in the manorial court rolls. In general, although wife killing was the most common intrafamilial homicide, it accounted for only about 1 percent of all homicides. The sexes were equal in instances of committing suicide. Only one case hints at depression arising from a quarrel. Isabel, wife of John Aylgard, was going into town with her husband when she told him that the fire had not been covered. He told her to return hastily and cover it. Perhaps his words were very rough, for she returned and hanged herself.[46]

Although men and women may have contributed equally to the household economy, each in their separate spheres, it is difficult to determine who made the major economic decisions. The moralist writing "How the Good Wife Taught Her Daughter" recommended that women not gad about to foreigners, who, in most instances, transported the slave out of the community. The first figure then, provides some idea of the Ragusan market for slaves, and it was twice the size of the export market. A wide variety of persons bought and sold slaves. Verlinden, in studying the Ragusan charters, believed Ragusans specialized in the export of slaves.[20] A more thorough analysis of the trade of these merchants casts doubt on his conclusion. These merchants followed the slave trade as a sideline. They were as interested in supplying the town with slaves as in exporting slaves—often, in fact, more interested in the former endeavor. Among slave vendors and purchasers were a large number of women, numerous artisans, and persons of the professional class—in all, a wide diversity of persons. The slave charters suggest a brisk internal market for slaves, a high turnover rate in sales—154 in a 39-month period in a town with a population of possibly 3000—and a relatively high slave density.

Sale charters were brief, terse documents but they do reveal something about the nature of the institution of slavery. In the late summer of 1281 Dominus Jacobus Guillelmus of Venice was visiting Ragusa and was interested in purchasing a slave. He bought one named Dabriça, from a noblewoman, Slava, the wife of Marinus Bincola.[21] The purchase price was ten *hyperpera*, a typical price for the day. The former owner turned around the next day and purchased a new household slave named Dragosti. She was a newly arrived slave from Bosnia, and the price was exactly what the noblewoman had received for the slave sold to the Venetian. While the ages of the two slaves are not given, the likelihood is that Slava de Bincola had traded a trained slave who was older for an untrained rural girl from Bosnia. Whether as a sideline or an intentional vocation, Slava de Bincola, a noblewoman, was training slaves for the export market. Many variants of this story may be found in the charters.

Residents of the Italian towns who sought newly imported slaves complained frequently about the deplorable habits and outlandish language and customs of slaves imported from the east. Slaves who had served in Ragusan households increased in value when they had shed their country ways and become somewhat familiar with the demands of the urban domestic household. These households were, of course, labor intensive, especially when they combined residence and business functions. A Ragusan slave, once trained in such a household, was a valuable commodity for the Italian market. In this light Slava de Bincola's transaction makes sense.[22]

A woman sold into chattel slavery in a Ragusan household could expect some further specialized training if she adjusted and satisfied her owners. The *Liber Statutorum* mentioned the *ancilla babiça*, the mammy or wet nurse of the Ragusan household, specifically. By law she was to be rewarded with manumission on the death of her owners, although her offspring remained slaves of the household.[23] Ragusans referred to their chattel slaves and servants by a bewildering series of terms, which, in sum, suggest varying gradations according to rank, free or unfree status, function, and probably favoritism. *Servus* and *ancilla*, the proper legal terms, were common, but certain persons were termed *nutrix* and *baiula*, that is, wet nurse and governess. *Homo*, in the sense of *Bogdan, homo Mergnani*, signified a heterogeneous category of dependent male servants, free or unfree. Others, again both free or unfree, men and women, were called *servientes*, while a further group waited on citizens of the town, in the sense of *dedi me ad serviendum* or *ad standum*. In the fourteenth century *famuli* and *famulae* occurred; women were frequently referred to as *famulae*, an obviously personal, even affectionate, designation. In other instances *pueri* and *puellae* were used in the traditional sense of persons in dependence rather than as a classification of age.[24] The variety of terms for household servants connoted more than an acquired level of skills or economic function. A complex ranking system lies revealed in servile nomenclature. It is surviving evidence of a system of favoritism with prerogatives and rewards, which allowed the householder to maintain a hierarchy of servants within the household. Even the critical distinction of free and servile was blurred by these common terms of reference. By employing them a householder avoided the stark terms of chattel slavery, in a sense obliterating its harsh truth from the day-to-day transactions that were necessary for the smooth ordering of the household. Additionally the euphemisms or "gentling terms" helped create a reward system based upon recognition and rewards from the slave owner. This could encourage docility and hard work and in that sense it served to emphasize that dependence upon the urban household extended beyond chattel slaves to a range of free but dependent household servants.

Ragusans favored women as slaves overwhelmingly. Nearly 90 percent of the slave charters recorded sales of women. The mountainous land above the Dalmatian coast suffered levies on its manpower from Roman times through the era of Turkish domination. This thirteenth-century levy differed from the others only in that it drew upon the women of the region, not the men. The women, like the men impressive in their size and strength, suggest by their greater numbers that urban domestic slavery was considered to be as well, or better, served by female laborers. Women might be housed within the domestic establishment. They stood in ranking order to the *ancilla babiça, nutrix,* and *baiula* of the household. They were thought more docile and tractable than men, and, deprived of a family network of their own, probably proved so in day-to-day life. The needs of a domestic household meshed readily with those of the commercial establishment housed with it. The enslaved mountain women could lift bales, clean, wrap, sort, and process exportable wax, skins, and other goods with no more complex skills than those they were acquiring to serve domestic needs. Equal to the work, they appeared to be easily controlled and motivated through a system of incentives and rewards.

Nevertheless, townsmen manifested a long-standing anxiety over the policing of their system and spent considerable effort in council to secure the return of fugitive or runaway slaves. Charters often stipulated that a vendor guarantee a slave was docile. A fine on the return of the purchase price if a slave ran away figured in the text of numerous contracts.[25] Statute law provided elaborate measures to guarantee an owner's right to pursue a runaway slave and to punish any who might harbor or abet a fugitive.[26] Proclamations of recent runaways were common occurrences in the town. From July 1322 until March 1323, thirteen fugitives were reported to the count and Small Council: two were *servi* or male slaves; all the others were *famulae* or *famuli*, family servants, the most common euphemism for slaves or manumitted, dependent free men and women.[27] One was the runaway daughter of the slave of an artisan. Roughly half the fugitives in this nine-month period were males, although males constituted little more than one-tenth of the charters for slave sales and a similarly small percentage of the free but dependent servant population of the town. Men were enslaved and used in traditional male pursuits, in retinues for ambassadorial missions, in caravans, on shipboard—in other words, in situations that offered opportunity to flee.[28] Women slaves domiciled in the town, sometimes encumbered by their offspring, tied to the household and rewarded through a complex system for industrious, docile behavior, were, evidently, less likely to flee and therefore preferable.

The free householders of the town remained apprehensive about the servile population nevertheless. The town's Great Council was dismayed by the possibility of gangs or groups of servants entering the homes of nobles and the *cives de populo* and doing harm. "Considerantes quod per fragilitatem et maliciam servitialium multa enormia pericula accidere possunt" (very great danger can exist from the frailty and mischief of servants), so the Council forbade public assembly to male servants.[29] And Ragusan slave owners kept no more males than absolutely necessary. Even female slaves were forbidden from congregating at the sites of fires or other urban disturbances. A tractable, almost invisible corps of nonskilled persons housed in scattered households represented an urban ideal.

The noble families of the town, that is, the highly successful merchant aristocracy, had such a suitable source of nonskilled labor in the institution of slavery that it is remarkable that they dismantled the system in the early fourteenth century. Yet they did, in response to market problems. Merchant aristocrats had never been the sole market for valuable imported slaves. Trade with foreigners augmented local demand, and Ragusans allowed their recruited skilled artisanal population to acquire slaves of their own. Among the slave owners in the late thirteenth-century charters were a barber, a stonemason, four tailors, the wife of a dock superintendent, a notary, his wife, a master of the arsenal, a physician, an officer of the town militia, and four goldsmiths.[30] Six other purchasers were titled "Magister"; they were evidently professional men in the community.[31] Such a diversity of *cives de populo* and foreign *habitator* slave owners would cut into the supply of slaves, of course, but slaves suited Ragusa's unique recruitment system for skilled labor in such a significant fashion that this situation was tolerated.

The conjunction of a recruitment policy for itinerant bachelor artisans and the importing of female slaves insured urban order and a degree of tranquility but simultaneously exacerbated the market problem. Female slaves provided some bachelors with a domestic establishment, sex, and companionship. The traveling years, when young men made their fortunes abroad in prospering towns like Ragusa, were being lengthened in these decades, and loneliness accompanied by alienation was a possible source of civic disturbance. A temporary household with a slave remedied this problem. Francho Sacchetti, the son of a Florentine in residence in Ragusa in the early decades of the fourteenth century, may have had a slave girl named Maria for his mother. His birth predated his father's marriage considerably, although he was an accepted member of his father's married household. As Eugene Genovese has remarked about such relationships, they were commonplace in slave systems and to be expected in the atmosphere of intimacy encouraged by domestic slavery.[32] Yet few offspring of such liaisons fared as well as Sacchetti.

Sharing with nonnoble households scarce, newly enslaved rural peasants could not alone provide cause for dismantling domestic slavery, yet it added its own strain and constantly nudged the prices of slaves upward. The real problem for the noble Ragusan slave owner lay in the attractiveness of domestic female slaves to foreign, long-distance merchants. Over a period of years Ragusa's success in utilizing domestic slaves in a wide variety of functions forced the noble household into a dilemma. Incentive multiplied to sell domestic slaves to foreigners at attractive prices. Each of these sales left a need for labor unfilled, so that it was necessary to replace urban slaves sold abroad. Noble households, then, increasingly balanced off the advantage of the quick profit of a slave sale against the need to purchase a new and untrained slave. In response prices spiralled upward.

Slaves, by certain comparative indicators, were expensive in the late thirteenth century. The average price for a female slave was a little less than ten *hyperpera* (five ducats, to state the price in a well-known currency of the day). In 1284 one could purchase a cow for two *hyperpera*.[33] In this decade a young man wishing to live outside his father's home after his father's remarriage could demand of his natal household twelve *hyperpera* for a year's expenses and another six *hyperpera* to provide for a servant of his own.[34] A slave's average price, then, amounted to over three-quarters of a year's expenses for a person of noble or *civis de populo* status. Around the turn of the century a Ragusan could purchase a modest house for six *hyperpera*.[35] A female slave was more expensive than a residence for skilled artisans and other working people.

If slave prices are compared to communally paid wages, a different picture emerges. The *Protomagister arsenatus* was hired by the commune for 100 *hyperpera* in 1333, 160 *hyperpera* in 1347, and 240 *hyperpera* in 1357.[36] Even allowing for a steady rise in slave prices in the fourteenth century, slaves were comfortably affordable for men earning such high communal wages. Young noblewomen who married in the late thirteenth century typically brought a slave and 400 *hyperpera*, or 200 ducats, as their dowries to their marriages. The price of their slaves amounted to a mere one-fortieth of their dower wealth.[37] Slaves were both expensive, if the price of other commodities is considered, and relatively inexpensive, if communal salaries and the private wealth of the noble families are used as a measuring rod.

Prices did increase over time. The pressure on slave sales may be understood by assessing seasonal variations in prices in the best-documented years, that is, 1281, 1282, and 1283. In all three instances there was intense activity in trading slaves in the last six weeks of the summer season. In 1281, 32 percent of the total year's sales took place in this six-week period; in 1282, 35.8 percent.[38] During the late summers the preponderance of sales involved foreign purchasers. Traders from Venice were frequent purchasers but so were traders from Apulia and other Adriatic communities. Traders from more distant lands, particularly from Crete, suggest that the Venetian fleet was in port during these weeks. In 1281 the average price paid for a slave showed a slight increase during this late summer period. The mean price from 1280 to 1284 was 9.5 *hyperpera*; the price in this six-week period in 1281 was 9.8 *hyperpera*.[39] In 1282 the average price paid for a slave in the same six-week period jumped to 11.7 *hyperpera*.[40] A smaller and less reliable sample of charters for the late summer of 1283 saw the price reach the inflationary average of 13.3 *hyperpera*.[41]

During these periods of heightened activity, sales from Bosnian traders to foreigners do not seem to have met the demand. Foreign merchants bought directly from noble Ragusan households; they purchased slaves from noblewomen, possibly slaves who were dower slaves, and they even purchased the domestic slaves of artisans who owned at the most one or two. Even at this early date slavery was pricing itself out of the market as a cheap and convenient method for supplying nonskilled labor to the urban community, not only because of limited and decreasing supplies from the interior, but also because of demand from overseas.

Thus women enslaved at Ragusa, trained, and then sold to foreigners prefigured the large-scale sea-borne migration of unskilled laborers that became such a striking feature of modern times. They were sought and their price bid up by affluent householders of Italy's trading cities. Labor shortages in Italian cities seriously affected the pool of cheap household wage labor, and trained slaves from abroad were an obvious, obtainable alternative. Women slaves trained at Ragusa became a high-priced commodity of Mediterranean trade by the close of the thirteenth century. Ironically, enslavement for women represented one of the best opportunities for geographic if not social mobility. A *schiava* (slave) from Ragusa commanded a price in a higher range than a rural Greek, Tartar, or Russian slave who lacked training as a domestic.

By the turn of the century the number of recorded sales charters for slaves had diminished at Ragusa. By the early years of the fourteenth century, sales were all but replaced by contracts for labor arranged with the rural peasantry of Bosnia, the Herzegovina, and other nearby territories.[42] These contracts were neither new nor unique: they required an initial payment of money to an individual (or the parents of that individual) in return for a stipulated period of work. The person who would supply that work, or, more frequently, the parents or guardians of that person, received the sum in full or in part, the remainder on the fulfillment of the contract. The contract might or might not contain a number of provisos: conditions if the laborer ran away, stipulations about the lodging, feeding, and clothing of the worker, clauses promising the laborer the opportunity to learn a skill (for male workers primarily), and the conditions under which the contract would become null and void.[43] The fact that these contracts had come to predominate over sales of slaves registered at the Ragusan chancellory represents a significant reorganization in the mode of supply for the labor demands of Ragusan households, but little change in the actual conditions of laborers supplying that need.

One obvious difference, of course, lay in the tenure of the labor contract. Since contract laborers were not legally chattel slaves, they could not be resold, hence exported overseas. A foreigner might make a contract with a rural peasant for labor and then return to his homeland with the laborer to fulfill the term, but laborers recruited by Ragusans to work in Ragusa would remain there.[44] The council confirmed the distinction by requiring all slaves transported abroad to be accompanied by a charter stating that they were legally the chattels of their owners. Consequently, a person working in Ragusa under a contract was protected from being transported out of the town.[45] Neither the slave trade nor the use of slaves in the town was abolished, but the overseas trade was deprived of substantial numbers of slaves. Whether the contract labor system meant a more humane method of treatment for women supplying work to the household is another matter.

It is important to reemphasize at this point that the distinction between the chattel slave and the legally free but dependent servant of the household had always been unclear. Chattel slaves had realistic expectations that they would be manumitted during their lifetimes. Noble wills and last testaments freed not only dower slaves and the *ancilla babiça* of the household but whole groups of slaves. Noblewomen were fond of dowering their former slaves and servants as an act of piety. In one instance a noblewoman offered a grant to a freedman of the town if he would marry her former servant, the gift amounting to nothing more than a bribe.[46] Households were served by chattel slaves, by freed slaves, by contract laborers, by the offspring of former slaves, and by persons who received wages.[47] Ragusans were not above allowing an occasional slave to purchase freedom, a good indication that the individual had been allowed to learn a skill and accumulate capital while in servitude. One slave won her manumission by finding a fellow countrywoman to be enslaved in her place.[48] Masters and slaves dickered and negotiated, a condition that may have humanized the institution for slaves and freed slaves but that reveals the inherent weakness of the system. If slavery had been practicable because it was suitable to the domestic household, it did not always supply hard-working labor without an elaborate system of rewards and incentives.

The elimination of chattel slavery from the varying conditions of dependence current in the Ragusan household in the early fourteenth century represented little substantial change for workers in the household or the complexion of the domestic household itself. Households that contained slaves had assumed responsibility for a slave's old age, either in the form of manumission with gifts suitable for sustaining a person beyond the working age when enfeebled, or food and lodging at the household's expense in the years when the slave grew old beyond the capacity to serve. Contracts with young persons allowed the urban householder to make the best of the vigorous, most productive years—terms of five, ten, even twenty years— without the obligation to see to old age or other provisions. An unwilling contract laborer could be returned to the countryside after a term of labor and a hard-working laborer rewarded with the same rewards and incentives that had made chattel slavery practicable. In that sense the new reliance on contract labor did not mean a more humane system but a less expensive one when chattel slavery began pricing itself too high. Work contracts for twenty years' service ranged from two to five *hyperpera* for female workers and up to ten or eleven *hyperpera* for males.[49] In the early fourteenth century the price of a slave had risen to twenty *hyperpera* on average, and would rise higher in subsequent decades.[50] For certain young rural women, whose parents received the initial sum for the contract and who served twenty years, the fourteenth-century contract may have meant a more exploitative method of rendering their labor to the urban economy than the slave system which had operated in former decades.

The Ragusan councils legitimized the household's authority over the bewildering variety of free, quasi-free, and wage laborers of the household in a very convincing manner in 1348. The legal conditions pertaining to the rights of surveillance over *servus* and *ancilla*, that is, persons legally bound in servitude, were to be, henceforth, applicable to *servicialis* (servants).[51] This law insured civil tranquility in the fearful months when the plague raged, but it also served to tighten the household's control over domestic servants. Numerous other factors combined to assist the noble householder in maintaining control. Few opportunities for wage laborers existed outside the orbit of the household, although some did exist and wage labor always remained an alternative method for rendering service for a few.

As chattel slavery influenced the nature of contract labor in the town, so did both influence the complexion of working-class society in the community. The few men earning wages for unskilled labor were severely restricted in their choice of marriage partners. Those servants or former slaves who had won approbation, the reward of manumission and, possibly, a dowry, represented their best available choices outside the few free-born daughters born to established working-class families. Former servants or slaves married late in life. No figures on family size are available for this urban segment, but late marriage is a well-known brake on fertility. By contrast, upper-class women married young and were encouraged to produce large families, as Irmgard Manken's reconstructed genealogies prove.[52] Balancing the following generation of townspeople to favor the affluent families numerically could be achieved by this relatively simple expedient.

A more subtle but no less important social consequence lay in the attitudes toward authority engendered in those manumitted women who married and settled in Ragusa. These women were the former servants or slaves of the households whose sons and fathers dominated civil government. They were the ones who had proved most tractable, hard-working, and, above all, deferential to the highborn. Their reward was a rare and valued opportunity to establish their own families in town. These circumstances imparted a particular complexion to Ragusan urban life, which was placid and peaceable in contrast to the tumultuous urban conditions prevalent elsewhere. Ragusans boasted of their outstanding record of civil tranquility. A quiescent, industrious, and deferential group of unskilled working-class families would have been viewed locally as highly desirable, if, in fact, town leaders gave any thought to the matter at all. The training of household servants was not brought to the level of articulated social policy; it merely served as underpinning for the town's smooth-running social life and commercial development. It represented a traditional way of life.

The conjunction of the institution of slavery with households capable of monitoring servants and a close, available supply first of slaves and then of contract laborers, proved workable. In this equation the critical factor may have been the preferential use of women as slaves and servants rather than men. Most outlets for hostility and revolt were precluded by individual households negotiating privately for laborers. Women absorbed into the household in this fashion were deprived of the support of family, friends, and neighbors; their options were defined by the households in which they served. Little choice remained but to serve and improve one's condition through striving for the incentives and rewards the noble household offered. Deference was the face of it, but the substance was a lack of viable choice.

## Notes

1. Moses Finley, *Ancient Slavery and Modern Ideology* (New York, 1981).

2. Yugoslav medieval historians have demonstrated a great interest in this issue. For that reason most of the documents pertaining to the slave trade have been published. Not only is slavery one of the better documented forms of medieval trade, but the interest of historians reflects a concern with the moral, social, and economic ramifications of a historical tradition where slavery bodes large. See Gregor Čremošnik, "Izvori za istoriju roblja i servcijalnih odnosa u našim zemljama sr. vijeka," *Istoriski-pravni Zbornik* (Sarajevo) 1 (1949): 146–62; and "Pravni polozaj naseg robilja u sredjem veku," *Sarajevo Zemaljski Muzej u Bosni i Hercegovini, Glasnik*, n.s.2 (1947): 69–73; as well as the major collection of documents on slavery, *Kancelariski i notarski spisi, 1278–1301* (Belgrade, 1932), henceforth referred to as Čremošnik, *Spisi, 1278–1301.* Vuk Vinaver, "Trgovina Bosanskim robljem tokom XIV veka u Dubrovniku," *Dubrovnik Anali* 2 (1953): 125–47. M. Dinić, *Iz Dubrovaçkog Arhiva*, 3 (Belgrade, SAN, 1967), contains documents pertinent to the slave trade for the period after 1301. Many other works by Yugoslav historians touch on the question of slavery in a more peripheral manner. These works will be cited where appropriate in the notes. Most recently, see J. Luçić, *Obrti i Usluge u Dubrovniku* (Zagreb, 1979), pp. 139–59, which provides a good comparative scale of service occupations for the household.

3. There are a number of valuable works by Verlinden to be consulted. For a general introduction, see *L'Esclavage dans l'Europe medièvale*, 2 vols. (Paris, 1955, and Ghent, 1977). See also "Orthodoxie et esclavage au bas moyen âge," *Melanges Eugene Tiserant, Studi e Testi* 235 (1964): 427–56. See also, for matters pertaining to the Adriatic and Crete, "Le Recruitment des esclaves à Venise aux XIV et XV siècles," *Institute Historique Belge de Rome* 39 (1968): 83–202, and "La Crète, debouche et Plague tournante de la Traite des Esclaves aux XIVe et XVe siècles," in *Studi in onore Amintore Fanfani* (Milan, 1962), pp. 594–669. On religious issues

related to Patarines and Bogomils, see "Patarins ou Bogomiles Reduits en Esclavage," *Studi e Materiali di Storia delle Religioni* 38 (1967): 683–700. Beyond the works of Verlinden cited above, see A. Teja, "La schiavitu domestica ed il traffico degli schiavi," *Revista Dalmatica* 22 (1941): 33–44; A. Tenenti, "Gli schiavi di Venezia alla fine de Cinquecento," *Rivista storica italiana* 67 (1955): 52–69; Iris Origo, "The Domestic Enemy: The Eastern Slaves in Tuscany in the Fourteenth and Fifteenth Centuries," *Speculum* 30 (1955): 321–99. See as well the correspondence between Datini and his wife concerning domestic slaves in I. Origo, *The Merchant of Prato* (London, 1960), p. 195. See also Wilhelm Heyd, *Histoire du Commerce du Levant au Moyen-Âge*, Supplement I, 2 vols., 6th ed. (Amsterdam, 1855), pp. 555–63. Most recently, see Pierre Dockès, *Medieval Slavery and Liberation*, trans. Arthur Goldhammer (Chicago, 1982). The work is largely theoretical and does not rely on the extensive documentation in Charles Verlinden's work.

4. *Liber Statutorum Civitatis Ragusii, compositus anno 1272, Monumenta Historico-Juridica Slavorum meridionalium*, vol. 9, ed. V. Bogošić and C. Jireček, (Zagreb, 1904), Liber IV, c. 2, 3; Liber VI, c. 42–53. Slaves are described as "*ancilla de perchivio,*" or dowry slaves, in dowries and wills. For example, Čremošnik, *Spisi, 1278–1301*, docs. 169, 180.

5. The full formula for thirteenth century sales reads as follows: "Die secundo novembris. Ragusii etc. Moysa, serviens Dobraueci, tepci domine comitisse de Chelmo, presentem et consentientem ancillam suam Jurislauam de Vecerich vendidit Petro de Sauere de Regio ementi nomine et vice Nicole Balbi de Venetiis pro s. dr. gross. septem et dimidium diffinite ad mortem, etc. Testis Marinus de Pesegna, iudex et Elias Blasii de Rasti." Čremošnik, *Spisi, 1278–1301*, doc. 42, p. 39. The agent for the sale in Ragusa was the son of the notary, who was purchasing a slave from a Bosnian dealer who had obtained the slave from the household of the Countess of Chelmo (Hlum or Herzegovina).

6. Constantine Jireček, "Die Bedeuting von Ragusa in der Handelsgeschichte des Mittelalters," in *Almanach der kais. Akademie der Wissenschaften in Wien,* 49. Jg. (Vienna, 1899), pp. 365–452.

7. *Dubrovnik State Archives* (henceforth DSA), fr. 985. *Pismo Kneza Crnomira Knezu Opstini Dubrovackoj.*

8. For a recent review in English on heresy and the Bosnian church, and an exhaustive bibliography of the subject, see John Fine, *The Bosnian Church: A New Interpretation* (New York: East European Monographs, 10, 1975).

9. For example, Čremošnik, *Spisi, 1278–1301*, doc. 10, p. 22, and doc. 101, p. 58. One slave belonged to the ban and was sold, the other was a gift from his household to a visiting merchant.

10. Malcolm Burr, "The Code of Stefan Dusǎn," *Slavonic and East European Review* 28 (1949–50): 202.

11. Serbs as well as Greeks did reach the slave market in the fourteenth and fifteenth centuries. See Verlinden, "Orthodoxie et esclavage au bas moyen âge," and "Le Recruitment des esclaves à Venise aux XIV et XV siècles."

12. See Irmgard Manken, *Dubrovački Patricijat*, pp. 91–102, for the collected grants of citizenship and right of inhabitance at Ragusa in the fourteenth century.

13. C. Fisković, "Dubrovački Zlatari od XIII do XVII Stoljeca," *Starohrvatska prosvieta* 3, ser. 1 (1949): 143–249. Lučić found thirty-five active in the late thirteenth century alone (*Obrti i Usluge u Dubrovniku*, pp. 67–70).

14. *Monumenta Ragusina*, ed. Fr. Rački (Zagreb, 1879–97); henceforth to be referred to as *MR*.

15. On the grain trade at Ragusa and the distribution system for the communal grain supply, see D. Dinić-Knežević, "Trgovina žitom u Dubrovniku u XIV veku," *Godišnjak Filoz. Fakultet, Nov Sad* 10 (1967): 79–131.

16. J. Tadić, "Le port de Raguse au moyen age," in *Le navire et l'economie maritime du moyen âge au XVIIIe siècle* (Paris, 1958), p. 18.

17. Dinić-Knežević, "Trgovina žitom u Dubrovniku v XIV veku," pp. 128–29, bases an estimate of population, which is somewhat higher than this figure and derives from the early fourteenth century, on the imported grain purchased. The import of her work however, lies in the estimated rise in grain consumption by the late fourteenth century from 10,000 *ster* to 20,000 *ster*. If this represents real increase rather than accidents in the preservation of documents, substantial population growth occurred after the Black Plague. However, the author admits that private persons purchased grain on their own initiative to augment supplies obtained by the *massarii bladorum* (officials of the grain office) throughout the century.

The issue of population reveals a split in opinions of historians familiar with the holdings of the Ragusan archives. A "small" population school exists, which follows the general opinion of Tadić that the town grew to no more than 7,000 people in its greatest period of prosperity. Others follow the opinion of P. de Diversis, *Situs aedificorum, politae et laudabilium consuetydinem inclytae civitatis Ragusii* (Zara, 1899), that Ragusa was a considerably larger community, importing massive amounts of grain as early as the fifteenth century. This study favors the "small" school, since all the evidence on social composition of the community bears out Tadić's estimate and his own credentials for a trustworthy estimate of population are among the finest for those who have worked in the Dubrovnik State Archives in the twentieth century.

In 1330 city households were allowed from 2 to 20 *ster* of grain, to last one-third of a year. Two *ster* (the smallest allotment) by council estimate could feed 2 or 3 persons for that length of time. Larger households could draw up to 20 *ster*. In all, 2,000 *ster* were allotted. At most, 1,000 would draw 2 *ster* each. Assuming a woman and child for each male drawing, the population would have been approximately 3,000. *MR* V, 293.

18. For comparison, see Verlinden, *L'Esclavage dans l'Europe medièvale*, vol 2, p. 743–64. Figures in Table 1 almost exactly duplicate Verlinden's findings; both estimates are substantially lower than those suggested by earlier Yugoslav historians.

19. The registrations of slaves at the chancellory are enigmatic documents. Slaves presented themselves, consenting and willing, to be the chattels of their owners; hence the tendency on the part of historians to refer to these as "self-enslavings." What they may represent are periodic checks on the slave population of the town. When no sales contract was available to verify a person's enslavement, these registrations may have been necessary so that the civil government could distinguish between the free and the unfree. In the late years of the thirteenth century the civil government appears to have been involved in developing a system of surveillance over the domestic use of slaves in the community.

20. Verlinden, "Le Recruitment des esclaves à Venise aux XIV et XV siècles," and "La Crete, debouche et Plague tournante de la Traite des Esclaves aux XIVe et XVe siècles." See also Verlinden, *L'Esclavage dans l'Europe medièvale*, vol. 2, pp. 750–59. He identifies certain Ragusans like Bogdanus Volcassio as long-distance slave traders. He believes Ragusans persisted in the trade through the fifteenth century.

21. Čremošnik, *Spisi, 1278–1301*, docs. 127 and 128. Dominus Jacobus Guillelmus had purchased another slave named Radosclava on August 21, 1281 (ibid., doc. 126).

22. See Origo, "The Domestic Enemy: The Eastern Slaves in Tuscany in the Fourteenth and Fifteenth Centuries," pp. 321–99.

23. *Liber Statutorum*, L. VI, 51.

24. Lučić, *Obrti i Usluge u Dubrovniku*, pp. 136–60.

25. For example, when Pasque Felicis de Grado purchased a slave named Tollislava de Sana from Michael de Syraca in 1282, he added a clause to the charter that the contract was valid only if the slave did not run away for seven years. If she did run away, the purchase price of nine *hyperpera* was to be refunded. Čremošnik, *Spisi, 1278–1301*, doc. 190.

26. *Liber Statutorum*, L. VI, 44. A Ragusan seeking a runaway presented himself before the count and Small Council and made a public statement of his loss. This was acclaimed publicly, transferring at least some of the responsibility for the recovery of the loss to the community at large. Čremošnik, *Spisi, Thomasina de Savere*, doc. 288, provides a case in point. Čremošnik, *Spisi, 1278–1301*, doc. 342, notes an instance when a barber obtained an agent to find his fugitive slave for him.

27. *MR*, I, pp. 122, 123, 124, 125, 126, 127. All thirteen cases fall between July 4, 1322, and March 22, 1323. The public acclamation of a runaway was so common in the fourteenth century that a search for a dozen or so slaves at any given moment would appear to have been common for the communal government. If the fugitive returned to the countryside, recovery would prove almost impossible.

28. When two Ragusan ambassadors were sent to the court of the Emperor of Serbia in 1360 to celebrate his wedding they were accompanied by eighteen persons listed as *famuli*. Ten accompanied them on horses and eight on foot. This amounted to a significant retinue. *MR*, III, pp. 40–41. On servants in caravans to the interior, see M. Dinić, "Dubrovacka Srednjevkovna karavanska trgovina," *Yugoslavenska Istoriski Časopis* 3 (1937): 132. Statute law provided that a slave on board ship had rights to a share of the profit from the ship (but his profit was the share of his master upon the completion of the voyage), just as did other mariners. However, if a slave were captured or fled, the master was not entitled to payment from the ship's owner. He might, however, continue to have the slave's portion. *Liber Statutorum*, L. VII, 19. Slaves were involved in short-distance hauling, particularly water carrying. *Liber Statutorum*, L. VI, 47. Hauling was important; for example, a slave "qui portat calcem cum asinis," Čremošnik, *Spisi, 1278–1301*, doc. 385.

29. *Liber Statutorum*, L. VI, 33 (4).

30. Čremošnik, *Spisi, 1278–1301*, docs. 41, 46, 58, 160, 169, 179, 186, 217, 224, 255, 276, 300, 323, 337, 342, 431, 463, 469.

31. Ibid., docs. 71, 164, 173, 241, 345, 445.

32. Dusanka Dinić-Knežević, *Polozaj Zena u Dubrovniku* (Belgrade, 1976), pp. 135–46; see also Eugene Genovese, *Roll, Jordan, Roll* (New York, 1974), pp. 413–31.

33. Čremošnik, *Spisi, 1278–1301*, doc. 363. On the other hand, the inflation in slaves appears to have kept pace with the inflation in the price of horses. In 1372 a female slave was exchanged for a horse at par. M. Dinič, *Iz Dubrovačkog Arhiva*, III, doc. 65, p. 27.

34. *Liber Statutorum*, L. IV, 9.

35. DSA, *Diversa Cancellariae*, IV, f. 20.

36. *MR*, V, p. 328; *MR*, I, p. 254; *MR*, II, p. 179.

37. Čremošnik, *Spisi, 1278–1301*, docs. 375, 387, 391, 395, 424, 430, 432, 541, 554, 582, 610, 622, 677, 697, 714, 722a, 727, 742, 743, 902, 919.

38. In 1281, 35 out of 106 slave sales; in 1282, 29 out of 81 slave sales.

39. Mean av. price 1281 = 9.5 *hyperpera*, 35 late summer sales = 9.8 *hyperpera*.
40. Twenty-nine summer sales, 1282, mean av. 11.7 *hyperpera*.
41. Seven late summer sales, 1283, mean av. 13.3 *hyperpera*.
42. Čremošnik, "Izvori za istoriju robilja," pp. 151–62. See also Vinaver, "Trgovina Bosanskim robljem," p. 141. The shift from slave sales to contracts may be seen in DSA, *Diversa Notariae*, Vol. I, a substantial collection of contract charters in the archives.

| 1310 | 128 contracts for labor | 10 slave charters |
| 1312 | 203 contracts for labor | 6 slave charters |
| 1322 | 198 contracts for labor | 9 slave charters |

43. For example, Radoanus was to serve Nicola, the tailor, for a term of ten years. He would receive his food and clothes, would learn "arnisia artis, que dantur secundom usum Ragusii" (Čremošnik, *Spisi, 1278–1301*, doc. 41). By contrast, a nonspecialized contract for a woman contained the following: Stana, a laborer from the mining site of Rudnik, was contracted to work three years. Two-thirds of a *hyperpera* was given to her mother, and one and a third more would be given to her mother at the end of the daughter's term. The mother was responsible if the daughter ran away (Čremošnik, *Spisi, 1278–1301*, doc. 79).

44. Persons from abroad could contract with families from the interior for servants, whom they would then transport to Apulia or elsewhere on the Italian mainland for the duration of their term of service, but they could not pass off a contract laborer as a slave. See, for example, DSA, *Diversa notariae*, V, f. 35v. See also R. Samardzić, "Podmladak dubrovačkih trgovaca i zanatlija u XV i XVI veku," *Zbornik studentskih strucnih radova* (Belgrade, 1948): 64–78.

45. Vinaver, "Trgovina Bosanskim robljem", p. 133.
46. DSA, *Testamenta*, V, 13–13v.
47. Čremošnik, *Spisi, 1278–1301*, doc. 154.
48. Ibid., docs. 193, 193a.
49. For example, DSA, *Diversa Notariae*, I, f. 2a and 2b. A male contracted for a period of twenty years for 11 *hyperpera* in 1310. The price of slaves having doubled since 1284 from an average price of 9.5 *hyperpera*, the contractor was receiving twenty years of labor for a little more than half the price a slave might have cost him in 1310. This was a considerable saving for the local labor market. Two women contracted for periods of twenty years for the price of 2 *hyperpera* and 5 *hyperpera* respectively, and another male, same term, for 6 *hyperpera*. These prices indicate that the contract labor was significantly cheaper than slavery, since the terms tended to cover the most productive years of a slave. The records of 1310 have been published in abbreviated form by Čremošnik, "Izvori za istoriju roblja i servicijalnih odnosu našim zemljama sr. vijeka," pp. 151–62.

50. Vinaver, "Trgovina Bosanskim robljem," p. 142.
51. *Liber Statutorum*, L. VII, 93; see also L. VI, 33 (4), a law from August 27, 1366. Among domestic servants there can be distinguished chattel slaves, contract servants, nurses and housekeepers, *homines, pueri, puellae, famuli* and *famulae, servitales, servicialis*, and those in attendance (*ad standum* or *ad serviendum*). Terms were imprecise and overlapping.
52. Manken, *Dubrovački Patricijat*, Part II (Genealogies).

# Women Servants in Florence during the Fourteenth and Fifteenth Centuries

W as the *Quattrocento* a golden age for female servants? The question arises when one sees the men of the time working obstinately to give value to the domestic activities of their wives and daughters. The fifteenth century is also a period in which the demographic and economic conjuncture greatly improved the conditions of salaried employment. Did these factors have an impact on the work done by female outsiders in Florentine families and on the importance accorded them? Richard Goldthwaite pointed out recently that servants "do not [make] much of an appearance in the imaginative literature of the period."[1] The absence of servants in literary, if not artistic, representations invites consideration of the place and function of women who entered into service with families in Florence in the fourteenth and fifteenth centuries.

I would like, therefore, to take up again the problem of domestic work in a slightly different light from that in which many works, whether recent or earlier, have placed it.[2] It seems to me that the necessary attention has not been given to the ideological and cultural context of Italian domesticity at the end of the Middle Ages. And yet, the *famiglia*[3] of which these male and female servants of all origins and conditions become members constitutes a universe comprising a cluster of values in a manner that may be artificial since it is imposed by the *padre-padrone*. Nevertheless, this cluster is enlightening because the household head has the power to make it formally respected. It seems indispensable to me to look again at the models offered by Florentine employers to evaluate correctly the reactions, even the resistance, of their domestic servants.

Women's work at the end of the Middle Ages is much more difficult to discern and evaluate than men's. Even when women worked for larger profits in industrial enterprises, spinning or weaving cloth, their work was

56

too often hidden in the shadow of particular houses or in the bosom of their familial activities. While historians have begun to study salaried employment in the fourteenth and fifteenth centuries in the trades that have documentation, such as construction or even the textile industry, or in charitable institutions that have left us abundant archives,[4] one must usually be contented with a few disparate notes on salaries or hiring contracts and brief literary allusions in dealing with feminine salaried employment, especially domestic employment. These documents do offer material for quantitative history. The history of these working women has been left in the picturesque half-light of accounts of the "private life" or of "manners," where the historians of the preceding century had ingenuously confined it.

This historiographic relegation is difficult to defend. First, domestic salaried employment is part of a job market in which women are in direct competition with men, seeking work for themselves that is not otherwise considered specifically feminine.[5] The respective salaries given for these unspecialized domestic workers are, therefore, probably the only ones that, compared over the course of the time, somewhat illuminate the sex differentiation that prevailed in the job market. In this period, other sectors of economic activity give us very little information on female salaried employment. Second, an exclusively feminine task, the nursing of infants, permits us to distinguish a sort of qualified aristocracy at the heart of female salaried employment. Is it not correct to consider the group of domestic nurses as truly "skilled laborers" and to compare them with all female servants who do nonspecialized service? Such a comparison could bring a counterargument to the observations made on the respective salaries and living standards of qualified and unqualified male workers.[6] Finally, the existence of domestic slavery, still very much present at this time, brings a supplementary element of competition in the job market whose effects we must measure.

These preliminary observations permit us to suppose that internal hierarchies structured the narrow universe of domestic life. If such hierarchies exist, both at the level of working conditions and at the level of contemporary representations, do they rest entirely on economic criteria? Do not values of another kind come to gauge the routine daily tasks within the walls of the private houses? In addition to a financial evaluation of the work done, I shall try, finally, to look beyond the judgments passed upon female servants in order to disentangle the particular social values that were fundamental to that society and that era.

## La Padrona Serva

"Nature wills that what a man brings to his house, his wife maintains. The wife, locked up in the house, should protect these goods and herself in complete tranquility, but also in fear and vigilance."[7] A place, a role is peremptorily given to the wife. Alberti, who holds this opinion in his turn, espouses, of course, very old traditions. The models for the female roles he proposes to his contemporaries hardly deviate from the *topoi* inherited from authors of late antiquity.[8] One cannot, however, relegate his philosophical reelaboration of the familial and conjugal ethics to the world of ideas or to the simple plagiarism of good authors. The pages he devotes to the division of male and female roles sound right; they call to mind many texts telling us more ingenuously the daily relations between spouses and the way in which they share the economic and familial responsibilities in Tuscan society. Alberti offers the theoretical framework for the sexual distinctions of these roles, but his recommendations agree with the Florentine practice we see in domestic literature.[9]

   Three areas are the province of the wife: the management of goods that are in the house (what Alberti calls the *masserizia*), good manners and the climate of amity that should rule the relations of all the members of the house (the *costumi*), and finally the children.[10] These are three themes on which she will converse with her husband, who reserves for himself the outside world, the activities conducted "among men outside, in public."[11] The master nevertheless maintains the right to oversee domestic management; the wife acts by delegation. She is given responsibility, certainly, but she is still dependent.[12] Her domestic power does not associate her, according to Alberti, with her husband's "major and own affairs": she does not even have to know where the "valuable papers" are locked away, the "secret commentary" that enlightens the tangled web of his transactions;[13] and it is not she who keeps the accounts of domestic administration from day to day.[14]

   One essential post, however, is assigned to her.[15] Always in the breach, she must "take care of the family, maintain and use well the goods of the household."[16] But our *padrona serva* was not educated to do all the housework; her husband, first of all, would keep her from lowering herself to that. A wife of the merchant class should maintain her rank of "padrona e maestra di tutti."[17] Her mother taught her only how to spin and to sew; when she arrives at her husband's house, she barely knows how to tidy her chests. It is up to the vigilant husband to teach her almost everything.

   That Alberti repeats here the pedagogical principles of his time, the early fifteenth century, on the education of daughters of good family is certain. It suffices to cite Francesco da Barberino, who, at the very beginning of the fourteenth century, arranges the content of the education of daughters according to their status. A knight's or lawyer's daughter learns from her mother how to "make purses, sew or spin" only in order to avoid boredom, to "keep from becoming depressed" in her reclusive state.[18] The sole object of having her taught by "some servant" how to "cook both ordinary and more refined dishes" is to endow her with an exceptionally feminine art, to serve at the table and to satisfy "a *gourmand* lord who knows the choice morsels."[19] Serving at table, an art that the Florentines prize so highly in the woman who learns it, is again a class distinction: it is certainly not a matter for a woman in these spheres to have her life revolve around her ovens.[20] On the other hand, Francesco da Barberino multiplies the household tasks to which the daughters of merchants or petty bourgeois have to initiate themselves. If it is "blameworthy" that they learn to read and write, they have to know how to perform "many more domestic tasks created by the management of households."[21] Even lower yet, daughters of the working classes should clearly know how to "sew and spin well, cook the best that they can and keep house, putting all their attention and effort, as good servants should, into the care of their families."[22]

To act "as good servants should" is not, therefore, the proper function of a woman of Alberti's class; the domestic servants assist the mistress of the household, whose apprenticeship consists mainly of learning to distribute the household work among them, to control the execution of it, in short, to make the house run while seeing to it that none of its cogs get jammed.

One compliment often recurs in the writings of men in the fourteenth and fifteenth centuries. Thus, Donato Velluti, writing a little before 1370, qualifies many of his relatives as *buono massaio, grande massaia*.[23] As opposed to the *cortesia* of squanderers, this quality is associated with "wisdom." Knowing how to rule one's self is the same as ordering one's domestic world. Alberti establishes the link very explicitly: in her function, the wife simply applies to the house the same precepts that the man must respect outside it.[24] The functions that lead to good government of the family may vary because of the sex of the person in charge; still, the execution of these tasks will be judged by the same standards of economy, of self-control, and of authority. To be fully acknowledged in her position, the mother of the family, imbued with her dignity, will sometimes appear at the open door of her house—at the frontier between inside and outside—"observing a sedate attitude, which will make her recognized and praised by the neighbors as a prudent wife and make her respected all the more by her servants."[25]

## Women Servants

Who are the "unmannerly and incompetent people"[26] who assume under the mistress's surveillance the feminine and household duties that her rank forbids her to perform? In the period (1300–1530) covered by the observations that we have been able to glean from the Florentine family books (*ricordanze*), only 14 percent of domestic women servants are not of Tuscan

## TABLE 1
### Origin of Female Domestics in Florence (1300–1530)

| Origin | 1298–1349 | 1350–1399 | 1400–1449 | 1450–1499 | 1500–1529 | Total |
|---|---|---|---|---|---|---|
| Unspecified | 16 | 14 | 43 | 31 | 9 | 113 |
|  | 84.2% | 53.8% | 55.8% | 27.2% | 31.0% | 42.6% |
| Tuscan | 3 | 11 | 27 | 57 | 17 | 31 |
|  | 15.8 | 42.3 | 35.1 | 50.0 | 58.6 | 43.4 |
| Italian |  | 1 | 5 | 7 | 2 | 15 |
|  |  | 3.9 | 6.5 | 6.1 | 6.9 | 5.7 |
| Foreign |  |  |  | 2 |  | 2 |
|  |  |  |  | 1.8 |  | 0.8 |
| Slaves and former slaves |  |  | 2 | 17 | 1 | 20 |
|  |  |  | 2.6 | 14.9 | 3.5 | 7.5 |
| Total N | 19 | 26 | 77 | 114 | 29 | 265 |
| Total Percent | 100.0 | 100.0 | 100.0 | 100.0 | 100.0 | 100.0 |

origin. The others are equally distributed among country and city women, if we accept the hypothesis that the women who do not explicitly acknowledge a particular place of origin live in the city. A noticeable rise in country women can be seen after 1450 (Table 1). To these nurses and servants, we must add the hundred or so male servants (cf. Table 4), who are especially numerous in the first two periods.

The tasks that devolve upon all these menials are, therefore, those that are too hard, too "vile," or too constraining for the mistress, but that make up part, in theory, of the *masserizia*. Drawing water and stoking the fire; cooking, housekeeping, washing; maintaining the chicken coops and the stables; spinning the flax, wool, and hemp; and washing, suckling, and watching over the children are the tasks that fall on those persons brought perforce into the family as slaves or those attracted by the lure of a salary. The valets (*fanti* or *famigli, ragazzi,* and *garzoni*) add to their tasks the job of accompanying the master on his trips and serving as messengers in and outside of Florence.[27]

When the master hires a female servant, he sometimes specifies one of her obligations or exempts her expressly from one.[28] That women servants can negotiate with masters, especially at the beginning of the fifteenth century, for the freedom from very hard tasks such as the washing, suggests that the power ratio favors women. This ratio is, first of all, determined by the general scarcity of workers. It is false to say, in effect, that medieval houses abound in domestic servants, even in the middle class, and that these servants constitute "one of the most numerous social components of the town in the late Middle Ages."[29] Even rich families are contented with a very small number of male and female servants during this period. Having four or five domestic servants and slaves seems at this time to be the exception, and the majority of households of Florentine high or middle class have only one or two.[30] Only the richest couples can maintain a nurse in the house, and, after 1400, parents evidently prefer to send their children to a nurse in the country.[31]

Another factor that works to the advantage of female servants is that men yield to them positions in domestic employment during a large part of the fifteenth century. The ratio of male to female servants clearly goes down after 1400. To judge by the hiring shown in account books, female servants, excluding nurses, make up only 37 percent of domestic servants before 1400, but 65 percent between 1400 and 1450, and 78 percent between 1450 and 1500 (cf. Table 4). After 1500, however, the hiring of male servants accelerates and leads to a more marked competition with the female servants, whose proportion seems to shrink in salaried domestic work.

In the fifteenth century, therefore, women hold more firmly to the market in domestic employment than they were able to do in the fourteenth century. If they are simple, "unqualified" servants, they have better chances than before of finding where to hire on. If they are biologically qualified as nurses, they have, to be sure, to deal with the competition of rural wet nurses, but they are assured of always finding enough rich people willing to open their houses and trust their children to them.

Another aspect that reveals the better conditions of female domestic employment is the transient nature of many of the services. At the beginning of our observations—the end of the thirteenth century—and until 1450, the wages were, with one exception, uniformly annual (Table 2).[32]

This arrangement did not mean that the servant would be obliged to fill out the year of service in order to be paid, or that her master could fire her whenever it suited him after having paid her. The vast majority of servants quit in the middle of the year. Advance notice of two weeks, to which an agreement reported by the *ricordanze* obliged the servant,[33] was perhaps customary and not worth the trouble of mentioning; in any case, a few masters remark in their accounts about the disagreeable surprise a *fanti* gave them by quitting the house without a prior agreement.[34] Although the *ricordanze* rarely give us the real reasons for quitting, the impression remains that the initiative came most often from the woman. If the servant was not an obvious thief, the master would prefer to keep her as long as possible so as not to have to find somebody else.[35] The women, however, who rented

TABLE 2

**Types of Salaries Mentioned in the Hiring of
Florentine Female Domestics**

| Calculated salaries | 1298–1349 | 1350–1399 | 1400–1449 | 1450–1499 | 1500–1529 | Total |
|---|---|---|---|---|---|---|
| Yearly | | | | | | |
| —in florins | | 14 | 54 | 49 | 11 | 128  (76.6%) |
| —in *lire* | 14 | | 4 | 5 | 3 | 26  (15.6%) |
| Monthly | | | | | | |
| —in florins | | | | 1 | | 1   (0.6%) |
| —in *lire* and *soldi* | | | | 1 | 11 | 12   (7.2%) |
| Total | 14 | 14 | 59 | 66 | 14 | 167(100.0%) |

Note: The salaries of domestic nurses are not considered here.

out their services by the year remained free to leave the house whenever they wished, and they did not deny themselves this right after 1350.[36]

Richard Goldthwaite has properly noted the rapid turnover of domestic help within one family.[37] Within five years in the Rustici household, for example, eleven servants succeeded one another, each staying an average of only five months. There are other similar examples. It is worth noting, nevertheless, that such transiency of servants is above all a mark of the fifteenth century. In the time of the Black Death, Jacopo di Francesco Del Bene kept half of his servants between one and four years,[38] while Bartolomeo Sassetti could only keep two of the twenty-six servants mentioned in his account books of 1440 through 1477 longer than one year. Eight stayed less than a month and twenty-two more than six.[39] There was, therefore, a more frequent turnover of salaried employees.

Many of these servants had sufficient autonomy to make their own contracts with their prospective employers. It is difficult, however, to ascertain their marital status with certainty. In the fifteenth century married women or widows were usually given the title "Monna"; it is most exceptional if their employer, when he does not add that title to their name, specifies whether they are married or widowed.[40] For lack of better indicators, therefore, we can regard the absence of this feminine title as an indication of being unmarried. Another difficulty arises concerning the distinction between married women and widows among those women called "Monna" if the writer of the document fails to give a more precise indication. I have assumed that those whose first name is followed by a man's name[41] were women whose husbands were still alive, and I have subdivided the others

TABLE 3

**Distribution of Florentine Female Domestics According to Marital Status**

| Marital status | 1298–1349 | 1350–1399 | 1400–1449 | 1450–1499 | 1500–1529 | Total |
|---|---|---|---|---|---|---|
| Single | | | 5 | 17 | 5 | 27 |
| Presumed single | 12 | 9 | 11 | 31 | 3 | 66 |
| Total | 12 | 9 | 16 | 48 | 8 | 93 |
| | 85.7% | 64.3% | 23.5% | 52.7% | 33.3% | 44.1% |
| Married | 1 | | 8 | 4 | 1 | 14 |
| Presumed married | 1 | 2 | 24 | 19 | 8 | 54 |
| Total | 2 | 2 | 32 | 23 | 9 | 68 |
| | 14.3% | 14.3% | 47.1% | 25.3% | 37.5% | 32.2% |
| Widowed | | 1 | 9 | 5 | 1 | 16 |
| Presumed widowed | | 2 | 11 | 15 | 6 | 34 |
| Total | | 3 | 20 | 20 | 7 | 50 |
| | 0.0 | 21.4% | 29.4% | 22.0% | 29.2% | 23.7% |
| Grand Total | 14 | 14 | 68 | 91 | 24 | 211 |
| | 100.0% | 100.0% | 100.0% | 100.0% | 100.0% | 100.0% |

Note: Domestic nurses are not considered here.

according to existing accounts of women whose civil status is known (Table 3).

From Table 3, in which I distinguish between given facts and information interpreted in the manner described above, one can see the importance, among salaried servants, of the group of unmarried women in the fourteenth century and at the end of the fifteenth. In the first half of the fifteenth century, their participation in domestic service declined compared with that of the married women and widows. If the *Quattrocento* was a golden age for female servants, it was above all the category of older women that bene-fited. The general aging of the population increases the relative importance of widows and older women.[42] Furthermore, the demand for men of working age in diverse economic endeavors left the field of domestic service open to a group of adult female workers who, because of their daily or unforeseen needs, found themselves looking for employment, even for short periods of time.

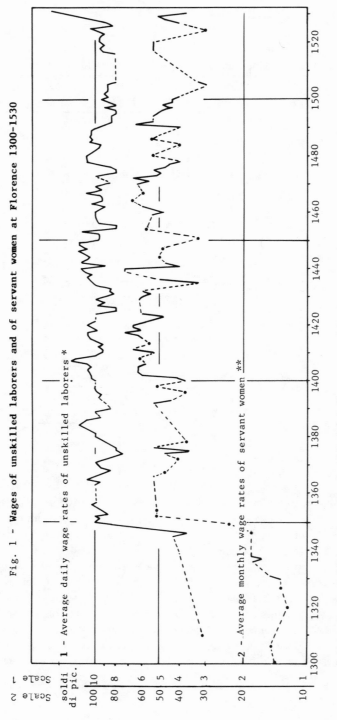

Fig. 1 - Wages of unskilled laborers and of servant women at Florence 1300-1530

1 - Average daily wage rates of unskilled laborers *

2 - Average monthly wage rates of servant women **

* From R. A. Goldthwaite - The building of Renaissance Florence, p. 318.

** From the Ricordanze.

## TABLE 4
### Decennial Averages of Monthly Salaries of Male and Female Servants and Domestic Nurses (in *Soldi "di piccioli"*)

| Decades | Male servants | | Female servants | | Nurses | |
|---|---|---|---|---|---|---|
| | number | monthly salary | number | monthly salary | number | monthly salary |
| 1298–1309 | 6 | 22.4 | 3 | 14.2 | | |
| 1310–1319 | | | | | | |
| 1320–1329 | | | 2 | 12.9 | 3 | 15.6 |
| 1330–1339 | 5 | 32.5 | 6 | 16.7 | 1 | 20.0 |
| 1340–1349 | 10 | 37.2 | 2 | 20.8 | | |
| 1350–1359 | 9 | 51.7 | 2 | 51.0 | | |
| 1360–1369 | | | 2 | 50.2 | | |
| 1370–1379 | 2 | 62.0 | 5 | 43.4 | 5 | 93.2 |
| 1380–1389 | 1 | 60.0 | | | | |
| 1390–1399 | 11 | 73.0 | 4 | 50.5 | 2 | 115.5 |
| 1400–1409 | 10 | 79.1 | 11 | 51.0 | 2 | 122.0 |
| 1410–1419 | 5 | 80.0 | 22 | 61.4 | 2 | 133.4 |
| 1420–1429 | 8 | 66.0 | 11 | 58.2 | 1 | 120.0 |
| 1430–1439 | 3 | 60.0 | 9 | 60.5 | 1 | 100.0 |
| 1440–1449 | 6 | 68.8 | 7 | 50.7 | 3 | 117.9 |
| 1450–1459 | 2 | 78.4 | 7 | 48.7 | 4 | 120.0 |
| 1460–1469 | 5 | 56.0 | 7 | 55.0 | 10 | 114.6 |
| 1470–1479 | 1 | 60.0 | 35 | 51.7 | 3 | 133.3 |
| 1480–1489 | 2 | 80.0 | 8 | 51.5 | 4 | 95.0 |
| 1490–1499 | 10 | 78.0 | 14 | 51.0 | 1 | 100.0 |
| 1500–1509 | 7 | 71.4 | 4 | 38.3 | 3 | 93.3 |
| 1510–1519 | | | 5 | 53.3 | 1 | 100.0 |
| 1520–1529 | 1 | 45.0 | 8 | 50.0 | 1 | 100.0 |
| Total | 104 | | 174 | | 47 | |

The salaries paid to female servants in the first half of the fifteenth century confirm how much the demographic and economic factors favored them. Figure 1 and Table 4 clearly show the improvement in the financial conditions of their employment during the years following the Black Death, especially after 1400 and up to about 1460 to 1470. The first effect of the Black Death was that salaries were calculated in florins (cf. Table 2). Even if a servant is actually paid in silver or copper coins, this new estimate of her salary works to her advantage by taking better account of inflation.[43] The salaries of female servants, in addition, more than double after 1348; they overtake those of male servants—a situation that will not occur again until the thirties and sixties of the next century. The wages of domestic nurses rise even more markedly after the Black Death. Whereas before that time, a servant would receive about 83 percent of the salary of a nurse *in casa*, the latter's wages would surpass hers constantly afterward, and, at the beginning of the sixteenth century, a servant would receive wages worth only 40 to 50 percent of those of a domestic nurse. In comparison with male servants, a female servant would maintain until 1470 a little better ratio than that of the early fourteenth century, with her salary staying at around 80 percent of theirs (fig.2).

After 1470, it is clear that this situation gradually worsens. The wages of female servants represent only 60 percent of those of their male coworkers. The population, which begins to grow again, soon throws into the job market young people who begin their service in the houses of well-off families. The demand for nurses remains strong, because this demographic upsurge begins at the base and increases the number of nursing infants. But the salaries of domestic nurses, mostly young women who themselves form a large section of the population, collapse also after 1480; a nurse in 1500 earns a salary one quarter less than her colleague in 1420–70. These setbacks are all the more perceptible since prices begin to climb in the 1470s. The graph of wheat prices published by Richard Goldthwaite shows only too clearly the disintegration of buying power of domestic and of other salaried workers.[44]

One of the gains made after the Black Death also loses its importance. For, whereas three out of four of the wages continue to be calculated in florins, these are taken for nominal money. While gold values climb in proportion to silver and this trend accelerates in the second half of the fifteenth century,[45] the rate of exchange of the florin, which serves as a basis for the computation of servant's wages, is held once and for all after 1440 at the level of before 1430 (that is, at four *lire* per florin).[46] As long as retail prices remain stable, servants and nurses hardly suffer; but after 1470, they obviously suffer more from the rise in the cost of living.[47]

It is true that domestic servants lived at the expense—*alle spese*—of their employers and did not have to deal from day to day with the price of bread and other foodstuffs. They also had secure lodging. Furthermore, in the fourteenth century, custom required that the employer give his servants the necessary work clothes, and the custom seems to have been perpetuated in the fifteenth, although many hiring contracts restrained the generosity of the employer to the gift of a shirt or a pair of shoes annually, to encourage the servant to fulfill the term of her year-long contract.[48] Clothing, however, remained in the servants' charge, and many employers had to consent to advances on wages in order to renovate servants' wardrobes. It was, besides the threat of departure, one of the ways domestic servants had at

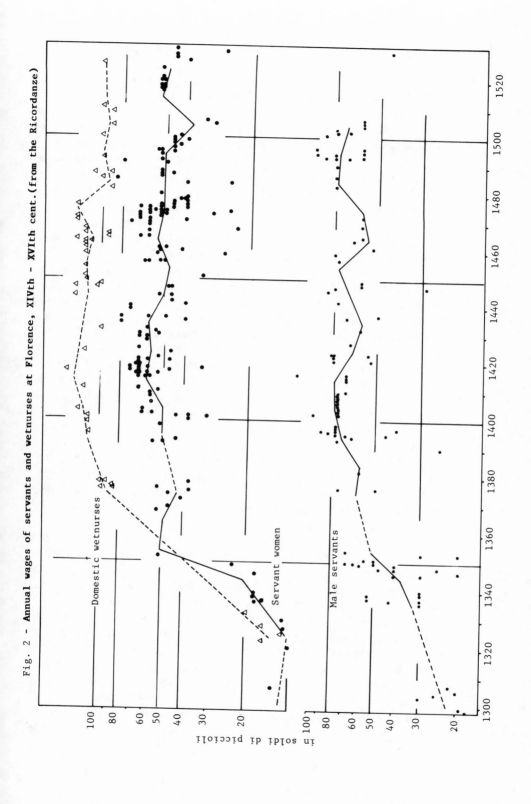

Fig. 2 - Annual wages of servants and wetnurses at Florence, XIVth - XVIth cent.(from the Ricordanze)

their command to get a part or a whole of their wages, payment of which rarely occurred at fixed dates.[49]

The problem of clothing also seems central in the hiring of a category of domestic servants that increases in the last third of the fifteenth century: young girls who have come to earn their dowries as servants. The hiring agreement for this child—or adolescent—worker demands that the young servant reside at the employer's house until her marriage if she wishes to receive her salary.[50] Arranged generally between a close relative of the child and her employer, the contract requires that after a variable amount of time—five to ten years, the average being eight[51]—the master, who also promises to feed and clothe the little girl, will pay her a dowry. The average dowry is eighty *lire* in the second half of the fifteenth century, a minimal dowry for that period, and usually consists mainly of clothing and bedlinens.[52] Allowed sometimes to determine the age at which it will be advisable to marry her,[53] like a true substitute for her father,[54] the employer appears all-powerful to the little girl of eight or ten who will grow up under his roof. If she quits before her marriage, she risks leaving with nothing but her ordinary, daily clothing or with whatever her employer judges good to give her.[55] In exceptional cases, the contract provides that she will be paid a prorated wage for the years of her service.[56]

In reality, this extraordinarily cheap female labor continued, under these conditions of work, for too short a period to gain the promised dowry. Of the thirteen girls whose time of arrival in a family we know, nine left before marriage. Only one fulfilled the promised time, but she later decided to become a weaver.[57] We know nothing of the fate of the last three.[58] This somber picture of the working conditions of young girls reinforces the impression of a deterioration and depreciation of female salaried employment in the last decades of the fifteenth century and the beginning of the sixteenth.

If one descends a step lower in the domestic hierarchy, one encounters the slaves imported from distant countries, individuals radically alien to the Tuscan culture, who remain marginal beings their whole lives. Their presence raises the question of the influence that this imported labor may have exerted on the job market. P. Guarducci and V. Ottanelli have recently insisted on the "political" character of the slave trade in the late Middle Ages, suggesting that employers encouraged the importation of slave labor to make an impression on the local workers who pushed their salary demands too far after the Black Death.[59] Their observation hits the mark, because the small number of domestic slaves (about 98 percent women) continues to grow smaller still in the fifteenth century and, therefore, cannot be regarded as a countermeasure designed to combat the rise of salaries—marginal salaries, in any case, because they are those of female domestic servants. This use of slavery as a measure of dissuasion has, nevertheless, given a certain flexibility to the heads of families who can acquire a slave. By purchasing or renting, they can remedy the scarcity of nurses that prevails in the first two-thirds of the fifteenth century: one out of ten domestic nurses listed in the *ricordanze* is a slave.[60] After a nurse has lost her milk, she works as a servant, or she is placed in other houses by her owner, who sees a good investment in this.[61] As her original price would reach at the highest no more than double or triple the annual wages of a free nurse, the investment brings in a good profit.

Because Tuscany was the terminus of Mediterranean traffic and less directly supplied than the large ports like Genoa or Venice, it had few slaves.[62] The *catasto* of 1427 shows only around 360. Households that kept more than one slave were rare: 323 Tuscan families accounted for these 360 women (261 Florentine families accounted for the 294 slaves in their city, and the 55 women enumerated in the Pisan *catasto* were distributed among 48 Pisan families).[63] These slaves certainly circulated from family to family, for they were rented, resold, loaned. Many more households were concerned with their presence, no matter how short a time, than the above-cited numbers would indicate. If we estimate that one-quarter to one-third of the families of Florence almost continually employed a servant, the slaves represent less than one-tenth of the effective force of female domestic servants in the first third of the fifteenth century.[64]

Assisted by all these women, the mistress of the household, we may state, has no other mission than the governing of her little world and the procreation of children. But even this latter function does not constitute a field reserved for her alone. The slave has to submit herself to all the requirements of her master and to the desires of his friends. How can she resist them, when she has no rights and finds herself included on his fiscal registers with the livestock? Florentine households shelter many illegitimate children born of these servile embraces. More numerous are the nursing infants abandoned at the foundling hospices, although born in the "servants' room" of the best houses.[65] A striking example of the sexual abuse of slaves comes to us from the hospice of San Gimignano, where abandoned infants were received.[66] Between 1434 and 1446, Stefano Moronti, one of the chief citizens of Florence, sent no fewer than four newborns, to whom his slave had given birth, to the hospice of Santa Maria della Scala. The Florentine *ricordanze* also show us these good family men at the hour of decision: should they keep and raise the children, even if only to make them domestic servants, or rather abandon them, because, being free, they are not negotiable like their mothers? I will cite only three cases, which well illuminate the attitude toward these most conspicuous illegitimate children. When his slave gives birth to a little girl in 1471, Jacopo Attavanti makes a hireling take the little girl to the hospice of the Trovatelli of Pisa, and he sells the mother two months later.[67] Guido Baldovinetti delicately avoids scandal for his fellow townsman, Jacopo Niccolini, who has just married but who had impregnated Guido's servant; Guido does not send the child to the hospice of the Innocenti until having it nursed for three months under his own name.[68] Giovanni Rucellai sends to Jacopo Attavanti his slave impregnated by Jacopo's brother in Naples; Jacopo covers all the costs of the childbirth, has the child baptized, finds him a nurse, and finally sends the bill to his brother.[69]

Not all the children of slaves were systematically rejected, and a certain number returned from the nurse to the household of their father or to that of their mother's owner. The legal spouse, as well as her daughters-in-law living under her roof, often pregnant, could not claim exclusive title to the sexual attentions of their husbands. Coming as young wives into their new household, they often found there sons that their husbands had with the household slaves. The wife of Bartolomeo Sassetti saw a bastard return from the nurse's home, a few weeks after the wedding, and her husband had a daughter by another slave a few years later.[70] Paolo Niccolini kept under his roof three sons born of his slave, one of whom was born after his marriage; in 1452, having produced eleven children by his first wife, and before having five more by his second, he had another natural daughter by a widow, and he welcomed her into his house as well.[71] By these liaisons and the anxieties caused by their pregnancies, these slaves, too submissive, constrained to accept the sexual advances of their masters, thus took revenge, whether they wished to or not, on the mistresses who daily dealt with their work and their unhappiness.

## The Price of Honor

The hierarchy of salaries indubitably contributes to establish a hierarchy of authority and of importance in the small world of domestic servants. But does salary alone contribute to the inequalities? Better paid than any male servant, the nurse is at the top. She is followed by male domestic servants, whose salaries fall between hers and those of other female servants. Close to the master, the male servants participate to a certain extent in his authority and in his superiority over the female group. Among female servants, the first large division is between adults and girls working for their dowry, between women who can negotiate their wages and leave, and little girls who look upon their employer as a second father. Within the group of the salaried, one may conjecture that the lowest salaries (four to eight florins a year), lower than the salary standard put forth by the statutes of the city in 1415 (nine or ten florins), were paid before 1450 to older or less reliable women.[72] But the employers of this period are not stingy if they wish to hire sturdy servants, and they often enough offer wages that are clearly higher than those required by the statutes.[73] After 1470 the salaries of adult women seem to cluster around seven to eight florins, and discrimination in terms of their strength plays less of a role in differentiating among them. The wages of former slaves working mainly on their own account in a new master's house or at their former owner's house match the contemporary average for domestic servants.[74] At the bottom of this salary ladder are the little girls, little working hands that never grasp the first penny, because their employers act as their bankers until their marriage.

The slaves are outside of this salary pyramid. An important demarcation, however, divides this group. As others have pointed out, Mediterranean slavery had major gradations. They were tied to the initial judicial document that put the women in servitude.[75] Many Ragusans living in Florence were sold by a close relative or sold themselves for an appointed time. Different from lifelong slaves who were procured through raids or war and who were bought without conditions, the Ragusans and Dalmatians had hopes of finishing their servitude at a precise date. In fact, among the twenty-four sale contracts found in the Florentine *ricordanze*, six place limits on ownership by the master, either time limits or conditions of resale.[76] Even if the Florentines do not seem to be conscious of the problem that the distinction between lifelong and temporary slaves creates, they seem to respect faithfully the obligations that they themselves or previous buyers have undertaken.[77]

The confusion and overlapping of judicial conditions resulting from the ambiguous character of this type of contract encouraged employers and owners of slaves to merge the conditions of employment of women who served them. Half-slaves and servants of long-term contracts, servants hired on the recommendation of a third party, and slaves rented out by their owners, who received the earned wages, all must have seen the shadings of servitude and service dissolve into the grayness of everyday contact. Toward the end of the fifteenth century and the beginning of the sixteenth, servants replaced slaves, now less numerous, in supplying the hospices with abandoned newborns.[78] Even the contemporary vocabulary reflects this confusion in describing more often as *serva* those slaves or servants who perform the function of *fante*.

Neither the salaries nor the judicial conditions totally account for the divisions separating the groups of domestic workers. Rather than concentrating on the moral qualities expected of servants by their employers, qualities completely imprinted with the same standards of propriety that we noted above in regard to the wife,[79] I will insist on a less obvious discriminating factor. The respect that employers show their servants depends largely on the relationship that the servant has to the marriage and to one of its conditions, sexual honor. Obviously, the nurse is not only better paid, but pampered, well fed, and sheltered from the attentions of the master of the house because the survival of the child who has been entrusted to her depends on her own health. I have shown elsewhere with what vigor masters react to an unforeseen pregnancy of their nurses.[80] Their confidence in her betrayed, they declare themselves ridiculed when the crime is accom- plished in their house, where surveillance over her chastity is easier and within their province. The nurse who becomes pregnant, much as the adulterous wife, sullies the honor of the father in not respecting the con- tract that obliges her explicitly to remain chaste. The role of substitute mother that she plays in regard to the child necessitates her proving that she has the same moral qualities as the wife, because she will transmit them, along with her physical qualities, to the child she nurses. The good side of the coin is that she enjoys a respect that places her clearly above all the other domestic servants. Even if they are not openly stated, the refer- ences to the survival of the line and the sexual honor of the Florentine wives are determining factors in the wages paid her.

An analogous criterion for sexual purity doubtless keeps the employer from attacking too rudely the young girls who are working for their dowry. Entrusted since childhood to the family, they are as vulnerable as the employer's own daughters, and in a certain way, they risk jeopardizing his honor by behaving too wantonly. Different from the adult servants who are judged responsible for their actions even when they have to submit to the violence of their employer or his sons, these girls are jealously watched and dismissed if they do not behave well. The act is equivalent to shutting up in a convent well-born daughters who have lost their reputation. The painter Neri di Bicci dismisses a young girl of thirteen, who, after four years of service, "refused to show herself obedient and attentive to proper, seemly things."[81]

At the other pole of domestic sexual values, the slave's body is a matter of property to her master. To make her pregnant does not injure her master's honor; rather, it damages his property. Liable to litigation, such an offense is usually settled by monetary compensation, as one can see from the sad story of Caterina, a Circassian "with black hair." While her master, Francesco Giovanni, entrusted the house and the children to her in his absence, Caterina (whom he had bought nine years earlier and who is now eighteen) invites a young man one night into her bed. The lovers are caught in the act. Francesco seeks recompense privately to cover for the losses that an eventual pregnancy would cause; left without response, he lodges a complaint. The father of the guilty party concedes and his son swears to have given Caterina, "who asked it of him, a cheap little brass ring." For her part, the poor girl says that "he gave her the ring as a promise of marriage." The token and the promise of marriage, in which the wooer certainly did not believe for a second, are nevertheless taken as a new "insult" by Francesco: not only for the fraud that they are in reality, but because he sees in them another threat to his legitimate property. Marriage is equivalent to freedom, and thus to the misappropriation of goods; in short, it is a theft. Francesco argues so well that the judge rules that the guilty party must promise to buy the slave if in the next three months she should prove to be pregnant.[82]

To all the players in the story, it seems quite ordinary that a young man should extort sexual favors from an ingenuous girl in return for a small gift. But it is the attitude of the owner that interests us here. Not for a moment does Francesco talk about outrage or injury to his own honor (though when a monastery wants to take one of his sons who wishes to enter religious life, it is exactly that with which he concerns himself!).[83] The injury to his goods, which is represented by the seduction of his slave, is here measured completely in terms of profits and losses, of property damage, and financial compensation. For Francesco to wish to ameliorate this grievous situation using the rules of courtship and preparation for marriage (no matter how perverted by the seducer) is simply unthinkable. Lacking sexual honor herself, how could a slave envision marriage and risk sullying her master's honor at the same time?

"Condemned to definitive celibacy" for the most part, the slaves who had not been sold on a fixed-term contract are freed too late to start a family. The Circassian Giuliana can count herself lucky to be an exception. After six months of work, this former slave left her master, Neri di Bicci, taking with her for her salary—and undoubtedly for her trousseau as well—a few paltry clothes, "having married a few days earlier Giovanni, the slave who turns the wheel."[84] A slave who finds some semblance of freedom only through her master's will can at least hope to spend her days in the bed he willed her or in a small dwelling in the shadow of his house to which she can retire.[85] Cateruccia of the Strozzi, who knew all the house secrets and could not be sold without risk,[86] "complains incessantly about her health, takes refuge in her room, sometimes spinning a little for [her mistress] and sometimes attending to her own business." Grumbling and hostile, she makes her masters pay dearly for the celibacy that they imposed on her after having done nothing but abuse her too much in her youth. Forbidden chastity, forbidden an honorable marriage, she is the exact opposite of the woman whom the Florentines revere.

The favorable conjuncture of demographic and economic factors certainly improved the working conditions of female domestic servants after 1350. The hold on domestic service that women procured for themselves at the end of the fourteenth century and that was accompanied in the first two-thirds of the fifteenth century, at least, by better salaries and by a mitigation of the constraints of their work was, in fact, an interlude. This interlude does not take on its full sense until we can set these scraps of history of women's work into a larger picture. We cannot interpret the evolution of domestic salaried employment until we know better the conditions in which women could work in various Florentine enterprises, in the workshops and small businesses. The impression gained from the texts and still sparse studies is that women withdrew from many sectors of work after the middle of the fourteenth century and seemed to retreat to domestic service, in which they acquired a major place in the decades following the Black Death. This finding suggests that women of the fifteenth century, hiring themselves out more easily to families of the town and changing employers at a rapid pace, were less interested in security than in gaining some profit from the scarcity of masculine labor (which was attracted to the better-paid salaried jobs), using the situation to obtain higher wages and to adjust their jobs more closely to their most urgent needs.

The predominance of married or widowed servants, adult or elderly, between 1400 and 1470 reveals an important aspect of feminine salaried employment in the Middle Ages, namely, its unusual character, which tied it closely to women's cycles of life. It was the unique demographic and economic factors of this century that created the demand for female labor. In spite of the accepted social norm that women's place was in their own homes, not elsewhere, these exceptional opportunities for profit induced wives and older women to serve in large numbers under someone else's roof, deserting their own families. And, if it was common that a poor girl entered into the *famiglia* of a bourgeois in order to earn the dowry indispensable to her honorable marriage, this situation, however short-lived, was still regarded as a last resort. At least the employer, if he fulfilled his role correctly, would maintain his place as "father," and the service of the young girl would result in a return to the natural order, to marriage and to her settlement in her husband's house. But it was better for the former servant, now a wife, to draw the curtain over this episode of her life, in which she put her honor in peril. The adult and forewarned woman who voluntarily exposed herself to this danger was in return very suspect.

Paying a woman for her services classes her at the far edge of the group of respectable women, even when her labor gives her access to matrimonial respectability. The suspicion attached to the condition of the salaried worker reflects the fundamental divisions between sexual roles in force in Florentine society, the basis of which is that the wife maintains the domestic property, indeed the money, that her husband brings in. Permitting a needy woman to accumulate earnings while performing the tasks of the housewife is to mix these roles. Who could completely trust these women who come from elsewhere, who will leave with some of the familial substance? The need to employ these poor women does not remove the stain that marks them. Is it then so surprising that employers are unwilling to pay their servants their salaries? Undoubtedly, they would prefer to operate with the appearances of charity rather than to remunerate an activity that confuses their values.

Only the nurse escapes these condemnations to a certain degree. She has taken for herself the lion's share in an aging, declining population in which, however, childbirth remains high. She profits in particular from the shrinking supply of young women. And she arouses discussions as rich and abundant as those held in regard to the choice and functions of the wife. It does not matter, in the last analysis, that she has her milk from an illegitimate union; there was too much need of her to look too closely. Different from the servant, who is ever under scrutiny as an impenitent thief, the nurse, who brings to the family not only her labor but also the precious substance of her milk, is the "good" image of the maternal woman; and it is that which has given her a predominant place in the domestic hierarchy, even if, like the servant, she usurps one of the roles that the well-born Florentines, indeed, denied to their wives.

*Translated by Nancy Elizabeth Mitchell*

## Notes

1. R. A. Goldthwaite, *The Building of Renaissance Florence, An Economic and Social History* (Baltimore, 1980), p. 108.

2. N. Tamassia, *La famiglia italiana nei secoli decimoquinto e decimosesto* (Rome, 1911; reprinted 1971), pp. 351–72. J. Heers, *Esclaves et domestiques au moyen-âge dans le monde méditerraneén* (Paris, 1981). P. Guarducci and V. Ottanelli, *I servitori domestici della casa borghese toscana nel basso medioevo* (Florence, 1982).

3. In the ancient sense taken up again by L.-B. Alberti, *I libri della famiglia* [ca. 1433], ed. R. Romano and A. Tenenti (Turin, 1969), p. 226: "E' figliuoli, la moglie, e gli altri domestici, famigli, servi."

4. F. Melis, *Aspetti della vita economica medievale. Studi nell'Archivio Datini di Prato* (Siena, 1962). C. de La Ronciére, *Prix et salaires à Florence au XIVe siècle (1280–1380)* (Rome, 1982). R. A. Goldthwaite, "I prezzi del grano a Firenze dal XIV al XVI seccolo," *Quaderni storici* 10 (1975): 5–36, and *Building of Renaissance Florence*. G. Pinto, "Personale, balie e salariati dell'Ospedale di San Gallo," *Ricerche storiche* (1974): 113–68.

5. Guarducci and Ottanelli, *I servitori domestici*, pp. 33–34.

6. La Ronciére, *Prix et salaires*, pp. 257–454. Goldthwaite, *Building of Renaissance Florence*, pp. 287–350.

7. Alberti, *I libri della famiglia*, p. 265.

8. M.-L. Lenzi, *Donne e madonne. L'educazione femminile nel primo Rinascimento italiano* (Turin, 1982). G. De Piaggi, *La sposa perfetta. Educazione e condizione della donna nella famiglia francese del rinascimento e della controriforma* (Abano Terme, 1979). G. Bochi, *L'educazione femminile dall'umanesimo alla controriforma* (Bologna, 1961).

9. Domestic literature is represented by account books and *ricordanze*, family chronicles, etc., described by M. Pezzarossa, "La tradizione fiorentina della memorialistica," in *La "memoria" dei mercatores*, ed. G.-M. Anselmi, F. Pezzarossa, L. Avellini (Bologna, 1980), pp. 39–149.

10. Alberti, *I libri della famiglia*, p. 269.

11. Ibid., p. 264.

12. De Piaggi, *La sposa perfetta*, p. 13. M. Pereira, "L'educazione femminile alla fin del medioevo. Considerazioni sul De eruditione filiorum nobilium di Viazo di Beauvais," *Quaderni della Fondazione G. Feltrinelli* 23 (1983): 109–23. P. Riché, "Sources pédagogiques et traités d'éducation," in *Les entrées dans la Vie. Initiations et apprentissages* (Nancy, 1982), pp. 15–29.

13. Alberti, *I libri della famiglia*, pp. 267–69.

14. Account books or *ricordanze* kept by women are rare; on the teaching of reading and writing given to girls, see C. Klapisch-Zuber, "Le schiave fiorentine di Barbablù: L'apprendimento della lettura a Firenze nel XV secolo," *Quaderni storici*, n.s., 57, no. 3 (1984): 765–92.

15. The metaphor is Alberti's: *I libri della famiglia*, p. 270.

16. Ibid., p. 279.

17. Ibid., p. 295.

18. Francesco da Barberino, *Reggimento e costumi di donna*, ed. G. E. Sansone (Turin, 1957), p. 17. Pereira, *"L'educazione femminile."*

19. Barberino, *Reggimento e costumi*, p. 17.

20. Giovani Morelli, in his *Ricordi*, ed. V. Branca (Florence, 1969), p. 179, praises his sister Mea in the following manner: "arebbe servito a una mensa d'uomini o di donne così pulitamente come giovane uso e pratico a nozze o simili cose." R. C. Trexler, *Public Life in Renaissance Florence* (New York, 1980), pp. 237–38.

21. Barberino, *Reggimento e costumi*, p. 19.

22. Ibid., p. 20.

23. D. Velluti, *La cronica domestica*, ed. I. Del Lungo and G. Volpi (Florence, 1914), pp. 94, 102, 106. Alberti, *I libri della famiglia*, pp. 272, 297.

24. The husband says to his wife: "Moglie mia, acciò che a questo e agli altri domestici bisogni non manchi le cose, fa in casa come fo io nel resto fuori di casa." Alberti, *I libri della famiglia*, p. 289.

25. Ibid., p. 295.

26. Ibid., p. 280.

27. Lello da Onti promises on June 5, 1396, to his master, a jurist, Ricciardo Del Bene, "servire in casa di ciò bisongnia e portare e' libro se bisongnasse e governare e' ronzino e andare in villa a piè se bisongnerà." Archivio di Stato di Firenze (abbreviated as ASF; all further references to archives without other indication are to these archives), *Carte Del Bene*, 37, f. 81r. See Heers, *Esclaves et domestiques*, pp. 148–49, on the legal contracts of servants comparable to those of apprentices.

28. "E dee lavare e reburattare," *ricordanze* (abbreviated as ric.) of Niccolo

Guidalotti, Archivio degli Innocenti, *Estranei*, 562 f. 53v, 13 Jan. 1372. "E dee lavare i panni picholi," ric. of Ser Jacopo Landi, Biblioteca Nazionale Centrale, Florence, *Palatini*, 1129, f. 87r, 15 Sept. 1401. "E debbe fare ongni chosa ecietto che lavare i buchati" and "salvo che lavare il buchato," ric. of Terrino Manovelli, *Strozziane*, II, 14, f. 15r, 3 Oct. 1429 and f. 16r, 2 Dec. 1429. Another restriction on the master's will: the female servant accompanying him outside of Florence is better paid; ric. of Antonio Rustici, *Strozziane*, II, 11, f. 13r, 24 Sept. 1417.

29. Guarducci et Ottanelli, *I servitori domestici*, p. 9.

30. Heers, *Esclaves et domestiques*, pp. 147–48, citing B. Casini, *Il catasto di Pisa del 1428–29* (Pisa, 1964), pp. 65–69, on servants in Pisa in 1428. The richest taxpayer has one *garzone* and five female slaves in his service; the fifteenth richest taxpayer (Simone da San Casciano) has one female servant, one male and one female slave; Mariano di Pancaldo, in the fortieth to fiftieth richest taxpayer group, has no one in his service, whereas the judge Urbano da Cigoli (around sixtieth) has a *garzone* for general housework.

31. C. Klapisch-Zuber, "Parents de Sang, parents de Lait. La mise en norrice à Florence (1300–1530)," *Annales de démographie historique* (1983), Table 1.

32 .The one exception among eighty-seven cases is dated 1431. Monthly wages are more frequent from 1450 to 1529.

33. Ric. of Uguccione Capponi, *Conventi soppressi, San Piero a Monticelli*, 153, f. 8r, 20 July 1440.

34. "E non disse nulla . . ." or also "sanza dire adio . . . ," ric. of Guido Baldovinetti, *Acquisti e doni*, 190, 3, f. 29r, 2 Jan. 1476 and f. 32r, 3 Feb. 1478. Young men seem to leave their employers in a more carefree manner, but this is probably noticeable because their contracts more closely resemble the contract of apprenticeship than do those of female servants. See above, n. 27.

35. Servants dismissed for their lack of discretion in the ric. of Manno Petrucci, *Strozziane*, II, 17, f. 40v and 63v, 1 Oct. 1444 and 27 Jan 1447; ric. of Bartolomeo Sassetti, *Strozziane*, V, 1749, f. 211v, 21 May 1470, and 1751, f. 172v, 12 Jan. 1475; ric. of Ser Andrea Nacchianti, Arch. Innocenti, *Estranei*, 633, f. 99r, 7 June 1491. These few cases (five out of about 200 servants considered here) scarcely justify the congenital mistrust of Florentine employers toward their female servants, assumed from the first to be potential thieves.

36. They freely take vacations for personal reasons, returning to their families or lending their services (as nurses to the sick, midwives, etc.) to other Florentines. See, for example, Monna Masa, servant of Bernardo Strozzi, who cared for six women in childbirth in the space of nineteen months; *Strozziane*, III, 347, f. 113r, 27 June 1430.

37. Goldthwaite, *Building of Renaissance Florence*, p. 107 and n. 49.

38. *Carte Del Bene*, 47.

39. *Strozz.*, V, 1749–51.

40. There are only four such cases, one from the first half of the fourteenth century and the other three from the first half of the fifteenth. The interpretation is more difficult in the beginning of the fourteenth century, where the title of "Monna" seems less widespread in the lower classes.

41. For example, "Monna Lena di Maso Cecchini da San Martino da Pagliuccio di Mugello," where it is not specified whether Lena is wife (*donna di . . .* ) or widow (*donna fù di . . .* ) of this Maso; Arch. Innocenti, *Estranei*, 633, f. 100r.

42. C. Klapisch-Zuber, "Célibat et service féminins dans la Florence du XVe Siècle," *Annales de démographie historique* (1981). On the age structure of the Floren-

tine population in 1427, see D. Herlihy and C. Klapisch-Zuber, *Les Toscans et leurs familles. Une étude du catasto florentin de 1427–1430* (Paris, 1978), pp. 370 ff. English translation: *Tuscans and Their Families. A Study of the Florentine Catasto of 1427* (New Haven, 1985), pp. 183–85.

43. Goldthwaite, *Building of Renaissance Florence,* pp. 301–17, 331–42.

44. Ibid., p. 318.

45. Ibid, pp. 429–30, for a table on the value of the florin. See also pp. 301–304, 315–16.

46. The first mention of the florin at four *lire* is in the *ricordanze* of Uguccione Capponi, *Conventi soppressi, San Piero a Monticelli,* 153, f. 8, 20 July 1440. There are multiple references after 1460. In 1494 and 1495, Ser Andrea Nacchianti offers eight florins to his servants, specifying "di fiorini di serve, cioè a ragione di lire 4 per fiorino come s'usa"; Arch. Innocenti, *Estranei,* 633, f. 110r and 113r.

47. On the standard of living in the fifteenth century, see Goldthwaite, *Building of Renaissance Florence,* pp. 331–50.

48. There are four cases of these annual gifts of clothing between 1400 and 1449, four from 1450 to 1499, and two after 1500.

49. Pinto, "Personale, balie e salariati," p. 124.

50. See Heers, *Esclaves et domestiques,* pp. 150–51, on this type of contract.

51. There are thirteen cases well described by the *ricordanze.*

52. The dowry is made up mainly of clothing but almost always includes a net sum. Ric. of Guido Baldovinetti, *Acquisti e doni,* 190, 3, f. 9r, 20 June 1482. Ric. of Tribaldo dei Rossi, Biblioteca Nazionale Centrale, Florence, II, II, 357, f. 47r, 14 Aug. 1488.

53. Ser Giovanni Bandini takes into his house a sickly eight-year-old orphan entrusted to him by her uncle on March 30, 1454: "e vogliola maritare quando mi parrà el tempo ragionevole." The child likes it and refuses to leave in 1458; the dowry is, therefore, fixed at a minimum of 80 *lire* after seven years of service; *Conventi soppressi,* 102, 82, f. 16v. In the same way, Ser Andrea Nacchianti will judge the sum total of the dowry (between 80 and 100 *lire*) "secondo e' sua portamenti"; Arch. Innocenti, *Estranei,* 633, f. 99v, 1 Feb. 1492.

54. Jacopo Attavanti marries under his roof a sawyer dependent on the fortress of Pisa to his servant "raised in our house"; on June 17, 1460, she admits having received, "da me in luogho di padre," the 100 *lire* of her dowry; Arch. Innocenti, *Estranei,* 55, f. 17r.

55. Jacopo Attavanti welcomes in 1461 the ex-concubine (*femina,* surnamed Gioia) of a deceased Pisan who threatened to turn wicked. He promises to "condurla a onore," to marry her well, if she conducts herself well. Nearly two years later, the girl leaves, taking nothing but her clothes and her linen, in order to work elsewhere; Arch. Innocenti, *Estranei,* 55, f. 15v. See another example in the *ricordanze* of Bonaccorso Serchelli, *Conventi soppressi, San Piero a Monticelli,* 185, f. 119r, 22 Nov. 1476.

56. Ric. of Bartolomeo banderaio, *Conventi soppressi, San Piero a Monticelli,* 185, f. 126rv, 1 Nov. 1503. The little girl should be clothed through his efforts, "like any other *servi,*" and receive after eight years or give to her husband 100 *lire* "e queli panni arà a suo dosso e quegli denari e panni sono per sua dotta per detto servito e per amore di Dio." If she leaves before that time, the employer will pay her for the time spent in his house 12 *l.,* 6s., and 8d. a year. Bartolomea leaves after two years and four months in order to work elsewhere.

57. Ric. of Tribaldo dei Rossi, Biblioteca Nazionale Centrale, II, II, 357, f. 47r, 3 June 1499.

58. Other *ricordanze* often give the description of the marriage of a servant under the patronage of her employer, but one does not know what proportion of the hiring totals these matrimonial successes represent (documents in 1300, 1414, 1428, 1430, 1459, 1470, 1480, 1502, 1511).

59. Guarducci and Ottanelli, *I servitori domestici*, pp. 79–80. On medieval slavery in the Mediterranean, see also Heers, *Esclaves et domestiques*. For Florence, the older works of A. Zanelli, *Le schiave orientali a Firenze nei secoli XIV e XV. Contributo alla storia privata* (Florence, 1885); R. Livi, *La schiavitù domestica nei tempi di mezzo e nei moderni. Ricerche storiche di un anthropologo* (Padua, 1928); I. Origo, "The Domestic Enemy: The Eastern Slaves in Tuscany in the Fourteenth and Fifteenth Centuries," *Speculum* 30 (1955): 321–66.

60. C. Klapisch-Zuber, "Parents de sang, parents de lait," Tables 2 and 3 (years 1377, 1378, 1447, 1449, 1450, 1453, 1456, and 1471).

61. On hiring of slaves *cum lacte*, see Heers, *Esclaves et domestiques*, pp. 203–204.

62. Heers, *Esclaves et domestiques*, takes up the earlier work of C. Verlinden.

63. B. Casini, *Aspetti della vita economica e sociale di Pisa dal catasto del 1428–1429*, Biblioteca del "Bollettino storico pisano," Collana storica, 3 (Pisa, 1965), pp. 18–19. G. Cherubini, *Signori, contadini, borghesi. Ricerche sulla società italiana del basso medioevo* (Florence, 1974), pp. 434–35. Herlihy and Klapisch-Zuber, *Les Toscans et leurs familles*, p. 142.

64. Remember that the population of Florence was around 40,000, divided among fewer than 10,000 households in 1472. This population remained stable until the 1470s. See Herlihy and Klapisch-Zuber, *Les Toscans et leurs familles*, p. 183 (p. 74 English ed.) also R. M. Smith, "The People of Tuscany and Their Families in the Fifteenth Century: Medieval or Mediterranean?" *Journal of Family History* VI (1981): 118.

65. According to Origo, "The Domestic Enemy," p. 347, at least 14 percent of the children who entered the hospice of San Gallo and the Innocenti between 1395 and 1485 were children of slaves or servants. R. C. Trexler, "The Foundlings of Florence, 1395–1455," *History of Childhood Quarterly* 1 (1973): 266–68, estimates that a third of the children who entered the Innocenti in 1445 were slaves' children. Pinto, "Personale, balie e salariati," p. 126, n. 55, reports seven children of slaves who came to San Gallo around 1400.

66. L. Sandri, *L'ospedale di S. Maria della Scala di San Gimignano nel Quattrocento. Contributo alla storia dell'infanzia abbandonata*, Società storica della Valdelsa (1982), pp. 93–94.

67. Arch. Innocenti, *Estranei*, 55, f. 5v.

68. *Acquisti e doni*, 190, 3, f. 28v (in 1474).

69. Arch. Innocenti, *Estranei*, 55, f. 17rv (1459–60).

70. *Strozz.*, V., 1749, f. 160, 164, 184 (1447–54).

71. G. Niccolini da Camugliano, *The Chronicles of a Florentine Family, 1200–1460* (London, 1933), pp. 112–13.

72. Some are kept through charity alone; see the ric. of Bernardo Rinieri, *Conventi soppressi*, 95, 212, f. 154r, 161v, 6 Jan. 1459; ric. of Manno Petrucci, *Strozziane*, II, 17, f. 60v, 10 Dec. 1446; ric. of Ser Andrea Nacchianti, Arch. Innocenti, *Estranei*, 633, f. 8r, 18 Sept. 1471.

73. Although 8.5 percent of male servants' contracts forecast a salary higher than

that of the 1415 statutes, only 7 percent of female servants make more than the female scale indicates. In total, 36 percent of female servants are paid at a level equal to or higher than that of the statutes, while 51 percent of men equal or surpass the scale of the statutes.

74. Among our 200 or so female servants, we find a small group of about 15 foreign women, undoubtedly former slaves of diverse origins (2 Russians, 1 Circassian, 3 Ragusans and 1 *schiavone*, 1 Tartar, 2 "blacks," 1 Greek, 1 Albanian, and 3 of indeterminate origin). Their average salary is 8.3 florins a year.

75. Heers, *Esclaves et domestiques*, pp. 152–58.

76. The little *schiavone* Marga, bought from her father by Carlo Strozzi in 1502, could not be resold. Her owner married her fourteen years later. *Strozziane*, IV, 76, f. 132v, 152r.

77. On the Venetian distinction between slaves and *anime*, and on the corresponding legislation, see Heers, *Esclaves et domestiques*, pp. 153–54.

78. A communal law passed in 1468 establishes that fewer slaves but more women than before are seduced by Florentine men; in the future, these seducers will be prosecuted in the same way as suborners of slaves. Zanelli, *Le schiave orientali a Firenze*, p. 70.

79. On the literary evidence concerning the cupidity and dishonesty of female servants, see Guarducci and Ottanelli, *I servitori domestici*, pp. 63–67.

80. Klapisch-Zuber, "Parents de sang, parents de lait," pp. 58–62.

81. Neri di Bicci, *Le ricordanze*, ed. B. Santi (Pisa, 1976), p. 253, 7 Oct. 1465, and p. 325, 21 Sept. 1469. On the feared vulnerability of these young female servants in the sixteenth century, see, however, R. C. Trexler, "A Widows' Asylum of the Renaissance. The Orbatello of Florence," in *Old Age in Preindustrial Society*, ed. Peter N. Stearns (London, 1984), p. 141 and n. 82.

82. *Strozziane*, II. 16 bis, f. 4v, 4 Sept. 1454. We may also note the matter that opposes Morello, the brother of Giovanni Morelli, against their nephew, son of a sister, who impregnated his slave. He pardons the "insult" when his valuable human chattel escapes the childbirth unscathed. *Carte Gherardi, Morelli*, 163, f. 68v (1406).

83. ". . . Che gli piacessi avere riguardo all'onore nostra . . . ," *Strozziane*, II, 16 bis, f. 21v (1456).

84. Neri di Bicci, *Le ricordanze*, p. 347, 26 March 1470.

85. Marco Parenti frees Nastasia in 1493 after thirty-two years of service; after his death in 1497, she will be able to live in a little house near his and have there her clothes, a bed, and her furniture. Nastasia only enjoys her retirement for eight years, dying in a hospital in 1505. *Strozziane*, II, 17bis, f. 52v, 84r, 86rv. Cristofano Rinieri wills his old coat and a house to his slave in 1503; *Conventi soppressi*, 95, 200, f. 1v. Tommaso Minerbetti frees his black slave by his will of 1499, but she must still serve the widow and heirs for ten years at a salary that is reduced by the heirs as soon as the father is buried. The slave dies of *tisicho* four years later; Biblioteca Laurenziana, Florence, *Acquisti*, 229, f. 17v.

86. A. Strozzi, *Lettere di una gentildonna fiorentina del secolo XV ai figliuoli esuli* (Florence, 1877), pp. 104 and 474.

# PART III

## Occupations Related to Female Biology: Wet Nurses and Midwives

In some occupations either female physiology or social custom dictated that only women would be practitioners. The birthing process was exclusively a female ritual in the Middle Ages and the only professional attendant was a midwife. Thus social customs and long practice made this profession exclusively female. In the case of the wet nurse, biology was, of course, the chief determinant; the women involved had to be relatively young and to have had a child of their own so that they had milk. Nursing infants other than a mother's own could be carried on in a number of environments and could prove a useful supplement to a family's income. Among the noble and wealthy families of Europe it was uncommon for a woman to nurse her own child and thus she or more likely her husband would find a wet nurse to live in as a domestic servant, as we have seen in Florence, or the child would be placed in the home of a wet nurse in the country. Women without milk and babies whose mothers died while they were still at the breast would also need a wet nurse. Some cities, such as Montpellier, undertook the care of foundlings and orphans and hired wet nurses. It is this group and their careers that Leah Lydia Otis has investigated.

A profile of the municipal wet nurses shows them to be married women living within Montpellier itself, whose husbands were generally from the humble ranks of craftsmen or agricultural workers. For the vast majority of these women the role of wet nurse would be a once-in-a lifetime experience rather than a continued occupation. Even those who simply undertook the nourishment and rearing of municipal charity children usually did it only once. Perhaps one of the reasons for the reluctance to become a municipal nurse more than once was that the pay was so poor. While the initial salary, paid as it was on a monthly basis, must have looked appealing, when reduced to a daily wage it was about what a woman grape harvester could get. Furthermore, as the wages did not change over the fifteenth century, the real buying power declined. Demand for wet nurses grew, however, as population recovered in the sixteenth century, and as more families became increasingly impoverished women had to sell their milk to help the family economy. Here again we return to the theme of economic and demographic effects on women's labor. As one would expect, the demand for wet nurses increased along with the baby boom of the sixteenth century, but because the economy was unfavorable the nurses' real wages continued to lose value.

The municipalities of preindustrial Europe increasingly concerned themselves with the welfare of their population and sought to provide basic services of wet nursing for their foundlings and midwives for their mothers. In Nuremberg Merry E. Wiesner has shown that the city fathers took a more than ordinary interest in providing for the training, regulation, and payment of midwives who would offer their services to poor women at municipal expense. The council insisted upon an apprenticeship of four years and preferred to have widows or older single women as midwives because they were less distracted by family duties. The midwives' code regulated the amount they could charge clients of various status in the city, the types of drugs that they could administer, their duties in the case of baptizing a baby about to die, and the amount of refreshment, particularly wine, they could accept at a birth. Although the skills of midwifery were learned through apprenticeship, the women who practiced it were apparently literate, for the early sixteenth century saw the publication of an extremely influential manual by Rosslin on midwifery. The midwives of Nuremberg became famous for their skills and were paid salaries that put them among the elite of female workers. If one may talk about a fully professional career for women in preindustrial Europe, it is that of the urban midwife.

For midwives the increased population of the sixteenth century meant that their services were in greater demand: their wages were high, their numbers grew, and the council urged that they take more apprentices. Among female workers that we have seen so far, they were the only ones who profited from the changed economic and demographic conditions of the sixteenth century.

# Municipal Wet Nurses in Fifteenth-Century Montpellier

**M**uch of women's salaried work in preindustrial societies—and even many industrial societies—mirrors those tasks women have traditionally performed in the context of their homes. The domestic servants found in middle- and upper-class homes perform the tasks relegated to the housewife in humbler classes. Prostitutes provide a professional service equivalent to the conjugal debt of the wives in all strata of society. Nurses or child caretakers offer services normally rendered by mothers.

Studies of this kind of women's work in late medieval Europe are rare, owing largely to the difficulties encountered in trying to amass sufficient documentation, usually scattered in diaries and notaries' registers.[1] The fact that two of these normally private services—prostitution and wet nursing— were sometimes channeled through the municipalities in late medieval Languedoc makes it possible to approach the subject from one angle, relying on the documentation generated by municipal administration. The object of analysis in this chapter is information on wet-nursing contained in the municipal financial documents of Montpellier, the most important town of eastern Languedoc.

By the fifteenth century it was generally acknowledged in Montpellier that the municipality had the duty of caring for abandoned children.[2] The town had no institution serving as an orphanage, but relied rather on individuals who were paid to take care of the children in their own homes. These people were referred to as nurses or wet nurses (*nourrice* or *nutrix*), as their principal task was to feed (*nutrire*) or breastfeed (*lactare*) the children. There is little in the way of narrative sources concerning these special municipal employees, but the municipal account books, many of which have survived from the fifteenth century, list methodically the people hired and the payments made to them.

The nature of the sources exploited presents important methodological

83

problems. Only a handful of account books have survived from the first six decades of the century,[3] and from 1460 to 1498 there are five lacunae,[4] making systematic analysis of the material available difficult. The information presented is also frustratingly laconic, as is typical of account books. But uneven and sparse documentation is indeed the classic problem facing the medievalist interested in social history, and the information concerning this kind of work in particular is so rare for the Middle Ages that any source is precious. The financial documents give at least an indication of the kind of person who nursed for the municipality, and the nature of the work involved.

Municipal wet nursing was a booming business—or rather, an expanding service—in the second half of the fifteenth century. In the early fifteenth century, only an occasional mention is made of a person being paid to take care of a municipal foundling.[5] In the early 1440s, the payments become regular, but to only one employee, whereas by 1450 five women were hired. Throughout the 1460s an average of seven people a year were paid to nurse the children; by the 1470s the average had climbed to eighteen a year, and in the eighties, twenty-four a year. In the last decade of the century the average number of nurses hired annually reached twenty-six; forty were paid in the year 1496 alone.[6]

During the thirty-eight years studied, 305 people were paid for their services as nurses. One must refer to people rather than women, for out of the 305 persons listed, 30 are men with no mention of women. In the majority of cases, however, the men were probably only collecting the pay, whereas a woman—usually a spouse, but perhaps a sister or even a domestic servant—was actually rendering the service in question. We may take the example of one of the most frequently cited employees: William Blat, scribe, received a total of seventy-four payments over a twelve-year period (from 1472 to 1485) for caring for two little girls; only twice in all those years is reference made to his wife, Guillermina, whereas it is clearly she who was looking after the children.

Of the women listed (275), the majority (243, 88 percent) are identified as being married women at the moment of first payment, seven of whom were widowed during the course of their services. Twenty-five women (9 percent) were widows at the time of the first payment; most widows were "dry" nurses, but eight were paid for breastfeeding. Two women in the series are identified as mothers, and two as sisters.[7] Only rarely is a woman not identified as being married, widowed, or otherwise related to a man,[8] although the absence of the name of a husband or late husband does not necessarily mean that the woman in question was single. Most married women are identified by their first names, followed by the full names of their husbands, but some bear second or family names of their own, making reference to the husband's full name not essential in order to identify the woman. Thus a woman who began her child-care services in 1480 is often identified in the books as Thoneta Cabassude without mention of her husband, Peter Tyrasson.[9]

All but five of the people hired as nurses in Montpellier in the fifteenth century were residents of the town. Three women were from the outskirts of Montpellier: one from the village of Laverune, three miles west of the town,[10] one from Teyran, eight miles north of Montpellier,[11] and another from Castelnau, a mile and a half east of the town.[12] Two other child caretakers were from the diocese of Nimes.[13]

In almost two-thirds of the cases listed in the municipal account books (192 out of 305), the social status of the nurse is indicated. They were generally of humble status. Frances Pojada, spice seller (speciayre), probably the most socially prestigious person mentioned, was paid only once, in December 1472, and that for feeding the daughter of a carpenter who died of the plague that year,[14] not for caring for an abandoned child.

Among those whose profession—or whose husband's profession—is indicated, there is a roughly equal number of craftsmen (eighty-seven) and agricultural workers (cultor or lavorador, eighty-one),[15] whose presence within city walls was typical of southern French towns. One may assume that most of the unidentified persons were engaged in one of these two professions. In general, scribes tended not to forget to specify the status of an important person in society. One may note, moreover, that in the decade of the 1470s, when all but three persons out of seventy were identified professionally, the above-mentioned spice seller and a master craftsman are the most socially prestigious persons mentioned.

A large number of crafts (thirty-one) were represented; nurses and nurses' husbands included six bakers (fornier), six stone cutters (peyrier), five tailors (sartor), and five dyers (textor). Municipal wet nursing seems to have been an activity particularly popular among the wives of carpenters (fustier), for considering that these craftsmen were by no means the most numerous in Montpellier, a disproportionately great number (fifteen) of them are found in the list of municipal nurses.[16] Most of the craftsmen mentioned were of a relatively humble status, as only two are referred to as Master (magister):[17] the painter Nicolas Leonard, who cared for the girl Johanna and eventually adopted her in 1480, and who was paid by the municipality for his work in the great church Notre Dame des Tables,[18] and the master carpenter Vincent Boyer, whose widow, Johanna Fornière, nursed a certain Johanna for five months in 1480.[19]

If one analyzes the professions by decades, one notices that whereas agricultural workers and their wives outnumbered craftsmen in the 1460s and 1470s (fifteen to twelve in the first case, thirty-four to twenty-seven in the second), the opposite is true in the last two decades of the fifteenth century: there were twelve craftsmen and only seven agricultural workers in the 1480s, and thirty-seven craftsmen as opposed to twenty-three agricultural workers in the 1490s. It would be tempting to see in this trend a pauperization of craftsmen's wives, who turned increasingly to rounding out the family budget by engaging in this rather ill-paid work. The presence of numerous unidentified persons in the later decades makes it impossible, however, to confirm such a trend, and reduces it to the level of speculation.

Members of what might be called the medieval "tertiary sector" were also represented among municipal nurses and husbands of nurses. It is not surprising to find four "hospitalers:" Gilleta, wife of William de Veytoris, hospitaler of St. James in 1403,[20] Marguarita Clamadella of the hospital of St. Martha in 1461,[21] Anthonia, wife of Master Alardin du Ponchel of St. Eloi from 1488 to 1491,[22] and the wife of John of Dijon of the hospital St. James in 1493 and 1495.[23] What is perhaps surprising is to see no more than four such people, as hospital work and charity were closely connected in the Middle Ages; the small budget for municipal wet nursing in the Provençal town of Tarascon, for instance, came from hospital coffers.[24]

A scribe (novel scriptor de lettra formada) and five sergeants are included among nurses' husbands. The largest category of the tertiary sector represented is that of municipal employees: nine "squires" (scutiffer) of the municipality are listed as having nursed, or having had their wives nurse, municipal foundlings. This social group enjoyed a greater than average "longevity" in this service: in only one case was the child kept less than a year and in two cases "squires" and their wives kept the same child for more than four years.[25] They also seem to have enjoyed a somewhat preferential salary.[26]

Nurses were usually assigned only one child at a time. Only in two cases were two children assigned simultaneously to the same woman. In 1490 Margarita, wife of Thadeus Michie, breastfed two boys (duos pueros) for a month; she was paid no more, however, than the standard rate for breast-feeding one child.[27] Anthonia, wife of the agricultural worker John Ferreyres, on the other hand, was paid for the keep of each of the children she looked after simultaneously from November 1493 to June 1494: Columbeta, whom she breastfed, and Bartholomew, whom she simply nourished.[28] In all other cases, only one child at a time was taken care of by a municipal nurse.

Of all the municipal nurses recorded in the financial documents of the fifteenth century, the vast majority (279 out of 305, 91 percent) took care of no more than one child. Only 17 nurses cared for two children, 7 for three, and 1 each for four and five children successively. For most of the employees involved, municipal child caretaking was a once-in-a-lifetime venture.

The majority of municipal nurses not only limited their engagement to one child but cared for that child for a very short period of time. One can calculate the period of time for 266 of the 279 nurses who cared for only one child; 174 of them (65 percent) kept that child for less than one year, the shortest time being a mere eight days.[29] Fifty-six (21 percent) kept them from between one and three years, only 26 (10 percent) for between three and five years, and a mere 10 (4 percent) for more than five years, the record being over eight years.

Even those people taking on two children successively usually did so for a short period of time. In sixteen out of seventeen cases the length of time can be calculated; ten nurses cared for the children for a period totaling less than one year; four for a period from one to four years, one for seven years, and one, Guillarmina, wife of the scribe William Blat, for eleven years and two months, in a veritable career that spanned thirteen years.

Of the seven women looking after three children successively, five worked for a total of less than three years (in only one case did the "career" span more than three years). Anthonia, wife of the agricultural worker James Melet, worked for a total of six years and seven months, taking care of three girls successively in a career spanning ten years, from 1473 to 1483,[30] and Peyronella, wife of the bolter (baralerius) John Bux, nursed two girls and a boy for ten years and ten months over a fifteen-year period, from 1478 to 1493.[31]

Anthonia, wife of the agricultural worker John Aygalene, had the longest career; over a nineteen-year period, from 1479 to 1498, she spent ten years and nine months caring, successively, for three girls and a boy.[32] Anthonia, wife of Alardin du Ponchel, nursed five children successively, but only for short periods (a total of one year and nine months) over a short span of time (three years).[33] This short but intense bout of municipal nursing was certainly related to the fact that Anthonia's husband was master hospitaler of St. Eloi, Montpellier's most important municipal hospital. The number of women to have taken on several children over a long period of time was very small; even they were not employed constantly, but often waited several years before taking on a new municipal child. They may perhaps have engaged in private wet nursing during those interims. And for the vast majority of women, taking on only one child for a brief period, municipal nursing was a very short-lived venture, not a veritable career.

The laconic nature of the documents makes it difficult to detect the attitude of municipal nurses to their charges. It would seem natural that nurses should have taken an emotional as well as financial interest in their work, especially those who kept the same child for a number of years. It would seem to have been fairly common for the children to be named after the nurse or nurse's husband through the 1460s,[34] but this custom seems to have died out afterwards. There is only one example of a nurse adopting his charge: In 1480 Nicolas Leonard, master painter, adopted Johanna, whom he had looked after for almost two years.[35] One may also note that taking care of abandoned children was an activity that could be engaged in by volunteers as well as by paid professionals, as is often the case in charity work. In 1496, the child John, who had been kept for twenty-four days by Katherina, wife of Sebastian Dict, was handed over to Master Peter Amelet and his wife, Alexandra, who promised to take care of the child "for the love of God."[36]

Such a case was exceptional, however; caring for municipal foundlings was generally salaried work. Two important developments can be observed concerning the wages of wet nurses: the decline in income throughout the century, to some extent in absolute terms, but more strikingly in real wages; and the distinction made by the consuls between wages for those women breastfeeding children and for those using other means of nourishing them.

It was during the 1460s that the consuls developed the custom of usually paying nurses one of two fixed sums, according to whether the child in question was breastfed or not. Typically the breastfeeding woman was paid 17s. 6d. a month,[37] whereas the person feeding the child other foods received only 12s. 6d. a month. This distinction would seem to indicate a recognition of the value of mother's milk for children, and/or the need for nutritional supplements to the lactating woman. It was only in the 1470s, however, that the municipal scribes began to note more carefully whether the activity of the nurse was to breastfeed (*lactare*) or merely to feed (*nutrire*).[38]

Thanks to this distinction, it is possible to get an idea of how long the municipal wet nurse breastfed, by studying those cases in which the transition from breastfeeding to other food is recorded. There are thirty-eight such recorded cases of weaning; the time during which the nurse gave the breast ranges from one month to four years,[39] the median length of time being one year, nine and a half months. In twelve of the above thirty-eight cases, however, the child had already changed hands during the breastfeeding stage. The accumulated lactation period in these cases ranges from ten months to two years, ten and a half months, the median being two years, one week. If one readjusts for these twelve cases, the median for the thirty-eight rises from one year, nine and a half months to one year, ten and a half months.

Were the children newborns when given to a wet nurse for the first time? Indication of age is given only rarely, but the introductory paragraphs to the lists of nurses that are present in the account books starting in 1479 indicate that the consuls took only those children "whose parents were unknown" (*quorum parentes ignorantur*), a policy that made it difficult for a resident of the town to deposit on the town-hall steps a child who was already a few months or years old. So one can conclude with few reservations that the typical lactation period of somewhat less than two years corresponds more or less to the age of the children at weaning.

Although the two-tier system of wages (17s. 6d. for breastfeeding, 12s. 6d. for others) was typical in the late fifteenth century, other rates exist in that period, the rationale for which is nowhere explained. In two cases we see a transitional period of nine months after breastfeeding when the nurse was paid 15s. per month before falling to 12s. 6d. a month.[40] There are numerous cases of people being paid only 10s. a month; two where the sum was 8s. 9d., three at 7s. 6d., and two, a mere 5s. a month.[41]

The wages of nurses were low—even a woman grape harvester earned about 1s. 3d. a day in fifteenth-century Languedoc, and that wage itself was half of what a man earned.[42] The wages of nurses were not only low, however; they declined throughout the century. The decline was at first in absolute terms; whereas in the forties, fifties, and early sixties it had been common to pay nurses a *livre* or more a month,[43] by 1464 17s. 6d. was the maximal rate possible.

The decline was in relative rather than absolute terms in the later decades—that is, it was a decline in real wages or buying power. The two-tier system remained stable throughout the end of the fifteenth century and the first half of the sixteenth century, a time of inflation when food prices in particular were rising considerably. Real wages were falling for most workers in that time period, but the situation was particularly dramatic for these municipal employees, whose wages were absolutely frozen at the same level for exactly a century, from 1463 to 1563.[44]

One would like to know much more, but the financial documents reveal only the minimum, enough to give but a sketchy profile of the typical municipal wet nurse in fifteenth-century Montpellier. Usually a married woman, the wife of an agricultural worker or a craftsman of modest standing, and a resident of the town, the typical nurse engaged but briefly in municipal nursing activity, taking in only one child, for a very short period of time, usually several months. The pay she received was greater if she breastfed (which she probably did for no more than two years), but in cases of both breastfeeding and other feeding, the wages were low, and their buying power was steadily diminished by inflation. If increasing numbers of women were hired by the municipality in this capacity, it was not because of the financial attractiveness of the wages, but because of the demographic situation; whereas only three children were supported by the municipality in 1450, the number had risen to at least twenty-one by 1498. The increased number of abandoned children and the degradation in the real wages of the

women who cared for them are both indications of the trends of the times:
the demographic increase and the "pauperization" of a large portion of the
population. The early sixteenth century was "hard times" for many in
Languedoc, but hardest of all, it would seem, for women and children.

## Notes

1. On prostitution in late medieval Europe, see my *Prostitution in Medieval
Society: the History of an Urban Institution in Languedoc* (Chicago: University of
Chicago Press, 1985), which includes an ample bibliography. Domestic servitude
and wet-nursing are discussed in a book devoted principally to medieval slavery:
Jacques Heers, *Esclaves et domestiques au moyen-âge dans la monde méditerranéen*
(Paris, 1981). The bibliography on wet-nursing in early modern times is larger;
Elisabeth Badinter presents a synthesis of recent research in her *L'amour en plus,
l'histoire de l'amour maternel, XVII<sup>e</sup>–XX<sup>e</sup> siècle* (Paris, 1980), which has been translated into English.
2. I intend to study this municipal service and the children involved in a future
article. Richard Trexler has studied the care of abandoned children in Florence in
his "The Foundlings of Florence, 1395–1455," *History of Childhood Quarterly* 1
(1973): 259–84.
3. The following books have survived: 1403 (529), 1432 (530), 1441 (531),
1442 (533), 1443 (534), and 1450 (535). The dates indicate the year as calculated
in the fifteenth century in Montpellier, from April to March 31; thus the book from
1403 runs in fact from April 1, 1403, to March 31, 1404. The books are cited
henceforth by the medieval date, but any precise date given in the article has been
converted to the modern style. The books are written both in Latin and in Occitan-
ian ("Provençal").
4. The books missing at the moment of classification of the financial series
include those from 1466, 1467, 1475, 1484, and 1487. The books from 1486 (568)
and 1499 (582) have since been misplaced. That from 1489 (571) was misplaced
while I worked on the series; it has since been found. Not only was it too late to
incorporate it into my research, but the state of the book makes it virtually illegible
in any case. The whole series of books (housed in the municipal archives of Montpellier) was in fact water-damaged several years ago, and some passages are extremely difficult to decipher. The series is now temporarily unavailable to scholars,
pending restoration.
5. The children nursed were not always foundlings. In 1403, for example,
Johanna, wife of William Bonet, was paid for feeding one of the children of a
municipal employee who was a poor widower, Aymeric Pozata, *scutiffer* (529, 9v).
6. The number of nurses paid each year is as follows:

| 1403—2 | 1450— 5 | 1464— 7 | 1471—11 | 1477—21 |
| 1432—2 | 1460— 8 | 1465— 5 | 1472—12 | 1478—30 |
| 1441—1 | 1461— 7 | 1468—11 | 1473—20 | 1479—23 |
| 1442—1 | 1462— 5 | 1469— 5 | 1474—18 | 1480—23 |
| 1443—1 | 1463—10 | 1470— 7 | 1476—20 | 1481—24 |

| 1482—34 | 1488—17 | 1492—16 | 1496—40 |
|---------|---------|---------|---------|
| 1483—27 | 1490—16 | 1493—28 | 1497—30 |
| 1485—22 | 1491—12 | 1494—33 | 1498—34 |
|         |         | 1495—28 |         |

7. Thoneta, "mater Francie filie sue et magistri Berenge Cabirii," 579 (1496), 66v, breastfed Johanna for three months. Maiota, mother of Guillerta, wife of Thomas Mere, breastfed Augustin for twenty-five days in 1493 (576, 40r); her daughter had breastfed William for nine months in 1492–93 (574, 576 passim). Catherina, sister of Leonarda, married to the fish-monger Matthew Coty, breastfed little Anthoneta in her sister's stead during the latter's illness in 1474 (555, 34r). Margaret, sister of John Chauchardi, took over the care of little Anthony from her sister-in-law in 1497 (579, 99r); the child stayed a year and a half with the latter, then two and a half years with the former.

8. Only three women are listed independently, without further identification: Marguarita Clamadella, hospitaler of St. Martha in Montpellier, 537 (1461), 42v–43r; Johanna Clamadella, apparently related to the above, 537 (1461) 64v–65r, and Guillemerta Primilhohla, 577 (1494) 52v.

9. 561 (1480)–565 (1483) passim.

10. Johanna, wife of William Bonet in 1403 (529, 9v).

11. Dalphine, wife and then widow of Laurence Vedier, agricultural worker, from 1468 to 1470 (544, 546, 548 passim).

12. Blanche, wife of Peter Miquel, agricultural worker, in 1471–72 (550, 43r, 552, 3r).

13. John Teysser (530 [1432], 7r, 28r; 535 [1450], 14v) was a resident of Monoblet, near Le Vigan. Berengaria, wife and then widow of John Cornairet, who lived in Santairargues (559 [1478]–563 [1482] passim), cared for little Ludovic for four and a half years.

14. 552 (1472), 21v. They took her in only because they saw that no one else was willing to feed her: ". . . per lo noyrement d·una petita filha, lacal era de Jehan Rinoche, fustier de Montpelhier, local moric de l·empidimia; et sa molher et lodit Pojada, vezent que ladita filha moria de faim, et no s·y trobaria que la volgues alimentar, et la tenc per certain temps et la noiric."

15. Among the craftsmen are three ortolan (gardeners), whom one may choose to put in the category of agricultural workers.

16. For an indication of the number of members in each profession, see André Gouron, La réglementation des métiers en Languedoc (Thèse—Droit—Montpellier, 1957), pp. 95–101.

17. Masters were generally owners of their own shops, and the other members of the profession, valets and apprentices, their employees. For the hierarchy of the professions, see Gouron, Métiers, pp. 241–78.

18. 559 (1478), 26, 66v, 106v; 560 (1479), 58r, 62r.

19. 561 (1480), 50v–51r.

20. 529 (1403), 18r.

21. 537 (1461), 42v–43v.

22. 569 (1488), 572 (1490) and 573 (1491) passim.

23. 576 (1493), 70v; 578 (1495), 4r.

24. The financial series includes payments made to Leonarda Martina, wife of Anniel Terssa, by the rector of the hospital in August 1496 and January 1497 (AM Tarascon, CC 146).

25. Berengar Garmand was paid for one month's care of Peter in 1464 (542);

Anthonia, wife of Peter lo Mercier, kept the girl Mathea for four and a half years, from 1474 to 1488 (555, 556, 558, 559 passim); Anthonia, wife of Anthony Allegre, cared for young Anthony for four years and two months, from 1476 to 1480 (556, 558, 559, 560, 561 passim).

26. See below, n. 38.

27. 572 (1490), 7v.

28. She had breastfed Bartholomew until February of 1493. If her resuming breastfeeding nine months later was not a case of relactation, it would indicate that she was nursing another child (her own, or that of a private individual) in the meantime. 576 (1493), 2v, 52r, 70r, 76v, and 577 (1494), 50r, 54r, 60r.

29. The reader stands warned that the following statistics on "longevity" effectively underestimate somewhat the average length of child care, as the missing account books are not represented. (The only cases I have not considered are those from before 1460 and those beginning in 1498 which probably continued beyond that year, that is, where payment is made up to the end of the book.) The only other alternative would have been to eliminate all ambiguous cases (there are thirty-seven), that is, where a nurse was paid through the last month of the account book preceding a lacuna. These ambiguous cases concern, however, a much larger than average number of examples of long-term child care, so eliminating them would have had more or less the same effect on the statistics—shortening "longevity"—as the calculation based on available information. The distortion, at any rate, is minimal.

30. 553, 555, 558, 559, 560, 562, 563, 565 passim.

31. 559–563, 565, 567, 573, 574, 576 passim.

32. 560–563, 567, 569, 572, 576–581 passim.

33. See above, n. 22.

34. The presence of unusual names, such as Gilleta, Loyssa, and Dionisia, makes it possible to rule out pure chance.

35. 559 (1478), 26r, 66v, 106v; 560 (1479), 58r, 62r. "Dictus Magister Nicholaus Leonardi in presencia nobilis viri Johannis Noguerii consuli dicte ville obtulit acetero nutrire et alimentare dictam Johannam eiusdem Leonardi propriis sumptibus et non sumptibus ville aut alterius, de quo dictus consul pro se et aliis consulibus fuit contentus de quibus."

36. 579 (June 1, 1496), 70r. ". . . quam diem consules tradiderunt Alexandre uxori magistri Petri Ameleti, qui Ameleti promisit lactare et nutrire facere amore dei et sua causa."

37. The first time this sum is mentioned is in June 1463, when Johannetta, wife of the *scutiffer* John Ayon, was paid 17s. 6d. a month for keeping Berengran (541, 8v and passim). The abbreviations *l.*, *s.*, and *d.* stand for *livres*, *sous*, and *deniers* (1l. = 20s.; 1s. = 12d.).

38. When the nurse was usually paid every three or four months, a transition within that period was noted, for instance, in 1484 Margarita, wife of the agricultural worker Deodat Galibert, was paid 30s. for two month's work: "scilicet pro mense martii xviis. vid. quod lactabat, et pro mense aprilis, xiis. vid." (565 [1483], 29v). There seem to have been some exceptions to the rule, however, as in the case of Anthonia, who nourished (*nutrire*) Anthony for four years and two months at the rate of 17s. 6d. (from 1476 to 1480). The privileged rate was probably due to the fact that her husband, Anthony Allegre, was a municipal employee (*scutiffer*). We see the wife of another *scutiffer* (Anthonia, wife of Peter lo Mercier) paid the same amount for the simple "nourishing" of the girl Mathea from 1474 to 1479 (see above, n. 25).

39. The latter is quite atypical, the second longest period recorded being only two years, eight months.

40. Jaumeta, wife of the agricultural worker William Chaneau, and Katherina, wife of the locksmith Peter Colaric, were both paid at this rate from June 1474 to February 1475 (555, passim).

41. Payments of 5s. a month were made to Dionisia la Banastiera, wife of the agricultural worker William Calmel, in 1463 and 1464 (541, 542 passim), and to Gailhard Alboyn in 1482 (563, 63v, 67r).

42. On women's wages, see Emmanuel Le Roy Ladurie, *Les Paysans de Languedoc* (Paris, 1966) I, pp. 276–79, and II, p. 859.

43. The highest rate recorded was that paid to Johanetta, wife of John Pegorier, in 1450: 1l. 2s. 2d. a month (535, 4v). The last woman to have been paid 1l. per month was Florencia, wife of the carpenter Peter Medici, in September 1463 (541, 64r).

44. Le Roy Ladurie uses Montpellier's wet nurses as one example of female "pauperization" in this period (*Paysans* I, pp. 276–79).

Merry E. Wiesner 6

# Early Modern Midwifery:
# A Case Study

The most important occupation in which women were involved during the medieval and early modern period, in terms of impact on society as a whole and recognition by government and church authorities, was midwifery. The midwife's vital role is often overlooked by modern historians, however, as they consider her only in passing while focusing on other developments. Medical historians tend to limit themselves to examinations of the development of obstetrics and gynecology, tracing the advances in the field made by university-trained physicians beginning in the early modern period, viewing the midwife as superstitious and bungling. They often skip from the theorists of ancient Greece to the Chamberlen brothers (who invented the forceps) in seventeenth-century England.[1] This ignores the fact, however, that the midwife's practices and methods during the intervening 1500 years were no more bizarre or occult than those of contemporary physicians, and were based on beliefs about the body and bodily processes current during the time period in which she worked.

Historians have noted the frequent identification of witches as midwives and have seen a decline in the status and role of the midwife during the sixteenth and seventeenth centuries because she was tainted with witchcraft, particularly in France and England. They point out that witches and midwives were often members of the same social group—poor, elderly women, often widows, with some knowledge of herbs and charms. This decline in midwifery, they feel, allowed for the entrance of male midwives—accouchers—and physicians into the field.[2] One wonders if the cause and effect relationship here is not the reverse, however, i.e., that the entrance of men into the field pushed the female practitioners out, as was the case in so many other fields. In addition, the very identification of witches and midwives shows that the community recognized the power which the midwives had— they *were* able to make the difference between life and death, just as witches

94

were perceived to. Even during the period of "decline," cities and rulers took as great care with the regulation of midwives as they did with the regulation of physicians and surgeons. They did this because the midwife had an extremely important role, not only handling nearly every birth, but also performing additional medical services, distributing public welfare, serving various religious functions, and giving testimony in legal cases.

Her multifaceted role can be seen clearly in a close examination of midwifery in one community. For this I have chosen the city of Nuremberg. Nuremberg had a system of midwives which was the envy of and later model for those in many other parts of Germany. Although there are no means of determining their actual effect on infant mortality, the fact that Nuremberg's midwives were sought by other cities and rulers indicates that their skills and teaching were highly regarded. Unfortunately, there are no diaries or case books from Nuremberg midwives, so it is difficult to perceive how they saw themselves or defined their own role, but the activities in which they were involved were so varied and their testimony taken so seriously that they are clearly seen as able and trustworthy. This despite their low social position, evidenced by the fact that they are always referred to by first name in court records, city council minutes, and private diaries.

## Historical Background

Nuremberg's population grew from about 23,000 in 1430 to about 54,000 in 1620, making it one of the three largest cities in Germany, along with Cologne and Augsburg.[3] A small city council (Rat) governed the city, making all decisions from the most important—foreign policy, declarations of war, religious change—to the most trivial—the permitted width of fur trimmings, the price of fruit and nuts, the proper method for washing clothing. Unlike most other German cities, there were no independent guilds, and all organized crafts had to swear an oath of obedience to the council. As a free imperial city, Nuremberg was not controlled by any secular or ecclesiastical prince, but swore allegiance only to the emperor.

During the fifteenth and sixteenth centuries, the city was a commercial and cultural center whose merchants and products were to be found throughout Europe. The work of her goldsmiths, artists, and printers was in demand everywhere, and the new ideas of humanism and later Protestantism found ready acceptance among the leaders of the city. The city council assumed control of public welfare and hygiene very early on, and Nuremberg's hospitals and system of poor relief would be emulated by other cities.

As in other social and intellectual concerns, the city stood in the forefront in the area of midwifery as well, first organizing and developing a system of midwives in the early fifteenth century. The first record of a midwife active in the city dates from 1381, and midwives first appeared as sworn city officials in the *Aemterbüchlein*, the list of all occupational groups required to take an annual oath before the council, in 1417.[4] Sixteen women were listed this first year; their number varied from eight to twenty-one over the next 200 years.

In 1463, the council instituted the office of *Ehrbare Frauen*, women from the patrician class given responsibility to oversee and control the midwives. They had no medical function, but assigned midwives and distributed food and clothing to indigent mothers, as well as disciplining women they felt were not living up to their midwives' oath. They were responsible for making an annual report to the city council immediately after Easter, reporting any problems or deficiencies among the midwives. The number of women in this office was surprisingly large, varying from seventeen when first established to a high of fifty-five in 1530, but then dropping throughout the sixteenth century to as few as nine by 1620, to two one hundred years later.[5] From about 1560 on, each year's *Aemterbüchlein* includes a note calling for the appointment of more *Ehrbare Frauen*, with no success. It appears that the office was no longer seen as prestigious by upper-class women.

Acting on the report of the *Ehrbare Frauen* and complaints by the midwives, the council created another office in 1549, the *Geschworene Weiber*.[6] These women were the wives and widows of craftsmen and minor officials who were to act as overseers, watching for the misuse of public welfare or any other infractions, and helping midwives in particularly difficult cases. Although no specific reason is given for the creation of the *Geschworene Weiber*, this was a period of more rigid social stratification in Nuremberg, leading one to speculate that the *Ehrbare Frauen* no longer wished to mix with the lowest classes, and called for this new office to deal with the poorest women.

The council paid the *Geschworene Weiber* twelve Rhenish gulden (fl.) annually, although the upper-class *Ehrbare Frauen* were not paid anything. The *Geschworene Weiber* were also given small tips by the midwives and the expectant mothers, but they were warned by the council not to demand or take too much "food, drink, or payment."[7] Their number varied from four to ten from 1550 to 1650.

The total number of women involved in the city's midwife system thus increased from sixteen in 1417 to a high of sixty-five in 1530 and then stabilized at forty to fifty for the next one hundred years. Of these, about one-third were active midwives.

As noted above, the population of Nuremberg during the late medieval and early modern period ranged between 25,000 and 50,000. Although a determination of the exact birthrate for any area before the advent of accurate record-keeping is impossible, several studies of preindustrial Europe have found the birthrate to be roughly 40–50 births per thousand population.[8] Thus one would expect somewhere between 1000 and 2500 births per year in the city.

With the number of midwives varying between eight and eighteen, the number of births per midwife would have varied between 60 and 300 a year. This latter pace—an average of nearly one birth a day—would have been very difficult to maintain and would not have allowed for any postnatal care, which midwives were also often paid to do. Thus one can understand the constant concern of the council that more women be trained, particularly whenever the total number of midwives in the city dropped below ten.

These figures may be somewhat high, because there were undoubtedly some women who gave birth without the aid of a trained midwife. If a woman had already had numerous children without complications, was generally healthy, and had friends and relatives who could attend to her, she may not have summoned a midwife. If the child was born prematurely, there may not have been time for one to reach her. Certainly women in the rural areas during this period did not expect the services of a midwife for each delivery.

However, given the fact that the council provided for the services of a midwife for every indigent mother, and carefully spelled out the proper charges for women of all social classes, one may assume that most births in the city itself were handled by a midwife. Three to five births per week was probably average for an experienced midwife.

## Fees and Regulations

Midwives' actual fees varied with the social class of the mother involved. Sebastian Welser, a wealthy cloth merchant and council member, recorded in 1534 that he paid the midwife 1 1/2 fl. for a delivery and 1 fl. more for the care of his wife during the three months after delivery.[9] Wives of craftsmen would generally pay half that, and wives of day laborers even less. In 1561, midwives were granted 42 pfennig by the council for caring for indigent women.[10] Midwives were also rewarded for medical services during times of an epidemic.

These payments compare relatively well with the salaries of craftsmen and journeymen, depending on how many births a midwife attended. Carl Sachs has determined the average salary for journeymen and apprentices in 1510 to be 15–33 pfennig a day, and that of a master 47–60 d, depending on the time of year and length of the work day.[11] Because of inflation during the sixteenth century, the payment granted to midwives for indigent mothers in

1561, 42 d, was probably very close to the average daily salary of a journey-man at that time. As one birth was all any midwife could physically handle in a day, the salaries are roughly comparable.

The council encouraged experienced midwives to move into the city by granting them free citizenship rights and often an initial salary as well. In some cases they seem to have paid the usual fee, but generally their entry in the new citizen lists (*Neubürgerlisten*) is accompanied by the note *dedimus*, i.e., granted free of charge.[12]

Only in very unusual cases was a midwife allowed to leave the city and render services elsewhere, despite the high position and prestige of those who requested one. In 1496, a woman was sent to Heidelberg to serve the wife of a Count Palatine; he had personally written asking for a midwife.[13] In 1506 the city of Ulm asked for one, and in 1541, Dorothea, the wife of Duke Albrecht of Saxony, did as well.[14] In the first case the council refused to send one, as it felt none could be spared.[15] The decision in the latter case is not recorded. The city of Heilbronn requested an experienced midwife to teach local women in 1606, and the council again refused, claiming a shortage in the city at that time would not allow it.[16]

The regulations governing midwives were promulgated in a series of ordi-nances, to be given to all of them annually before the oath-swearing. The first systematic ordinance was put forth in 1522, with amendments and alterations made as new problems arose.[17] From these ordinances, and the day-to-day cases before the city council, we can get an idea of the wide variety of activities in which midwives were involved. The most basic rules concerned their conduct vis-à-vis pregnant women. They were to treat all alike, rich and poor, and especially not to leave a poor woman to attend a rich one for whom they would be paid more. No birth was to be hurried; if a midwife needed rest during a particularly long or difficult birth, she was to call another sworn midwife, and not simply her maid. She could be fined five fl. and deprived of her office for leaving a woman in need. Excessive wine-drinking was repeatedly forbidden.

Midwives were not allowed to dispense strong drugs, only "common medicines, juices, nectars and the like, that cannot be mishandled easily but used safely every day."[18] These they could obtain from an apothecary, however, without referral by a doctor. If their patients could not pay for the medicine themselves, the city paid the apothecary.

The period of apprenticeship for a midwife was four years. Apprentices were required to stay with one mistress the whole period, or else prove that they had left through no fault of their own; this restriction is the same as those in other craft regulations. If the council found a maid had valid reasons for leaving her first mistress, such as cruel treatment, the maid would be assigned to another. As punishment, the old mistress could take on no new apprentices until her previous one had finished her training, even though she was now learning with another woman.[19]

Midwives were admonished to take on no "young, light-headed" girls. A later amendment forbade married women with families as well, for fear they would be too busy with their own concerns and housework. Apprentices could not be sent to any case alone until they had served one year, and then only to women who had already had several children. Unlike most occupations, there was no required grace period after one apprentice left before another could be taken on. On the contrary, the council asked that another be accepted within three months.

Bonuses were offered to encourage the acceptance of an apprentice. In 1483, four midwives were granted two to three lb. a year when they took on apprentices; the following year this was raised to five pounds.[20] In 1517, the council increased this even more: "From now on, the sworn midwives are to be given 32 lb. to teach each maid, but [payable] only when she has completed her instruction and sworn her oath."[21]

During the middle of the sixteenth century, the council called for even stronger measures to encourage the teaching of more apprentices: "Each midwife is to be told once again to be prepared to take on a qualified apprentice, or the council will punish her in earnest."[22] This did have some effect for several years.

Further changes were made in the seventeenth century, ordering midwives and their maids to report any miscarriages, forbidding the marriage of any maid during her training period, and suggesting more midwives be sent to the rural areas which the city controlled.[23]

A picture of the typical midwife, or at least one which the council hoped was typical, emerges clearly from these ordinances. She was a widow, or an older, unmarried woman, not especially well-off financially as she did not have her own household. The fact that admonitions against married midwives continued indicates that not all were of the marital status considered proper, however.

## Delivery Procedures

We must first examine the most important activities—delivery and child care. The regulations and ordinances give us little information about actual techniques and methods, but the early sixteenth century saw the publication of an extremely influential midwives' manual which does address these questions, and which covers the beliefs about gynecology and obstetrics which were certainly current in Nuremberg. This was Eucharius Rösslin's *Den Swangern frawen und hebammen Roszgarten* (The rosegarden for midwives and pregnant women). It was first printed in 1513 by Martin Flach in

Strassburg, with two more editions printed in Hagenau that same year. Nearly 100 additional editions were published during the next 200 years in various languages—English, French, Latin, Dutch, Italian, Spanish and Czech.[24] It was always illustrated with woodcuts and engravings, although these varied from edition to edition.

Although objections may be raised against using a printed manual as a source of popular beliefs, in the case of the *Rosengarten* this may be justified on three grounds. First, midwives seem to have been much more literate than has previously been assumed. In Nuremberg, for example, they were given printed copies of their oath and of baptism regulations so that they would be able to refer to them if questions arose; no provision was made to have these read to midwives who were illiterate.[25] The number of editions and widespread popularity of Rösslin's manual and its copies also point to a large body of readers interested in its advice. Second, although midwives actually learned through an apprentice system and never from a manual alone, the *Rosengarten* gives hints and tips for medicines and techniques that could easily have been adopted by the most enlightened midwives and then passed on to their assistants and apprentices. Third, although Rösslin names only classical authors as the source of his ideas, he also often adds the comment "as is widely known" or "as is known by wise women" after describing certain treatments; clearly he had talked to midwives and women about their practices while writing his manual.

The pictures and much of the text of the *Rosengarten* stem from classical authors; Rösslin himself lists Hippocrates, Galen, Averrois, Rhazes, Avicenna, and Albertus Magnus as his sources. He does not mention his most important source, however, a Latin translation of a gynecological text by Soranus of Ephesus, written about 100 A.D.[26] The translation from Greek was made in the sixth century by Muscio (Moschion), and usually bore the title *Gynaecia Muscionis;* numerous copies from the ninth to the fifteenth century are still extant. One copy of this book was in Heidelberg at the time Rösslin wrote the *Rosengarten,* and it may have been the copy he used.

The pictures which Rösslin adopted from Soranus of the baby *in utero* were not only included in further reprints and translations, but were copied by Jakob Rueff, Ambrose Pare, Jacques Guillimeau and others in their own works until nearly 1700.

The actual text begins with a discussion of the normal position of the baby in the uterus, the normal duration of pregnancy (40 weeks), and how to tell if a woman is likely to have a miscarriage or difficult birth. Expectant mothers are urged to watch their diets in order to prevent constipation (which was linked to difficult births) and maintain their strength.

Certain foods, such as broth, juices, fried apples, figs, goose fat, and linseed or fenugreek oil are advised to make the mother wider in the pelvis, and also warmer, moister, and more pliable, all of which aided in delivery. Warm herb baths also served this purpose. In no case was the woman simply to lie in bed, but keep to her normal routine of moving and working. Specific advice for the mother and midwife during labor and delivery was as follows:

> When the mother finds an increase in pain and some dampness that begins, appears and flows to her genitals, she should prepare herself in two sorts of ways. The first is to make a shortened descent and passage out for the child. The second way is a lessening of the accompanying pains and aches; she should sit down for an hour and then stand up, climb up and down the stairs crying loudly. The woman should also breathe heavily and hold her breath so that she pushes her insides down.
>
> The woman should also drink one of the medicines which follow so that she pushes the child out to its birth. When she discovers that the uterus has opened and the liquid is flowing freely, she should lie down on her back, but not completely lie down nor stand up. It should be midway between lying and standing with the head more toward the back than the front. In upper German lands and in Welfish countries the midwives have special chairs for use when the women bear. They are not so high, but are cut out in the middle.
>
> The chairs should be made so that the woman can lean back on her back. These chairs should be covered and padded at the back with cloths. When it is time the midwife should lift up the cloths firmly and turn the woman first onto the right side and then onto the left. The midwife should sit in front of her and pay careful attention to the movement in the mother's body. The midwife should control the mother's legs and movements with her hands which have been coated with white-lily oil or almond oil or the like. With her hands the midwife should also advise, instruct and direct the mother, nourish her with food and drink and encourage her with gentle words to exert herself so that she breathes deeply. She should also lightly press on the stomach above the navel toward the hips. The midwife should also comfort the mother with the happy prospect of the birth of a boy.[27]

In case of abnormal presentation, the midwife was first to attempt to turn the child around to bring about a head-first position by pushing the feet upwards. If this was impossible, a feet-first presentation was the next best, with care taken that the arms were at the child's sides, not alongside its head. The midwife could bind both feet together with a linen bandage in order to make delivery easier. Any other presentation, breech, knee, shoulders, or hand-first, was to be handled in this way as well, the midwife first attempting to effect a head-first presentation and then a feet-first if that was easier. In all cases she was to handle the baby carefully and gently.

The midwife was also to treat any postdelivery illnesses of the mother, which Rösslin felt came either from an incomplete cleansing and purification, which led to fever, or from a loss of too much blood. Barley-water, broth, and pomegranates are advised to bring down fever, as well as numerous potions and mixtures to alleviate pain. Bandages and cloths soaked in herb mixtures could be placed on the mother's vagina, or the mixtures poured directly into the uterus.

Rösslin next discusses premature births and miscarriages, and here his dependence on classical authors emerges most clearly. He cites both Avicenna and Hippocrates in giving reasons why a woman would miscarry: If she was too fat or too thin, ate the wrong foods, took too long or too hot baths, went out in the night air, suffered from diarrhea or constipation and took any strong drugs to alleviate this condition, was frightened or injured in any way. External factors could cause a miscarriage as well: unseasonal temperatures or other climatic conditions (especially an unusually cold summer), or meteorological phenomena such as eclipses or comets.

The midwife and the mother were to recognize the signs of an imminent miscarriage, particularly the collapse or shrinking of one of the mother's breasts. Again, following Hippocrates and Avicenna—"If the right breast shrivels then a boy will be miscarried, as normally a boy lies on the right side, and a girl on the left side."[28] Various methods are suggested to prevent miscarriages: mild laxatives, moderation in food and drink, bloodletting, no vigorous exercise, drugs that will make the mother's vaginal opening narrower.

Perhaps the most unpleasant task a midwife had to deal with was handling a baby which had died inside the mother. Rösslin lists twelve ways to tell if the child had died, some of which make sense—if the mother had great pain or a fever, or poor color, if she couldn't sleep or felt no movement. Others have no biological basis—if the mother's breasts shriveled, if her urine or breath stank, if the whites of her eyes turned brown or her nose or ears grew numb, stuck out or turned blue, if she wanted to eat and drink unusual things. (!)

Once it was determined the baby was actually dead, the midwife could either attempt to force it out by administering medicines or cut the child apart and remove it piece by piece. Medicines and treatments recommended vary widely: the woman could sit over a smoldering fire of donkey's dung so that the child would be smoked out; she could drink a brew made of figs, fenugreek, rue, and wild marjoram, which would make the child slip out; she could drink the milk from another woman who had borne a dead child before her; she could bathe in an herb bath made with rain water, and afterwards drink crushed date seeds and saffron mixed with wine.

If none of these, nor the numerous other recommended treatments worked, the midwife was forced to use surgery:

The woman should be laid on her back with the head down and the legs up. She should be lifted on both sides and her arms bound tightly so that she cannot pull away when the child is drawn out. Then the midwife should make the woman's opening wider with her left hand—which had been greased with white-lily oil or with something else that makes it smooth and slippery—with the fingers spread. Then she should reach in the opening of the woman and search for the limbs of the dead child, so that she knows where to put the hook and how to pull the child out. If the child is lying in its mother's body with the head toward the opening then the midwife should put the hook in one eye of the child, in the gums of the mouth, under the chin in the throat, in one armpit or in another part of the child where the hook goes in easily. If the dead child comes with its feet first then the midwife should force the hook into a bone above the pelvis of the child, as in the middle ribs, or in the bones of the breast or behind in the back. When she has forced one hook in she should lift with her right hand, but not pull, and reach with her left hand inside the woman and push another hook in on the opposite side of the dead child from the first hook. Then the midwife should pull with both hands together and not only one, so that the dead child will be pulled equally on both sides. She should jerk slowly and gently from one side to the other, and while doing this should grasp inside the woman with a well-greased pointer finger and loosen the child on all sides from the mother, moving it toward the opening and loosening it if it is stuck anywhere. She should do this until the child has been removed completely from the mother's body.

It may happen that the dead child has one hand forward without the other which cannot be easily pushed back in the mother's body because the opening to the uterus is too narrow. Then a cloth should be tied tightly around the child's hand so that it cannot slip off easily and the midwife should pull on the hand until the entire arm emerges completely and then cut off the arm at the armpit. The same thing should be done at the elbow when both arms of the dead child emerge and cannot be pushed down to their correct position.

When one or both feet appear and the body will not follow, they should be pulled out and cut off by the pelvis. The barber-surgeon or midwife should have special instruments or tools for this like scissors, iron tongs and iron hatchets so that such things are easily pulled out and cut. Then she should pull the rest of the dead child out wholly or in pieces until the dead child comes completely out of the mother.

If the head of the dead child is swollen or enlarged with evil fluid and liquid so that it cannot come out of the mother's opening because it is too narrow, the midwife should have a sharp little knife between her fingers and should rip open the head of the dead child. Then the head will shrink as the liquid flows out of the head.

If the head comes out of the mother's body and the chest of the dead child is too large or the passage too narrow and it won't emerge, then the breast should be squeezed and split and the armpits used to pull on it so it will come out . . .

In a case where the mother is dead, which one can tell by the normal signs of a dead person, and there is hope that the child lives, then the mother's mouth, uterus and vagina should be kept open, so that the child has air, as women normally know. Then the dead woman should be cut open on the left side with a shearing knife, because the left side is more open and free than the right because the liver lies on the right side. And when you have cut open this woman, reach inside with both hands and pull out the child. We read in the history of the Romans that the first emperor, named Julius, was cut from his mother's body. For that reason one who is cut from his mother's body is called a Caesarean.[29]

From Rösslin's text and contemporary woodcuts depicting women in childbed, one can get the truest picture of the normal activities of a mid-wife, and the usual methods of delivery. The mother was seated on the birthing stool, gripping the handles, with the midwife seated directly in front of her to assist in bringing about a normal presentation. Often a number of other women bustled about, preparing broth, wine, and other drinks for the mother, and a meal for the midwife. Normally a warm herb bath was prepared for the baby and care was taken to have clean swaddling clothes. The scene is usually shown as one of great joy and contentment, with the midwife often asleep beside the bed after her job has been success-fully completed.

Dr. Christoph Scheurl, a Nuremberg lawyer, pictures just such a scene at the birth of his son George:

> The birth occurred in the back of the house, in our normal eating room along Rosenpadt street. I was banished before the bed was prepared. Frau Margrethe Endres Tucherin, Ursula Fritz Tetzlin, the widow Magdalena Mu-genhoferin and Anna the midwife assisted her.[30]

The social position of the midwife can be seen from the fact that Scheurl refers to her by first name only, and to the other women of his own social class who were also present by their complete names.

Despite the pictures of happiness and calm, on reading the *Rosengarten* one can easily see why the slightest complication could so often be fatal, and why a period of rest three to six weeks in duration was recommended after childbirth. The chance of infection from the midwife's hands or the local treatments was great, as was the possibility of puncturing the uterus when using clumsy iron tools. No matter how skilled the midwife, her basic techniques and anatomical knowledge were the same as those used 1500 years earlier.

Thus it is readily, though unfortunately, understandable why Rösslin includes a section instructing midwives how to tell if a mother was dying:

> This can be recognized if she grows weak or falls unconscious, and becomes oblivious to the things around her and loses her memory; if her limbs become heavy and cannot be moved; when one calls to her or talks to her and she gives little or no answer, especially if she answers very weakly when one calls her with a loud voice; when her face clouds over and she won't eat anything; when her pulse grows fast and weak and her pulse twitches, flutters and beats wildly. Through these signs one knows that the woman cannot be helped and cannot be kept alive. Then she must be commended to God.[31]

## Other Medical Functions

Midwives often served as back-up medical assistants during outbreaks of the plague and other epidemics. In 1534, one was granted a special payment of one pound for services during a recent epidemic (Sterbslauf).[32] Fifty years later, another was removed from office because she was "such an unruly woman"; the next year this same woman was asked to take care of pregnant women in the Lazarett, the special infirmary set up for plague victims.[33] She was to be paid half a florin a year for this and reinstated in her office after the plague had passed.

One of the midwives or Ehrbare Frauen assisted in the Sondersiechenschau, the annual examination of those suffering from leprosy and other diseases, looking at all the woman to determine if they actually did have leprosy.[34]

Midwives were used by physicians in all vaginal inspections, as a physican never performed manual vaginal exploration.[35] As noted above, midwives also did caesarean sections on dead or dying mothers and removed babies which had died in the uterus. This probably led to their doing other minor surgery, such as the removal of boils or the opening of abscesses, especially if they were located in a woman's genital area.

The midwives were a vital link in the city's welfare system. They were responsible for handing out the Arme Kindbetterin Almosen (alms for poor expectant mothers), which consisted of bedding, bread, and lard, to needy women. The council found they were often misusing this, however, and requesting it for women who didn't need it once these women had agreed to call them and not another midwife. If this collusion was proved, the mid-wife was immediately removed from office.

Some authors have commented that the Almosen could actually include a bed and care in the home of one of the Ehrbare Frauen during the time of delivery.[36] This seems to be a misreading of the word Bett, however, which at that time could simply mean bedding, as in "feather-bed"; at any rate, no specific mention is to be found in the Ratsbücher of such a practice.[37]

## Baptism

It was the duty of the midwife to carry any child which she had delivered in its baptism ceremony. She was not to send her apprentice, nor bring along any other members of her family, and had to be sure that all babies were baptized and registered in the parish in which they were born.[38] Baptism was primarily a female affair; the child's father and godfather were the only men allowed at the church ceremony.[39]

The midwife was also held responsible if any sumptuary laws were broken at the baptism:

> All midwives should warn all new mothers that they should stay within the laws at baptism and other parties. If they don't tell the parents and guardians the limitations, and therefore help them to break them, or if they allow extravagances on purpose, they, as well as the parents, should be punished.[40]

With the coming of the Reformation, and the city's assumption of all church functions, closer attention was paid as to how midwives carried out emergency baptism. Initially Luther and other Protestant theologians had accepted the Catholic doctrine of baptism "on condition," which meant that foundlings and other children who had been baptized by lay people, if there was some question about the regularity of this baptism, could be baptized "on the condition" that they had not been properly baptized before.[41] This assured parents that their child had been baptized correctly, while avoiding the snare of rebaptism. In 1531, however, Luther rejected all baptisms "on condition" if it was known any baptism had already been carried out, and called for a normal baptism in the case of foundlings.

Andreas Osiander, the preacher at St. Lorenz, one of Nuremberg's two main churches, and a leader of the Reformation in Nuremberg, disagreed with Luther, and the issue was not discussed at all in the church ordinances of Nuremberg and Brandenburg from 1533, leaving the matter open. By 1540, however, most Lutheran areas, including Nuremberg, were no longer baptizing "on condition" and those who still supported the practice were occasionally branded Anabaptists.[42] As Gottfried Seebass notes, this avoided casuistry in dealing with problems of the validity of baptism, but it also made it much more important that midwives and other lay people knew how to conduct an emergency baptism correctly.

The midwives were examined, along with pastors, church workers, and teachers, in the visitations conducted by members of the city council and pastors of the main churches. The council found what it considered shocking irregularities, and ordered the pages from the baptism ordinance which dealt with emergency baptism (*Jachtauffen*) to be printed up and a copy given to each midwife.[43] The midwives were bound in their oath to perform all baptisms correctly; every time they swore the oath, the council was to make sure each had a copy of this ordinance. Later that year the whole baptism ordinance was actually published with the *Getrenksbüchlein*.[44] The midwives were all called together, given the pamphlet, and sworn to abide by it with the threat of punishment. If any midwife could not be at the meeting, she was to come some other time and get the rules. Interestingly enough, no provision was made for midwives who were illiterate; no mention is made that these women were to have it read to them. Given the popularity of midwives' manuals, perhaps the council could safely assume that all midwives in Nuremberg could read.

In 1578 the city published an entirely new set of baptism regulations (*Kindtaufbüchlein*) with a special section on emergency baptisms.[45] This was later revised, and the city council again stressed that "the midwives are to be bound in their oath to uphold the new set of baptism regulations and do or allow nothing which violates it."[46]

As baptism was an important social occasion and a chance for the flaunting of wealth and social position, an early emergency baptism was often hushed up if the child lived, so the whole normal church ceremony could be carried out. In areas of Germany where Anabaptism flourished, Anabaptist midwives were charged with claiming that they had baptized babies when they really had not. The opposite seems to have been the case in Nuremberg, where parents paid the midwife to conveniently forget she had baptized their child.

The problems with emergency baptisms continued throughout the seventeenth century. An addition to the midwives' ordinance from 1660 demands that they pay more attention to their oath "so that they do not commit such inexcusable mistakes in emergency baptisms." One from 1704 reads: "They shall be required to report all children who have had an emergency baptism immediately in the parish churches, so that they may be registered in the normal manner."[47]

## Abortion, Infanticide and Foundlings

Midwives appear most often in the city council records (*Ratsbücher*) in connection with criminal cases, particularly abortion and infanticide. Their oath required them to report immediately all illegitimate children—who the parents were, whether the child was alive or dead, where the mother was. The council recognized that illegitimate children would be those most likely to be aborted, killed, or abandoned, for there were no means of public support for them; the *Arme Kindbetterin Almosen* was only given to the wives of citizens or permanent residents whose children were legitimate. As noted above, the council punished midwives who did not make these reports.

A woman suspected of aborting or killing her child was taken in to the Loch, the city jail, where she was examined by a midwife to see if she had been pregnant, which generally meant only seeing if she had milk.[48] If the suspect was from a rural area, she was often brought into the city in chains, at night or in the early morning.[49]

The midwife also questioned her, as an admission of guilt was needed for capital punishment, particularly after the institution of the Carolina Constitution Criminalis, the set of legal procedures drawn up by Charles V and adopted by the city in the 1530s.[50] Her house was searched for anything suspicious like bloody cloths or clothes, and apothecaries and neighbors questioned as to her activities and purchases. Often the suspect was held for weeks or months while the investigation continued.[51]

A midwife and often a barber-surgeon were sent out to search for the body of the child, to examine it for signs of violence and an indication that it had been born alive. This occasionally involved an autopsy to see if it had drawn breath: "On the report of the sworn midwives as to how they had found the dead child with a piece of wood stuck in its mouth it is recommended that the child be cut open and examined further."[52]

The body was exhumed from the field, dung-heap, or cow-stall where it had been buried, examined, and then reburied with a simple ceremony conducted by the midwife.[53] In one particularly gruesome case, a woman had killed the child which had been conceived in incest with her father, but had not buried it deep enough and the body was dug up by the neighborhood dogs; the midwife was dispatched to bury what was left.[54]

The council usually called the midwives who were active in the area where the body was found to make the examination. If they conducted it alone, they sent a report to the council; if a barber-surgeon was also involved, the opinions of the midwives or Geschworene Weiber were included in his report.[55] Not until 1624 was the presence of a trained physician (Medicus) required at an autopsy, and then only if there was a suspicion of force in the death.[56] Even after this date, in the case of newborns, the testimony of midwives often stood alone.

The child's corpse was generally brought in to the mother in order to shock her into confession. Occasionally reports of this are particularly macabre. A child found three days after its death was shown to its mother:

> And then the midwife said, "Oh, you innocent little child, if one of us here is guilty, give us a sign," and immediately the child raised its left arm and pointed at its mother.[57]

The unfortunate mother was later executed by drowning.

The council did recognize that confessions were not always valid. In 1610 a woman accused of child-murder confessed out of fear of torture. Her confession proved untrue, as no bodies could be found where she claimed they were, and she was released.[58]

Great care was taken to prove that the child had actually lived and that the mother's actions had in fact caused its death. If this was at all in doubt, the mother was not executed, even if she had tried to abort or kill the child and failed.

Between the years 1533 and 1599, fifty-five cases of infanticide were reported.[59] More than half the women involved were not from Nuremberg, and most were pregnant outside of marriage.[60] Children were usually killed when they were only a few hours old, and most often by stabbing, strangling, or not tying the umbilical cord so that they bled to death.[61] The city executioner drowned or beheaded nineteen women for infanticide in the forty years between 1578 and 1617.[62]

Along with actual infanticides, midwives were often called in to give opinions in cases of suspected abortion. Various methods were tried to abort a child, including witchcraft and sodomy with farm animals, but the usual ones were draughts or douches of drug and herb mixtures. In 1614, a woman tried to abort her child with herbs, although she was unsuccessful. The council asked the Geschworene Weiber "whether one can abort a child with such herbs."[63] The dosage proved too weak, so the mother was simply given an imprisonment for fornication, although the council warned her that she would have been banished except for its mercy.

A midwife suspected of aiding in or covering up an abortion or infanticide was just as harshly handled as the mother was. One was banished for not reporting that an unmarried woman had killed her own child.[64] Another was imprisoned in the Loch for questioning, "because she has helped and advised Anna Müllner as to how she could kill her child."[65]

The council also wanted midwives to report all illegitimate births so that it could trace foundlings more easily. Popular sites for leaving foundlings were the gates to the city, church doorways, in front of the houses of clergy or wealthy citizens, and the doorway of the supposed father.[66]

All citizens were admonished to watch for mothers leaving children, and were rewarded for reporting this to the council.[67] City officials were also rewarded for finding a child's mother: "The mother should be followed and taken into custody and the watchman honored with a tip."[68] The council questioned those living near the place where a child had been set out, as well as friends or relatives of any suspect.[69]

If the mother could not be found, or if it was certain that she had left

Nuremberg, the child was taken into the orphanage or given to a wet nurse.[70] He or she was baptized immediately, and given a first name, often the saint's name of the day it had been found.[71]

Mothers who left foundlings were banished, with a slight fine often added, but were not punished corporally. There was no church punishment either before or after the Reformation for setting out a foundling, only for bearing an illegitimate child. Women were treated with increasing severity, however, throughout the sixteenth century, with the suggestion made in 1597 that any woman having a child secretly be banished, no matter what she had done with the child.[72]

Midwives were called in to examine any female prisoner who claimed she was pregnant, along with those charged with infanticide or abortion. In the fifteenth century pregnant women were not tortured, although this special treatment was gradually lessened during the sixteenth century. The council's medical counselors still advised a milder handling, for otherwise "they [the mother] could become unconscious and hurt the child in their bodies."[73] Corporal punishment was still used, however. Throughout the period, a woman who claimed she was pregnant and was found not to be so was dealt with more sharply. In 1581, a woman accused of repeated theft and other crimes was sentenced to death, but then claimed she was pregnant and demanded a stay of execution. The four midwives who examined her could not agree, so the council ordered that she be held in the *Loch* until they could be sure.[74] Three months later there were still no signs of pregnancy, and she was executed.[75]

Thus we find midwives active in a broad spectrum of medical, legal, and religious activities. Their opinions and judgments were taken seriously and their essential power over life clearly recognized. No other group of women received more frequent consideration by the city council or was more closely watched as to conduct, numbers, and skill.

At least in Nuremberg, then, the early modern period does not see a significant decline in the role of midwives. Their social utility continued to be recognized, and we find no male midwives operating in the city until the eighteenth century. Nuremberg may be a peculiar case, as it was so tightly controlled by a conservative city council, which was apparently quite satisfied with the system it had developed, and as it also had no executions for witchcraft during the whole period. One suspects, however, that the general thesis of the decline in midwifery with the advent of professional obstetrics needs to be modified, or at least pushed back several centuries. The early modern midwife was not viewed by her contemporaries as an anachronistic relic, holding to old techniques out of ignorance and fear, but as a woman on whose skills and knowledge they depended.

## Notes

This chapter originally appeared in *International Journal of Women's Studies* 6, no. 1: 26–43. All translations are my own.

1. See, e.g., Palmer Findley, *Priests of Lucina: The Story of Obstetrics* (Boston, 1939) or Irving S. Cutter and Henry R. Viets, *A Short History of Midwifery* (Philadelphia, 1964). For more balanced views, see, e.g., Audrey Eccles, *Obstetrics and Gynecology in Tudor and Stuart England* (Kent, Ohio, 1982) or Ann Oakley, *The Captured Womb: A History of the Medical Care of Pregnant Women* (London, 1984).

2. Thomas Rogers Forbes, *The Midwife and the Witch* (New Haven: Yale Univ. Press, 1966).

3. Rudolph Endres, "Zur Einwohnerzahl und Bevölkerungsstruktur Nürnbergs im 15./16. Jahrhunderts," *Mitteilungen des Verein für Geschichte der Stadt Nürnberg* (MVGN) 57 (1970): 242–71; Otto Puchner, "Das Register des gemeinen Pfennigs der Reichsstadt Nürnberg," *Jahrbuch für fränkische Landesforschung* 34/35 (1974–75): 909–48; Caspar Ott, *Bevölkerungsstatistik in der Stadt und Landschaft Nürnberg* (Berlin: R. Trenkel, 1907).

4. Friedrich Baruch, "Das Hebammenwesen in Reichsstädischen Nürnberg," (Dissertation, Erlangen, 1955), p. 8; Aemterbüchlein, Nuremberg, Staatsarchiv (StN), Repertorium 62, Nr. 1–139.

5. StN, Repertorium 62, Nr. 5–139.

6. StN, Ratsbücher (RB), Repertorium 60b, Vol. 24, fol. 299 (1549).

7. StN, Amts-und Standbücher (AStB), Repertorium 52b, Vol. 100, fol. 126.

8. Carlo Cipolla, "Four Centuries of Italian Demographic Development," in *Population in History*, ed. D.V. Glass (London: Edward Arnold, 1965) finds the crude birth rate in Lombardy in the eighteenth century varies between 37 and 45 per thousand. J.C. Russell, *British Medieval Population* (Albuquerque: Univ. of New Mexico Press, 1948) finds the birth rate in England to be about 53 per thousand. T.H. Hollingsworth, *Historical Demography* (London: Sources of History, 1969) determines the birthrate in England and Wales in the eighteenth century to be 44 per thousand, and notes this was the same in Spain and Prussia.

9. Nuremberg, Stadtarchiv, Quellen zur Nürnbergische Geschichte, Repertorium F5, Nr. 168 (unpaginated): "Abschrift des Journals des Sebastian Welser (1530–1539)."

10. RB 31, fol. 197' (1561). A short note on monetary values: The basic unit was the silver pfennig (d); 120 d made up one "new" pound, which was strictly a money of account. The gold Rhenish gulden (fl) was generally figured at two pounds, 12 d, although its value fluctuated. Over the fifteenth and sixteenth centuries, the value of the gulden increased as Bohemian silver created a glut on the market.

11. "Nürnbergs reichsstädtische Arbeiterschaft des Amtszeit des Baumeisters Michel Behaim," *Mitteilungen aus der Germanische National Museum* (MGNM), 1914/15, pp. 141–209.

12. AStB, Vol. 305–306 "Nürnberger Neubürgerlisten." The percentage of all new citizens that were women varied between 0 and 15%, although it was usually about 1%.

13. RB 6, fol. 155 (1496).

14. Baruch, p. 12.

15. StN, Briefbücher, Repertorium 6, Nr. 57, quoted in Baruch, p. 13.

16. RB 64, fol. 236' (1606).

17. AStB Nr. 100, fol. 180–182 & Nr. 101, fol. 100–103.

18. Baruch, p. 14, from a report by Joachim Camerarius, a doctor in Nuremberg during the late sixteenth century.

19. AStB; Vol. 100, fol. 182.

20. RB 3, fol. 265' (1483) & RB 4, fol. 54 (1484).

21. RB 11, fol. 102' (1517).

22. RB 29, fol. 268' (1556).

23. Baruch, p. 32.

24. A facsimile reprint of the first Hagenau edition was published in 1910 in Munich as volume 2 of the series *Alte Meister de Medizin und Naturkunde*, with accompanying notes by Gustav Klein. This reprint was the edition used here.

25. AStB 103, fol. 323', "Einer Hebamme auf dem Land verneuerte Pflicht."

26. Klein, *Rosengarten*, p. x, and Cutter/Viets, p. 217.

27. Rösslin, pp. 26–27. It was widely believed that the birth of a girl was more difficult than the birth of a boy, which partially explains the last sentence.

28. Ibid., p. 63.

29. Ibid., pp. 70–73.

30. "Schuld und Rechnungsbuch Dr. Christoph Scheurl," unpublished manuscript in the Germanische Nationalmuseum, fol. 10.

31. Rösslin, p. 70.

32. RB 16, fol. 148 (1534).

33. RB 43, fol. 53 (1584) & RB 44, fol. 106' (1585).

34. J.F. Roth, *Fragmente zur Geschichte der Bader, Barbiere, Hebammen, Ehrbare Frauen und Geschworene Weiber in der freien Reichsstadt Nürnberg* (Nuremberg, 1792), p. 12; Willi Rüger, "Die Almosenordnungen der Reichsstadt Nürnberg," *Nürnberger Beiträge zu den Wirtschafts-und Sozialwissenschaften* 31 (1932): 24.

35. Paul Diepgen, *Frauen und Frauenheilkunde in der Kultur des Mittelalters* (Stuttgart: Thieme, 1963), p. 224.

36. Roth, p. 42.

37. The *Arme Kindbetterin Almosen* was a charity fund totally administered by women. It was directed by a *Pflegerin*, an upper-class woman appointed by the city council, and received many contributions from wealthy widows. It continued as a separately endowed charity until the city was taken over by Bavaria in 1806.

38. Parish registration of baptism began in the 1540s; unfortunately no sixteenth-century baptism rolls survive.

39. AStB, Vol. 232, "Wandelbuch Ordnung und Gestez," fol. 165.

40. Joseph Baader, "Nürnberger Polizeiordnungen," *Bibliothek des litterarische Vereins Stuttgart*, 63 (1862): 69–70.

41. This issue is discussed fully in two articles by Gottfried Seebass: "Das Problem der Konditionaltaufe in der Reformation," *Zeitschrift für bayerischen Kirchengeschichte*, 35 (1966): 138–68, and "Die Vorgeschichte von Luthers Verwerfung der Konditionaltaufe nach einem bisher unbekannten Schreiben Andreas Osianders an Georg Spalatin vom 26. Juni 1531," *Archiv für Reformationsgeschichte* 62 (1971): 193–206.

42. Seebass, "Vorgeschicte," p. 195.

43. RB 27, fol. 360 (1554).

44. RB 28, fol. 53 (1554).

45. RB 37, fol. 176 (1578) & AStB, Vol. 250 "Kindtaufbüchlein."

46. RB 69, fol. 53' (1614).

47. Baruch, p. 39, quoting from *Hebammenordnung*.

48. StN, Ratsverlässe (RV), Rep 60a, 2908, fol. 108.

49. RV 1034, fol. 24' (1549).

50. *Kaiser Karl des fünften peinliche Gerichtsordnung* (*Carolina Constitution Criminalis*), ed. Reinhold Schmidt (Jena, 1835).

51. E.g., RV 1109, fol. 1, 3, 9, 25 (1554).

52. RV 1141, fol. 33'–34.

53. E.g., RB 29, fol. 354' (1557); RB 35, fol. 125' (1578); RB 56, fol. 507 (1597).

54. RB 33, fol. 219' (1568).

55. E.g., RV 1141, fol. 33' 34, 34'; (1556); RV 1496, fol. 32 (1583); RV 1538, fol. 2, 5 (1586).

56. Jurgen Dieselhorst, "Die Bestrafung der Selbstmörder in Territoriums der Reichsstadt Nürnberg," MVGN 44 (1953): 112.

57. AStB, Vol. 226a "Malefizbücher" (1549).

58. Achtbuch 1610, fol. 172, quoted in Hermann Knapp, *Das Lochgefängnis, Tortur und Richtung in Alt-Nürnberg* (Nuremberg: Heerdegen-Barbeck, 1907).

59. Karl Roetzer, "Die Delikte des Abtreibung, Kindstötung sowie Kindsaussetzungen und ihre Bestrafung in der Reichsstadt Nürnberg" (Jur. Dissertation, Erlangen, 1957), p. 86.

60. Ibid., p. 103.

61. Ibid., p. 97.

62. *Meister Franz Schmidts Scharfrichter inn Nürnberg all sein Richten* (Leipzig, 1913). This is Schmidt's own record of all the people he either executed or gave corporal punishment to during his period as city executioner (*Scharfrichter*), 1578–1617. Interestingly, Schmidt first convinced the council in 1588 to behead women rather than drown them. He reported that the Pegnitz River had been frozen several times when he was supposed to carry out an execution. The council accepted his reasoning and also came to the conclusion that a beheading had more shock value than a drowning, when no one could see the actual death. There were still those who argued that beheading was more difficult, especially in the case of women, as the victim often fainted or sank to the ground in fear, making it hard for the executioner to do his job with the first stroke (Knapp, p. 71). Until 1515, women had been buried alive, but the council decided at that time to switch to drowning "in consideration of what a horrible death being buried alive is for women and that such punishments are no longer being carried out in many imperial areas." (Knapp, p. 73, from *Nürnberg Kriminalrecht*, p. 56. This is also noted in RB 10, fol. 223').

63. RB 69, fol. 545, 549 (1614).

64. RB 12, fol. 96 (1522).

65. AStB Vol. 221 "Malefizbücher," fol. 48' (1514).

66. Roetzer, p. 97.

67. E.g., RV 1936, fol. 3; RV 1942, fol. 46; RV 1080, fol. 31; RV 1874, fol. 34.

68. RV 1140, fol. 14' (1557).

69. E.g., RV 969, fol. 3'(1544); RV 845, fol. 6 (1540).

70. RV 575, fol. 3 (1514).

71. RV 923, fol. 22 (1540).

72. Roetzer, p. 104.

73. StN, Repertorium 51, Ratschlagbücher, Nr. 10 (1530).

74. RB 40a, fol. 287' & 290'. (1581).

75. RB 40a, fol. 378' (1582).

# PART IV
## Urban Women in Work and Business

Whether in a small market-town with a population of three thousand such as Exeter or a large urban center such as Montpellier with forty to fifty thousand inhabitants, women played a role in the work force and in some businesses in the fourteenth century. Since both Exeter and Montpellier had a mixed economy of some crafts, local and long-distance trade, and the usual victualing trades, women would presumably have had a variety of opportunities to find work and practice business. When one looks at their actual participation, however, one finds them clustered in occupations that relate to their skills as housewives or to lighter crafts.

Kathryn L. Reyerson found that the most common apprenticeships for girls were to bakers and gold-thread spinners. Girls were not apprenticed to money changers, apothecaries, spicers, merchants, or drapers. When women did participate in a luxury trade such as silk selling, they were usually widows. Three notarial contracts show women investing in long-distance trade, but they were not engaging in the business themselves. Women did, however, constitute a fairly large part of agricultural trading, buying and selling grain, grapes, and livestock. Women also played a rather important role in real estate, both as passive investment partners in land purchases and as buyers and sellers of land. Women who bought land did so more frequently with cash rather than with credit and they tended to buy vineyards or houses. Their large role in real estate probably derived from the fact that their dowries and dowers were arranged in property. These women usually came from agricultural or craft backgrounds, the same groups that played a large role in the credit market. The pattern of their borrowing was consistent with their role as provider for their families, for they mostly borrowed for consumption and subsistence. Although the bulk of women's participation in credit transactions involved small amounts of money, some women did make investment deposits with bankers and showed through their transactions that they were cognizant of the mechanisms of medieval finance.

115

Medieval Exeter was considerably smaller than Montpellier, with somewhat less diversification of trade and crafts, but it did have some overseas trade, leather tanning, and cloth making. Maryanne Kowaleski found, however, that women predominated in the victualing and service trades. They brewed and sold beer; retailed eggs, butter, and cheese as well as staples such as flour; became servants and sometimes prostitutes. But women also found ready employment in the local cloth trade. Like the women of Montpellier, they were involved in the local credit market, usually entering into rather small loans. Legal disabilities limited women's participation in credit transactions. Since women could not be admitted to the freedom of the city, they were effectively barred from much of the commercial activity.

Kowaleski has made some observations on the nature of women's participation in Exeter's economy that have a more general applicability. First, women usually did not receive formal training (since they could not enter the freedom of the city they could not be apprenticed) and thus the type of work they did involved transferring skills learned within their family. Even when they did learn skills, as in cloth making, their employment tended to be in low-status, marginal positions. Women usually changed their economic activities to suit the various stages in their life cycle. Single women might start out working in cloth, but when they married and had families they were more likely to move into some aspect of victualing or to become involved in their husband's trade. Not only did women change their work to accommodate their life cycle, they also tended to work on more than one occupation. Only widows who continued their husband's trade showed a consistency of work patterns similar to that of men.

Kathryn L. Reyerson 7

# Women in Business in Medieval Montpellier

T he legal history of women in medieval Montpellier has been examined in several valuable theses and articles but the role of women in the economic life of this commercial and financial center of Lower Languedoc has not been the focus of investigation to date.[1] In this study I will treat the economic activities of Montpelliérins in the aggregate through the earliest extant notarial registers of the period 1293–1348.[2] Beyond the economic operations per se, analysis of the social background and marital status of women in business will help illuminate the nature of their participation, as will consideration of the influence of kinship ties in areas of commerce, finance, and real estate. The extent of sexual division of labor and the degree to which sex roles varied in different urban social and economic groups will provide further perspectives on women's roles. I will set my findings within the broader urban economy so that the activities of Montpellier women can be perceived in proper historical context.

Historians posit a decline in the status of women in Europe from the late eleventh century, with the beginnings of political reorganization and the growth of the bureaucratic state.[3] Although the Crusades offered women new responsibilities, and the halcyon days of courtly love still lay ahead, noble familiies increasingly obeyed patriarchal and patrilineal impulses, resulting in the shrinkage of opportunities—economic and other—for women to wield influence.[4] Further decline in women's status is generally assigned to the late Middle Ages, after the demographic catastrophe of the Black Death.[5] The period of the present inquiry falls between these two poles and coincides with the end of an era of urban expansion in medieval Europe.[6]

The urban environment was far removed from the noble feudal context and from the manorial agricultural setting. Within a town such as Montpellier, various social groups with differing economic status coexisted.[7] Women were confronted with many economic opportunities and numerous life styles. Before exploring the range of economic activities recorded for Montpellier women, and the distinctions among these, I want to sketch briefly the legal framework for women's participation in business. It will then be possible to investigate actual business practice as observed in the notarial registers.

Statutes of Montpellier, drafted in the years 1204–21, deal rather obliquely with the issue of women's economic rights.[8] Considerable space is devoted to the questions of dowry, inheritance, marriage, and the right to make a will. Much less local regulation of women's contractual potential in business can be found. However, it is clear from the existing statutes and from the use of renunciations of Roman law that the local law must be distinguished from that of Justinian in its treatment of women. The current notarial practice of renunciation of the *Senatusconsultum Velleianum*, one of the strongest Roman law protections limiting the legal capacity of women, and the statutory validation of obligations undertaken by a woman with her husband's permission removed barriers to her contractual participation.[9] The most elaborate statement of a woman's contractual rights came in article 38 of the 1204 statutes.[10] This statute concerned a woman's ability to act as an *fideiussor* (guarantor) in a contractual agreement, one of the keystones of business law in the Middle Ages.[11] A woman was effectively obligated if she exercised a trade and intervened by reason of it or if she acted according to the wishes of her husband. If women could bind themselves as surety for someone else, by implication they were able to contract obligations on their own behalf, and, of course, in actual business practice that is what one observes. With regard to real property transactions wives acted generally with their husbands' consent.[12] In other contexts, they often acted alone.[13]

Full contractual potential without a curator came at the official age of majority, which for girls, as for boys, was twenty-five years.[14] However, all pacts, agreements, and acquittals that girls made to their fathers and mothers at the time of their marriage, regardless of age, were valid.[15] In practice, girls reached a working majority at age twelve, boys at age fourteen.[16]

Dowry and inheritance were important sources of a woman's financial resources for participation in business. Dotal goods came under the control of the husband but could be alienated only with the consent of both spouses. Some wives retained control of their personal property, termed *bona paraphernalia*.[17] A dowered daughter could not expect a further inheritance from her father's or from her immediate family's estate if there were sons or unmarried daughters. The latter might hope to inherit. A father could, of course, leave a legacy to his married daughter, thus circumventing the statutory regulation.[18] Married women without children could not dispose of their goods through a will without their father's permission.[19] Women with children were free to frame their wills as they chose. At the dissolution of a marriage or at the death of her husband, a woman could, in principle, expect the restitution of her dowry.[20]

Married women with children who found themselves widowed were frequent participants in notarial contracts. While Roman law did not readily allow a mother to be the guardian of her children, in Montpellier such was often the practice.[21] One of the most prominent capacities in which women appeared in business transactions was as tutors or as curators of their children.[22] In these roles and as executors of their husbands' estates, they were involved in the payment of debts, acquittals and real estate acts, and in the apprenticeship of their children.

By and large women were absent from legal, paralegal, medical, and political roles in Montpellier during the era under study. In contrast, their involvement in a wide spectrum of business activities can be demonstrated in the surviving evidence. I will divide this discussion of women's participation in economic matters into five categories: apprenticeship, commerce, partnership, finance, and real estate. Women's activities will be set in the general context of urban business operations in these areas.[23] The following tables analyze women's roles in business in the context of the social categories of the town and according to their own varied backgrounds. These categories were developed in conjunction with a study of the diversity of the notarial clientele.[24] Underlying the participation of women in business in all five areas were the basic female roles of mother and provider of food and household maintenance for the family.[25] The details of women's work in the familial domestic context defy investigation given the lacuna of surviving records.

In the contracts of the notarial registers, women were usually identified by their husband's name and profession or by their father's name and occupation or by both.[26] Some women, presumably but not demonstrably single, were termed simply *habitatrix* (inhabitant) of Montpellier.[27] With very rare exceptions, women were not identified, as men were, with occupational designations of their own, though their geographic places of origin and residence were generally given.[28]

The medieval town of Montpellier enjoyed a great mixture of artisanal/industrial activities. In his study of guild organizations in southern France, André Gouron noted some evidence, particularly regarding Toulouse, that women were associated with men in trades.[29] In the case of Montpellier Gouron cited only the *caritat des fourniers* (a type of baker), whose regulations of 1365 made mention of women participants.[30] Later guild ordinances of the fifteenth and sixteenth centuries contained brief references to arrangements made for widows supported by the assistance of journeymen.

If the evidence for formal integration of women into guild structures is absent in Montpellier, the extant apprenticeship contracts offer a useful glimpse of women employed in the crafts and artisanal industries. Thirty of the 208 contracts surviving from before 1350 concern women.[31] The food trades, the specialized textile industry, and precious metalwork were the primary concentrations of female apprentices. In contrast to most towns in Languedoc by the year 1300, Montpellier had no substantial wool cloth industry; thus, many of the traditional female trades of the cloth industry such as spinning may have been practiced on a more informal, familial level in Montpellier than elsewhere in the south of France.[32]

Fourteen of the thirty female apprentices noted were in-migrants, drawn to the metropolis for purposes of training and employment. Of these the largest number in any trade—six—were destined to be bakers.[33] Five of them came from a radius of within fifty kilometers of Montpellier, the sixth from the region of Saint-Flour in the Massif Central. Women were not found as apprentices in the more prestigious commercial and financial occupations of Montpellier. The money changers, apothecaries, pepperers, merchants, and drapers recruited male apprentices, often from a distance of more than fifty kilometers from the town.[34]

Girls were apprenticed to both men and women and to couples, where, in most cases, the understanding was that the apprentice was to learn the wife's trade.[35] Fathers, mothers, parents, uncles, and brothers apprenticed their children, nieces, and sisters in trade, and husbands at times engaged their wives.[36] Widows, in keeping with their role as guardian of their children, regularly apprenticed their sons and daughters, alone or in conjunction with male relatives.[37]

Where ages of apprenticeship were given, girls were apprenticed at twelve and older, boys at fourteen and older. Local girls apprenticed at the beginner level had engagements of 4.3 years on the average; nonlocal girls spent 5.3 years in training. For local boys the average was 3.3 years, for nonlocal boys, 6 years.[38]

Trades related to the textile-finishing industry were important occupations for girl apprentices. Several contracts for the spinning of gold thread survive. In a typical apprenticeship contract, the daughter of a silversmith was apprenticed to a gilder for four years to learn the spinning of gold.[39] In a second example, the daughter of a furrier was hired by the widow of a grain merchant to spin gold for four years with a remuneration of 10 s. t. per year.[40] Here the hiree was already experienced. In yet another variation of terms, an oil merchant hired his wife out to the wife of a gilder for about a year at the rate of 4 s. t. per ounce of spun gold.[41] Part of this arrangement was a loan of 40 s. t. granted the oil merchant and his wife, with 12 d. t. to be deducted in repayment from the salary for each ounce spun. Gold thread was used in

embroidery, in cloth trimming, and in the making of brocade.[42] One apprenticeship contract described the instruction of the daughter of a cultivator by
the wife of a wood merchant in embroidery.[43] Girls were taught the making of
silk and linen corduroy and the tailoring art.[44] The mercery trade was also a
focus of female apprenticeship, although no woman in the notarial documents was termed a mercer, and the mercers' statutes of 1328 made no
mention of the participation of women.[45] The mercer's trade was one of the
most important retail/wholesale occupations of Montpelliérins. Montpellier
had a silk-finishing industry and a linen industry in which the above arts were
used.[46] The involvement of women in silk sales and purchases, an active
branch of Montpellier commerce, may have been connected to the silk-finishing industry.[47]

Additional skills taught to girls in formal apprenticeship conditions included basket weaving, painting, the marketing of old clothes, and the
polishing of silver cups.[48] Domestic service was another outlet for girls.[49] In
many other instances girls undoubtedly learned the skills of their mothers
without leaving home. The trades of women providing instruction might
differ widely from those of their husbands, as in the case of the changer's
wife who taught the art of making linen corduroy.[50] Women might, however, train girls in the same trades that their husbands exercised, as suggested by the apprenticeship of a fisherman's daughter to the wife of a tailor
to learn the tailoring art; here husband and wife worked at the same or
related trades.[51] By the same token, a daughter's instruction might bear
some relationship to her father's occupation. Thus, the daughter of a silversmith apprenticed to a gilder to spin gold was still handling precious
metals.[52]

With few exceptions women were apprenticed in crafts that might be
classified as women's work. These activities have left no trace of formal
guild organization. The prestigious occupations of the mercantile elite were
male-oriented. There were thus clear sex distinctions, which appear in the
apprenticeship evidence.

The notarial registers preserve scattered records of women's transactions
in the luxury trade and on the commodities market in Montpellier.[53] They
sold silks (Table 1) and wool cloths (Table 2). The accompanying tables
provide a view of these market sectors overall, with women's participation
broken down by social category. In the silk trade, the connection of wives
and widows with a particular branch of trade was directly related to their
husbands' occupations. Thus, the widow of a mercer made four sales and
wives of silk industry personnel, two. In the one instance where a woman
(the wife of a wood merchant) bought silk, she may have been acquiring
goods for her own enterprise, perhaps common to wood merchants' wives,
as the earlier apprenticeship example might suggest. Female participants in

TABLE 1

**Silk Transactions (Total Acts 57)**

| Social Category | All Sellers | | All Buyers | | Women Sellers | Women Buyers |
|---|---|---|---|---|---|---|
| | No. of Acts | % Total Acts | No. of Acts | % Total Acts | No. of Acts | No. of Acts |
| Merchants | 17 | 29.8 | 3 | 5.3 | | |
| Changers/Moneyers | 4 | 7 | 2 | 3.5 | | |
| Retail/Wholesale | 25 | 43.9 | 24 | 42.1 | 4 | |
| Nobles/Burgenses | 1 | 1.8 | | | | |
| Professions/Education | | | | | | |
| Jews | | | 6 | 10.5 | | |
| Royal Administration | | | | | | |
| Ecclesiastics | | | | | | |
| Women | 6 | 10.5 | 1 | 1.8 | n/a | n/a |
| Artisans/Service | 2 | 3.5 | 4 | 7 | 2 | 1 |
| Food Trades | | | | | | |
| Agriculture | | | | | | |
| Foreigners | 2 | 3.5 | 16 | 28.1 | | |
| Unidentified | | | | | | |
| Local | | | | | | |
| Other | | | 1 | 1.8 | | |

the luxury trade utilized credit recognizances in the capacity of buyer and seller, as did their male counterparts.[54] They generally employed procurators, as men did, to draft their contracts before the notary and to carry out their business. They might also be present in person in such matters.

Widows were most commonly noted as participants in the luxury trade, as can be seen in Table 3, but wives were also represented in greater numbers than single women. The luxury trade demanded capital and commercial organization, resources that married and widowed women may have more readily enjoyed. Single women without a large inheritance would have lacked the requisite capital for luxury trade investments. Widowed mothers were present with their sons as buyers in further transactions of luxury commerce (Table 4.)[55] Women were notably absent from the spice trade, sector *par excellence* of international trade. They were not mentioned as sellers of mercery of Lucca, the elaborate brocades and damasks of the Lucchese silk-finishing industry, a branch of the silk trade that enjoyed considerable marketing specialization in Montpellier.[56] However, among the clients of the most prominent specialists in mercery of Lucca, the Cabanis brothers, merchants and mercers, was a widow of Toulouse, who purchased this product in person in Montpellier.[57]

## TABLE 2
### Cloth Transactions (Total Acts 140)

| Social Category | All Sellers | | All Buyers | | Women Sellers | Women Buyers |
|---|---|---|---|---|---|---|
| | No. of Acts | % Total Acts | No. of Acts | % Total Acts | No. of Acts | No. of Acts |
| Merchants | 49 | 35.0 | 11 | 7.9 | | |
| Changers/Moneyers | | | | | | |
| Retail/Wholesale | 65 | 46.4 | 14 | 10.0 | | |
| Nobles/*Burgenses* | | | 7 | 5.0 | | |
| Professions/Education | 1 | 1.0 | 2 | 1.4 | | |
| Jews | | | | | | |
| Royal Administration | | | 1 | 1.0 | 1 | |
| Ecclesiastics | | | 5 | 3.6 | | |
| Women | 3 | 2.1 | 3 | 2.1 | n/a | n/a |
| Artisans/Service | 3 | 2.1 | 19 | 13.6 | | |
| Food Trades | | | 1 | 1.0 | | |
| Agriculture | | | 4 | 2.9 | | |
| Foreigners | 18 | 12.9 | 70 | 50.0 | 1 | 2 |
| Unidentified | | | | | | |
|   Local | 1 | 1.0 | | | 1 | 1 |
|   Other | | | 3 | 2.1 | | |

Note: Linen, cotton, and cloth mixtures such as fustian are not included in these calculations.

The agricultural market in Montpellier also witnessed the participation of women. In fact, they were present in considerable numbers in the commodity trade as buyers of grain and grapes (Tables 5 and 6). Women buying grain were concentrated in the more modest urban social and economic categories. Male buyers were more broadly representative of the population as a whole.[58] The foreign women noted in Table 5 were rural villagers who, like their numerous male counterparts, often purchased grain in Montpellier in years of bad harvest such as 1327 and 1333.[59] While few couples were present selling grain, thirteen were recorded in grain purchases (Table 4). By the same token, grain purchases were made by common action of men and women of different surnames from villages surrounding Montpellier; their relationship remains inscrutable in the documents. The involvement of women in grain purchases reflects the role of provider alluded to earlier. Bread was the staple of the medieval diet.

Women were also actively involved in the grape trade in a region where cultivation of the vine was as important in the Middle Ages as it is today.

## TABLE 3
### Marital Status of Women in Business

| Economic Sector | Single | | Widowed | | Married | | Unknown |
|---|---|---|---|---|---|---|---|
| | Sellers | Buyers | Sellers | Buyers | Sellers | Buyers | |
| *Luxury Trade* | | | | | | | |
| Spices | — | — | — | — | — | — | — |
| Silks | — | — | 4 | — | 2 | 1 | — |
| Mercery of Lucca | — | — | — | 4 | — | — | — |
| Woollen Cloths | 1 | 1 | — | 1 | 2 | 1 | — |
| Skins and Leather | — | — | — | — | — | — | — |
| *Commodities* | | | | | | | |
| Wool | — | — | 1 | — | — | — | — |
| Grain | 1 | — | 1 | 8 | — | 1 | — |
| Grapes | — | — | 4 | 8 | 2 | 5 | — |
| Animals | — | — | 5 | 1 | — | 1 | — |

| Economic Sector | Single | | Widowed | | Married | | Unknown |
|---|---|---|---|---|---|---|---|
| | Investors | Workers | Investors | Workers | Investors | Workers | |
| *Partnerships* | | | | | | | |
| Maritime Comanda | 1 | — | 2 | — | — | — | — |
| Maritime Societas | — | — | — | — | — | — | — |
| Land Comanda | — | — | 9 | 2 | 2 | — | — |
| Land Societas | — | — | 1 | 1 | — | — | — |

|  | Lenders | Borrowers | Lenders | Borrowers | Lenders | Borrowers | Unknown |
|---|---|---|---|---|---|---|---|
| *Finance* | | | | | | | |
| Money Exchange | — | — | — | — | — | — | — |
| Loans | 11 | 6 | 11 | 17 | 7 | 7 | — |

|  | Sellers | Buyers | Sellers | Buyers | Sellers | Buyers | Unknown |
|---|---|---|---|---|---|---|---|
| *Real Estate* | | | | | | | |
| Land | 4 | 1 | 29 | 9 | 23 | 16 | 2 |
| Houses | 5 | 3 | 3 | 7 | 11 | 3 | — |
| Land Rights | 1 | 1 | 7 | 4 | 2 | 2 | 3 |
| House Rights | — | — | 4 | 1 | — | — | 1 |
| Shop Rights | — | — | 1 | — | — | — | — |

|  | Lessors | Lessees | Lessors | Lessees | Lessors | Lessees | Unknown |
|---|---|---|---|---|---|---|---|
| Shop Rents | — | — | 10 | — | — | — | — |
| Land Rents | — | — | 6 | 1 | 1 | 1 | — |
| House Rents | 4 | 10 | 19 | 8 | 4 | 2 | 1 |
| *Accapitum/Emphyteusis* | | | | | | | |
| Houses | — | — | 1 | — | — | 2 | — |
| Lands | — | 1 | 8 | 8 | 1 | 9 | — |
| TOTALS | 28 | 23 | 118 | 80 | 57 | 51 | 7 |

## TABLE 4
### Kinship in Business

| Economic Sector | Total Acts[1] | Father/Son | Father/Daughter | Mother/Son | Mother/Daughter | Parents/Child | Aunt Uncle/Nephew | Uncle/Niece | Siblings | In-Laws[2] | Inter-family[2] | Same Name | Total Kin No. | Total Kin % | Couples |
|---|---|---|---|---|---|---|---|---|---|---|---|---|---|---|---|
| *Partnership* | | | | | | | | | | | | | | | |
| Maritime Comanda | 53 | | | | 11 | | | | 2W | 1 | 5 | 11 | 10 | 18.9 | |
| Maritime Societas | 2 | | | | | | | | | | 1 | | 1 | 50.0 | |
| Land Comanda | 38 | 11/1W | | | | 11 | | | | 1 | 4 | 11 | 9 | 23.7 | 3W |
| Land Societas | 22 | | | 1W | | | 11 | | | 1 | 6 | | 9 | 40.9 | |
| *Luxury Trade* | | | | | | | | | | | | | | | |
| Spices | 33 | | | | | | | | 3S | | | 2B | 5 | 15.2 | 2B |
| Silks | 47 | 1S/1B | | 1B | | | | | 1S/2B | | | | 5 | 10.6 | 2B |
| Mercery of Lucca | 13 | | | | | | | | | | | | 1 | 7.7 | |
| Woollen Cloth | 132 | 2S/4B | | 3B | | | | | 18S/9B | | | 4S/3B | 43 | 32.6 | 2B |
| Skins and Leather | 35 | | | 2B | | | | | 1S | | | 1S/2B | 6 | 17.1 | 3B |
| *Transport* | 43 | | | | | | | | 4C/1T | | | 1T | 6 | 14.0 | |
| *Commodities* | | | | | | | | | | | | | | | |
| Grain | 189 | 2S/6B | | 3B | | 4B | 1B | | 5S/6B | | 11 | 4B | 31 | 16.4 | 4S/13B |
| Grapes | 107 | 1S | | 1S | | 1S | | | | | | 2B | 5 | 4.7 | 18S/1B |
| Animals | 123 | 2S | | | | | | | | | | 2S | 4 | 3.3 | 2S |
| *Finance* | | | | | | | | | | | | | | | |
| Money Exchange | 64 | 2C | | | 1D | 1D | | 1D | 4C/5D | | | 4C/5D | 20 | 31.3 | |
| Loans | 375 | 1C/12D | | 10D | 1D | 1D | 4D | | 6C/11D | 5D | 11 | 1C/4D | 68 | 18.1 | 3C/58D |

*Real Estate*

| | | | | | | | | | | | |
|---|---|---|---|---|---|---|---|---|---|---|---|
| House Sales | 92 | 3S/1B | 1S | 2S | 10S | 1S | | 3 | 2S/1B | 24 | 26.1 | 14S |
| Land Sales | 249 | 5S | 9S | 3S | 9S/2B | 1B | | 5 | 0S/1B | 48 | 19.3 | 49S/3B |
| House Rentals | 136 | 4L/4R | 4L | 3L | 6L | 1L | | 1 | 1R | 25 | 18.4 | 5L/6R |
| Land Rentals | 36 | | 1L | | 3L | 1L | 1L | | 2L/2R | 10 | 27.8 | 1R |
| Rentals/Tables and Shops | | | | | | | | | | | | |
| Accapitum/ | 26 | | | | 2L | 2L | | | | 4 | 15.4 | 2R |
| *Emphyteusis* | | | | | | | | | | | | |
| Houses | 8 | | | | | | | | | | | |
| Lands | 107 | 12L/1R | 1L/1R | 3L | 1L 2L/2R | | | 1 | | 1 | 12.5 | 1L 3L/1R |
| Land Exchanges | 22 | | | | 1 | | | | 2 | 23 | 21.5 | |
| Sharecropping | 23 | | | | 2L | | | | | 3 | 13.6 | 9 |
| Rights of Use | 106 | | 1L 3S | 1L 3S | 6S | 1S | | | 3S/3R | 23 | 21.7 | 12S/2R |
| | | 1S | 2S | 1S | | | | 3 | | | | |

¹Figures do not include data from the Nogareti register for the Cabanis family, as these would have skewed the results.

²If there is no key symbol, contracts are between family members. In those cases where family members comprised *one* of the contracting parties in contracts of the economic sectors on the left, the specifics of the family relationship were broken down. In those cases where *both* parties to a contract were family, the fact was recorded under the category of "Interfamily" and the relationship not broken down.

KEY:

| | | | |
|---|---|---|---|
| W | = Workers | I | = Investors |
| L | = Landlords | R | = Renters |
| B | = Buyers | C | = Clients |
| S | = Sellers | T | = Transporters |
| C | = Creditors | D | = Debtors |

TABLE 5

**Transactions in Grain (Total Acts 190)**

| Social Category | Women Sellers No. of Acts | Women Buyers No. of Acts |
|---|---|---|
| Merchants | | |
| Changers/Moneyers | | |
| Retail/Wholesale | | |
| Nobles/*Burgenses* | | |
| Professions/Education | | |
| Jews | | |
| Royal Administration | | |
| Ecclesiastics | | |
| Women | | |
| Artisans/Service | | 2 |
| Food Trades | | 2 |
| Agriculture | | 1 |
| Foreigners | 1 | 4 |
| Unidentified | | |
| Local | 1 | |
| Other | | |
| Grain Merchants | | |
| TOTAL | 2 | 9 |

The distribution of women sellers and buyers varied somewhat from the male population of participants.[60] No women of agricultural background were noted selling grapes, while four instances of agricultural women purchasing grapes have been recorded (Table 6). Among men, sellers in agriculture accounted for 45.5 percent of all sales. Vineyard cultivation was a labor-intensive effort in which women may have been less active than men.[61] Women did, however, own vineyards, as the real estate acts show. Women bought and sold on the futures market in grapes, as did their male counterparts. Numerous couples were recorded selling grapes (Table 4). Widows and their sons were involved jointly in a few additional grape and grain purchases.

In yet another sector of the agricultural market, women were present in sales of animals of transport and burden (Table 7). They were primarily of rural background or from the group of cultivators of urban Montpellier. In this area of trade, as in the grape and grain transactions, widows were by far the most heavily involved buyers and sellers (Table 3). Here, as in the luxury trade, women used the same credit and financial mechanisms as their male counterparts. In general, women were modestly represented in the

TABLE 6

**Transactions in Grapes (Total Acts 112)**

| Social Category | Women Sellers No. of Acts | Women Buyers No. of Acts |
|---|---|---|
| Merchants | | 1 |
| Changers/Moneyers | | 2 |
| Retail/Wholesale | 2 | |
| Nobles/*Burgenses* | | |
| Professions/Education | 1 | |
| Jews | | |
| Royal Administration | 1 | |
| Ecclesiastics | | |
| Women | | |
| Artisans/Service | 2 | 4 |
| Food Trades | | 2 |
| Agriculture | | 4 |
| Foreigners | | |
| Unidentified | | |
|   Local | | |
|   Other | | |
| TOTAL | 6 | 13 |

luxury and commodities markets of the town. They were not noted in the extant transport contracts by which luxury goods in particular were shipped to markets at Paris and the Champagne Fairs or to Spain and Italy.[62]

Women participated in international and local commerce on another level through partnership contracts, an important form of investment credit in Montpellier. Four types of commercial partnership contracts have survived: the maritime *comanda,* the maritime *societas,* in which no women were participants, the land *comanda,* and the land *societas.*[63] The majority of female partners concentrated their activities in land trade as opposed to international maritime trade (Table 8). Out of fifty-nine surviving maritime contracts, women were mentioned in only three.[64] In one instance two sisters financed their brother's venture in the export of linen cloths to Cyprus and Armenia through a maritime *comanda* of 260 *l. t.*[65] They acquired 250 *l.* of linen cloth on credit and 50 *l.* in loan from a local merchant. In order to secure their debt to him they turned over a credit obligation that they held against a Jew of Montpellier for a house purchase. In a second act a draper's widow and daughter, who were subordinate investors in the export of French wool cloth and local cloths to the Byzantine Empire, contributed 65.2 *l. t.* to a total capital of 625.4 *l.*[66] It was not

TABLE 7

**Animal Transactions (Total Acts 124)**

| | All Sellers | | All Buyers | | Women Sellers | Women Buyers |
|---|---|---|---|---|---|---|
| Social Category | No. of Acts | % Total Acts | No. of Acts | % Total Acts | No. of Acts | No. of Acts |
| Merchants | 5 | 4.0 | 15 | 12.1 | | |
| Changers/Moneyers | | | 2 | 1.6 | | |
| Retail/Wholesale | 4 | 3.2 | 10 | 8.1 | | |
| Nobles/*Burgenses* | | | 2 | 1.6 | | |
| Professions/Education | | | 2 | 1.6 | | |
| Jews | | | | | | |
| Royal Administration | 1 | 0.8 | 3 | 2.4 | | |
| Ecclesiastics | | | 3 | 2.4 | | |
| Women | 5 | 4.0 | 2 | 1.6 | n/a | n/a |
| Artisans/Service | 17 | 13.7 | 20 | 16.1 | 1 | 1 |
| Food Trades | 7 | 5.6 | 7 | 5.6 | | |
| Agriculture | 40 | 32.3 | 45 | 36.3 | 2 | |
| Foreigners | 42 | 33.9 | 13 | 10.5 | 2 | |
| Unidentified | | | | | | |
| Local | 2 | 1.6 | | | | 1 |
| Other | 1 | 0.8 | | | | |

only women of the merchant class who chose maritime investment. An innkeeper's widow invested 50 *l. t.* in the trade of a grain merchant on land or on sea for one year.[67] Women were never involved in these partnerships as traveling partners in international maritime trade.

The main role of women in the surviving partnerships was, in fact, a passive one of sedentary investor. Even in the land-based contracts, women rarely played the working role. In one of the exceptions, a Franciscan friar was the investing partner in a land *comanda* with the widow of a cloth cutter who was the working partner.[68] In another instance, the widow of a silversmith accepted four and one-half marks of silver in *comanda* from a bachelor of canon law, perhaps to carry on the trade of her late husband's atelier.[69] Women and their sons might also be involved jointly as working partners.[70]

Women investing in land partnership contracts came from a broad spectrum of the local population, as shown in Table 8. In land *comande* widows predominated in nine of eleven instances, with wives present in two others.[71] Martha de Cabanis, widow of the mercer Guiraudus, acted as *curatrix* in a large bilateral *comanda* with a linen merchant as working partner.[72] Again, in the role of *curatrix*, Martha financed the largest surviv-

TABLE 8

**Women in Partnership Contracts**

| Social Category | Land Comanda Investors | Maritime Comanda Investors | Land Societas Investors | Land Societas Jr. Partners | Land Comanda Workers |
|---|---|---|---|---|---|
| Merchants | 2 | 2 | | | |
| Changers/Moneyers | 1 | | | | |
| Retail/Wholesale | 2 | | 1 | | |
| Nobles/*Burgenses* | | | | | |
| Professions/Education | | | | | |
| Jews | | | | | |
| Royal Administration | | | | | |
| Ecclesiastics | | | | | |
| Women | | | | | |
| Artisans/Service | 1 | 1 | | | 2 |
| Food Trades | | | | | |
| Agriculture | 3 | | | | |
| Foreigners | 2 | | | | |
| Unidentified | | | | | |
|   Local | | | | | |
|   Other | | | | 1 | |

ing land *societas* before 1350, capitalizing her partnership with a merchant through an investment of 1340 *l. t.*[73] Women and men united readily in partnership with one another at all levels of society. Family members joined together, as in the case of the fisherman who termed his mother-in-law, the widow of a shoemaker, *dicta socius mea.*[74]

In acts of partnership women were as versatile in their choice of partners as their male counterparts. Thus, the widow of a merchant financed fishermen in two *comanda* contracts, and the widow of a cultivator supplied capital for a silk merchant of Le Puy.[75] Interestingly, women were present in the only two extant *comanda* contracts that clearly show the conversion of real property into liquid capital for the purposes of partnership investment. In addition to the maritime investment by the two sisters noted above, a second act shows the widow of a man of Clermont-l'Hérault who had since migrated to Montpellier investing 20 *l.* from the profits of a home sale in Clermont in a *comanda* with a man of that town.[76] It may be that women's assets were often immobilized in real property, given the sources of their fortune in dowry and inheritance; record of moneyed dowries has, however, survived.[77] In another rare instance of financial practice, a woman demonstrated the negotiability of *comanda* credits by transferring them to a third party to offset a debt.[78]

The few international maritime investments by women were in the mainstream of the Montpellier export of wool cloths and linen to the Levant. The land *comanda* investments of women resembled investments by men in local trade and artisanal activities. Women were noted in substantial placement of funds. The main distinction to be underlined in partnership was the absence of women from the role of traveling merchant and the infrequency of their participation alone as working partners. Departure from the family home would have been more difficult for women at any stage in life—whether as mothers raising children and running a household or as young unmarried women or older widows—than for men. Factors mitigating against the activity of women as long-distance traders were the dangers inherent in travel—robbery and piracy—and the general hardship entailed by primitive roads and transportation systems.[79] Moreover, if no prescriptive literature regarding women's roles survives in medieval Montpellier, there is no reason to suggest that a woman's place as wife and mother was not the norm in local attitudes. This familial role was incompatible with long-distance travel. The career profile of the international merchant included a lengthy period of apprenticeship abroad, which resulted in late marriage for merchants of Montpellier.[80] In the majority of surviving marriage contracts, the man acted alone, a fact suggesting that he was probably at least twenty-five years of age.[81] This phenomenon was corroborated at all levels of society. Although there is no firm proof, given the absence of age statistics in marriage contracts, women may have married earlier. The fact that all obligations to their parents at the time of marriage, regardless of age, were declared valid by statute lends support to this contention.[82] Women contracted marriage in the majority of cases with the consent of both parents, one parent, other family members, or friends. Particularly in the case of merchant-class women, for whom dowry was no problem, marriage may have been early. Such factors would have weighed against the participation of women as traveling merchants.

Closely related to the urban commercial activities of Montpellier residents were those of banking and finance. The connections of foreign-exchange transactions to international trade can be amply demonstrated in the Montpellier evidence.[83] Women were not involved in extant foreign-exchange contracts, the domain of the merchant bankers and money changers.[84] In contrast, women were well represented in local lending activities.[85] They were recorded in 29 loans as lenders (7.6 percent of the total) and in 30 as borrowers (7.8 percent of the total) out of 384 surviving acts. Among the lenders women were rather evenly distributed across a whole range of social backgrounds; their fathers and husbands were changers, moneyers, members of the retail/wholesale trades, artisans, members of the service and food trades, and foreigners. Some women lenders were simply termed inhabitants of Montpellier by the notary. Women lent money to acquaintances and to their sons; especially in the case of widows, these loans were investments for profit.

The involvement of women in lending shows a somewhat different distribution of social groups than that of men. Merchants (12.2 percent of the total lenders) were the most frequently noted male lenders outside of the Jews. Women of merchant background accounted for only 3.4 percent of women lenders. Agricultural and artisan/service backgrounds were more heavily represented among women lenders than among men. While lending money was a common practice in Montpellier, in spite of ecclesiastical prohibitions of usury, women of the mercantile elite may have been less involved in this activity because of the lingering stigma attached to it and because their participation in business overall was a less necessary component of family survival than at other economic levels within society.[86]

Although female lenders and borrowers were of comparable numbers, borrowers were drawn from different social strata. Few mercantile and financial backgrounds were noted. Instead, artisanal and agricultural milieux provided women borrowers, as did the villages within a radius of fifty kilometers from Montpellier. This distribution was similar to that of male borrowers. Fifteen of the thirty women borrowers were not from Montpellier, though thirteen of those fifteen were from nearby. Most of the non-resident borrowers were clients for small loans—some in kind—from Jewish lenders at the end of the thirteenth century.[87] Women were noted further as borrowers in ten loans in association with their sons and in one case with a daughter (Table 4). The pattern of women's borrowing that emerges from these acts was one of consumption and subsistence, consistent with the traditional female role of family food provider. Much of the medieval population lived on the border of starvation.[88] Especially in the rural hinterland around Montpellier, bad harvests created real hardship, causing inhabitants to go into debt.

Single and widowed women were noted in equal numbers as money lenders (Table 3). Married women appeared less often in this role. In all likelihood, single women, after a certain age, and widows had more control over their resources than married women, whose dowries were assimilated with their husbands' goods.[89] Widows of humble background far outnumbered both single and married women as borrowers, suggesting the difficult financial straits of their status.

The activities associated with medieval banking and finance included foreign exchange, lending, and deposit banking. Women made investment deposits and accepted safekeeping deposits. Thus a changer secured the deposit of 200 l. melg. made to him by his widowed sister in 1301.[90] In the same year the daughter of a deceased draper requested the transfer of her deposit of 60 l., instituted by court order initially, from one party to another, with the expectation of receiving up to 6 l. (10 percent return) a year for her needs.[91] In 1343 a widow recognized before the notary that she held fifty Florentine florins *in custodia* for a master of medicine.[92] Deposit banking left relatively little trace overall in the Montpellier documents; hence, the participation of women is significant here. The degree of sophistication of operations by Montpellier changers, the traditional medieval deposit bankers, remains obscure, but there is no evidence to indicate that women were other than clients in the financial practices of changers.[93] In the related area of recovery and payment of debts, women were heavily involved, often as a reflection of their roles as administrators of the husbands' estates and as guardians of their children.[94]

Women were well represented in the complex real estate market of Montpellier, due undoubtedly to factors of dowry and inheritance.[95] They formed 21.8 percent of the sellers of land, a percentage higher than that of any one category of male sellers, and 10.7 percent of the land buyers; in these transactions women utilized credit infrequently and cash with regularity at rates that fall in the mid-range of male behavior. Less than one-tenth of women's sales of land were on credit while just under one-fifth of their purchases were with credit, an indication that women were perhaps cash poor. The male artisanal and service trades of Montpellier showed an even greater preference, relatively speaking, for credit purchases, with over one-third of their transactions so designed. In general, credit was less commonly employed in real estate than in the luxury trade of Montpellier. Over half of the sales and purchases of women were in vineyards, making them among the most active agents in this type of land sale. The climate of Montpellier and the pride of urban inhabitants in having their own *caves* made vineyards a common real estate investment.

House sales also drew women in impressive numbers, at 20.7 percent of the total participants, again a rate higher than that of any one male social group. Women bought houses with frequency, representing 14.1 percent of the total buyers. They recorded credit transactions in houses in numbers comparable to men. For no one group were credit sales an important facture of house transactions. Women's presence as proprietors of housing may reflect the composition of dowries and inheritance. Urban housing could be a profitable investment if rented out or exploited through one of the several methods described below. Housing management was less complex and less speculative than the administration of rural agricultural lands, whose yields might fluctuate enormously from year to year. Such facility may have been an attractive feature for urban women investors.

The social distribution of women sellers of land spanned a large cross-section of the population, with representation in all groups except nobles, *burgenses*, Jews, and royal administration. However, women of agricultural background were by far the most numerous sellers, accounting for 32.1 percent of female sales. In the general pool of the male population agricultural workers represented only 15.6 percent of the land sellers. Given the rigors and uncertainties of agriculture in the fourteenth century, it may be that many widows of local cultivators found themselves in need of converting land into cash.[96] Such an interpretation is consistent with their infrequent use of credit sales. Widows comprised the largest group of land sellers (Table 3). Married women were also present in important numbers; generally they stated that they had their husband's permission to act.[97]

Women selling and buying houses were more evenly distributed across the local social groups with the retail/wholesale and artisanal/service trades the sources of the largest numbers of women sellers. Buyers were uniformly representative of social groups with the exception of Jews and royal administration, groups absent from the pool of male sellers as well. Women were the only representatives of the category of nobles and *burgenses* to buy houses. For the reasons described above, housing could be a profitable and less burdensome investment than agricultural holdings. Women of the urban nobility were not active in commerce; their behavior may resemble that of a rentier class, for which nonspeculative, conservative investments were preferred.

In the exploitation of real property, women were again active. Many methods of deriving income from real estate were employed in this era: house and land rents, sharecropping, *accapitum* and *emphiteusis* tenurial arrangements.[98] Women were present in smaller numbers as lessees in these engagements. They were particularly dominant in the renting out of tables and shops in the markets of Montpellier, accounting for about one-third of the total transactions; they were never recorded as shop tenants. They were familiar with the means of generating real estate revenues from methods such as sales of rights in lands, houses, and shops for specific periods of time. One can also note their activity in land exchanges. Women as a group showed a preference for short- over long-term contracts in exploiting real estate holdings. This trend was especially marked among women from the artisanal/service trades and from agriculture. Women investors could be more responsive to market evolution and to adjustments for inflation and currency manipulation as a result. In sum, women had important interests in urban and rural property, demonstrating the full gamut of real estate techniques.[99]

As shown in Table 4, women acted with their children in land transactions. Couples were frequently sellers of land. Real estate sales were often accompanied by formal approvals of family members. In southern France, as elsewhere in medieval Europe, there was a strong predilection for families to guard jealously the kin's right of oversight in matters of property.[100]

After this rapid survey of women's participation in business in Montpellier, it is useful to highlight features of the urban environment that may account in part for women's economic roles observed in this study. In the sixty years preceding the Black Death of 1348, Montpellier had between thirty and forty thousand inhabitants, a significant population by medieval standards.[101] The population had reached a plateau by the end of the thirteenth century, and the economy was no longer in an expansive phase.[102] It did, however, demonstrate some resilience. In the uncertain economic conditions of the early fourteenth century, there may have been population pressure creating a tight job market, but the continued influx of foreign apprentices casts doubt on the magnitude of this pressure.[103] What, if any, competition for jobs existed remains unknown. No wage data permit comparison of male and female wages. That inhabitants were discontented is demonstrated by the unrest and factionalism of fiscal revolts in the 1320s and 1330s.[104]

The participation of women in an impressive variety of economic sectors is worth underscoring in light of these social and economic conditions. A cross-section of the urban population of women appeared in the notarial contracts. Distinctions of a social and economic nature among women's activities were more a matter of scale than of type. It comes as no surprise that women of Montpellier were not in the vanguard of international trade and finance, nor is it unexpected that they were not mentioned as traveling merchants on land or on sea. The long training in distant lands of the international merchant was irreconcilable with the demands of home, marriage, and family. Women were occasionally the recipients of local investment partnerships, but in most cases their role was one of sedentary investor. The remaining business contracts portray women as fully cognizant of the standard credit and investment mechanisms of the day. These business techniques were far from obscure; they were utilized by all social groups within the town. Women may have become familiar with these practices through observation of male family members or friends at work or through the advice of such individuals or even from the professional counsel of specialists such as the notary.

Women's work in industry and crafts was concentrated in areas typical of women's involvement throughout western Europe: the food trades, textiles, and precious metals. However, the absence of a significant wool cloth industry in Montpellier reduced the range of traditional textile roles for women. In Montpellier and elsewhere in Europe these women's trades were related to traditional female roles of provider of food, clothing, and ornament for the family. These occupations reflect a sharp sexual division of labor.

Real estate may well have been the sector in which women were most active. In this they shared some of the characteristics of a rentier class. Property was a conservative form of investment, in contrast to trade, where the risks multiplied with distance and difficulty of travel. Women did not specialize in speculative forms of capital investment such as foreign exchange. They lacked experience as changers and merchant bankers. While they were noted in international commercial investment, they seem to have favored economic stability over high profits. Widows often had responsibility for the welfare and support of children, preoccupations that could deter aggressive speculation. The widowed mother's role as guardian of her children was at the root of the frequent cooperation of mothers and sons noted in Table 4.

Widows emerge as the most active group among Montpellier women.[105] Because of their independence and potential means—they were free from their husbands' constraints and probably from their fathers' as well—widows were better equipped to participate in more diverse economic areas. Widows had an incentive not to remarry because the usufruct of their husbands' property was often dependent upon widowhood. The incidence of remarriage appears relatively low in Montpellier. Of the 132 marriage contracts surviving, only 7 instances of remarriage were recorded.[106]

Married women registered sufficient economic activity to vindicate the statutory posture that they might act with their husbands' consent or on their own responsibility if they exercised trades themselves. Their activities have almost the same breadth, if not the frequency, of widows' business operations. The demands of home and family could be reconciled with local economic ventures.

Single women were present in fewer numbers than either widows or wives. They had narrower investment options because without in-laws or children they had more limited contacts. They seem to have preferred reliable sources of revenues to preserve their livelihood. Single women appeared most often in real estate transactions and in loans, suggesting a conservative approach to business on their part. There is no way of knowing what proportion of the urban female population within Montpellier was single. However, the town can be characterized as one of merchants, jurists, doctors, university professors, students, and clerics, men who remained bachelors or married late in life.[107] Montpellier may not have been the most auspicious marriage market.

The notarial contracts of Montpellier portray women in active economic roles in the first half of the fourteenth century. Further work should test whether this relatively positive situation survived the era of the Black Death and the dramatic demographic changes that Montpellier experienced.[108] Before 1348 one possible explanation for women's participation in business could lie, somewhat ironically, in the weaker and less traditional configuration of the family in the urban setting. Urban families were more fragile than rural families because of the difficult living conditions in towns. Immigration itself caused disruption of family ties. Crowding in towns led to poor hygiene and rapid spread of disease. If much of women's influence in the rural setting, which characterized the early Middle Ages, had been through family channels, in some towns family structure, rather than evolving along patriarchal lines, tended to fragment.[109] Women were forced to assume more independence. The low incidence of kinship ties observed in business operations in Montpellier may have favored female activities.[110] There were times when women acted without a base in family enterprise, perhaps on behalf of their own trades. Women's economic involvement was not a direct parallel of men's roles, but the activities of Montpelliéraines were well integrated into the local business community and conspicuous within the urban economy of the pre-plague era.

## Notes

1. Thanks go to my colleague Sara Evans for her comments on this paper. Montpellier Law School doctoral theses that treat topics involving the legal status of women include Jean Hilaire, *Le régime des biens entre époux dans la région de Montpellier du début du XIIIe siècle à la fin du XVIe siècle* (Montpellier: Causse, Graille & Castelnau, 1957) and Louis de Charrin, *Les testaments dans la région de Montpellier au moyen âge* (Ambilly, 1961). Useful articles on the subject are by Edmond Meynial, "Des renunciations au moyen âge et dans notre ancien droit," *Revue historique de droit français et étranger*, ser. 3:25 (1901): 241–77, and Pierre Tisset, "Placentin et son enseignement à Montpellier. Droit romain et Coutume dans l'ancien pays de Septimanie," *Recueil de mémoires et travaux publiés par la société d'histoire du droit et des institutions des anciens pays de droit écrit*, fasc. 2 (1951): 67–94. By way of general background on the topic of this study, a somewhat anecdotal treatment of the urban woman in the Middle Ages is to be found in several chapters of Frances and Joseph Gies, *Women in the Middle Ages* (New York: Barnes & Noble, 1978).

2. Future studies will address the role of women through an investigation of the charter and cartulary evidence and in portraits of individual women's activities, which will flesh out the skeletal nature of this initial analysis. Data for this study were drawn from the notarial registers II 1–3 of the Archives Municipales de Montpellier (hereafter abbreviated A. M.) and II E 95/368–377 of the Archives Départementales de l'Hérault (hereafter abbreviated A. D.).

The notarial registers of Montpellier are collections of legally valid instruments written by notaries who had been licensed by public authority as recorders of public and private law transactions within medieval society. The notarial instrument might be a will, a contract, an act of litigation, an emancipation, an appointment to office, an acquittal, a statement or letter of one kind or another, solemnly registered by the notary in the presence of witnesses. The notary's register or cartulary served the purpose of a much expanded registry of deeds, preserving notations of engagements for which written proof might be needed in the future. These records provide a texture, depth, and range of evidence unequaled in the terse entries of the town chronicle of Montpellier and in the municipal statutes, and a consistency missing from the thousands of individual charters housed in the Archives Municipales de Montpellier. Notarial records furnish a practical laboratory for the study of business operations. On the use of this sort of evidence, see David Herlihy, *Pisa in the Early Renaissance: A Study of Urban Growth* (New Haven: Yale University Press, 1958), pp. 1–20.

3. Jo Ann McNamara and Suzanne Wemple, "The Power of Women through the Family in Medieval Europe: 500–1100," *Feminist Studies* 1 (1972): 136–38. One might note that queens such as Blanche of Castile were still able to exert tremendous influence in a later period. Another study suggesting decline is that of Marion F. Facinger, "A Study of Medieval Queenship: Capetian France, 987–1237," *Studies in Medieval and Renaissance History* 5 (1968): 1–48.

4. On strategies of family preservation, see Georges Duby, *La société aux XIe et XIIe siècles dans la région mâconnaise* (Paris: A. Colin, 1953).

5. Régine Pernoud, *La femme au temps des cathédrales* (Paris: Editions Stock, 1980), recently advanced the hypothesis that the position of women in France declined with the rise of the bourgeoisie at the end of the Middle Ages. A revisionist view of the fate of urban women in early modern Europe is provided by Judith C. Brown and Jordan Goodman, "Women and Industry in Florence," *Journal of Economic History* 40 (1980): 73–80.

6. On the downtrends in urban population in the later Middle Ages, see Harry A. Miskimin, *The Economy of Early Renaissance Europe, 1300–1460* (1969; reprint, Cambridge: Cambridge University Press, 1975), pp. 73–77.

7. On the diversity of the urban population, see my dissertation, "Commerce and Society in Montpellier: 1250–1350," 2 vols. (Ph. D. diss., Yale University, 1974), pp. 1–56. See also Louis J. Thomas, *Montpellier, ville marchande: histoire économique et sociale des origines à 1870* (Montpellier: Librairie Valat, Librairie Coulet, 1936).

8. Alexandre Teulet, ed., *Layettes du Trésor des chartes*, I (Paris: Plon, 1863), provides the most reliable editions of these statutes. For the tenth through the twelfth centuries, David Herlihy has argued for the high status of women in southern France. See "Land, Family, and Women in Continental Europe, 701–1200," *Traditio* 18 (1962): 89–120; reprinted in *Women in Medieval Society*, ed. Susan Stuard (Philadelphia: University of Pennsylvania Press, 1976), pp. 13–45. To date there exist few studies of women in contractual law and business. One work of interest, however, is Susan Stuard, "Women in Charter and Statute Law: Medieval Ragusa/Dubrovnik," in *Women in Medieval Europe*, pp. 199–208.

9. Meynial, pp. 264–67. On the *Senatusconsultum Velleianum*, see Adolf Berger, *Encyclopedic Dictionary of Roman Law* (Philadelphia: The American Philosophical Society, 1953), p. 700. By the *Senatusconsultum Velleianum* women were forbidden to assume liability for others. On marital authorization see Hilaire, pp. 118–32.

10. Teulet, p. 259: "Si mulier fidejusserit pro aliquo vel pro aliqua, tenetur in illis casibus in quibus leges permittunt. Nam secundum leges viget intercessio femine: creditoris ignorancia, obligantis se scientia, largitione, rei proprie racione, renunciatione, pignoris [vel] yppotece remissione, secundo post biennium cautione, coram tribus testibus in instrumento preemissa confessione, libertate, dote, et si

exerceat officium et gratia illius intercedat, vel voluntate mariti, efficaciter obliga-
tur." See also Tisset, p. 87.

11. For a discussion of the institution of *fideiussor*, see Mireille Castaing-Sicard,
*Les contrats dans le très ancien droit toulousain* (Toulouse: Imprimerie M. Espic, 1959),
pp. 379–403. For an important example of a woman acting as *fidejutrix*, see the case
of Mirabelle, wife of Johannes Andree, in my article "Commercial Fraud in the
Middle Ages: The Case of the Dissembling Pepperer," *Journal of Medieval History* 8
(1982): 63–73.

12. Hilaire, pp. 112–13.

13. E.g., A. D. II E 95/370, J. Holanie, f. 69r, for a woman acting without her
husband's consent.

14. Tisset, p. 80.

15. Article 90 of the 1204 statutes; see Teulet, p. 262.

16. See the discussion of apprenticeship contracts below.

17. Meynial, pp. 266–67, and Tisset, p. 86. See also Hilaire, pp. 102–17. It
should also be noted that the husband often made a marital gift to the wife in the
form of the *augment*. See Hilaire, pp. 192–201.

18. Tisset, p. 88, and article 12 of the 1204 statutes; Teulet, p. 256.

19. Tisset, p. 98, and article 54 of the 1204 statutes; Teulet, p. 260.

20. Hilaire, pp. 136–91. The issue of restitution was a complex one, often
governed by the specific clauses of the marriage contract.

21. De Charrin, pp. 118–22, studied the institution of the guardian in the
Montpellier evidence. I plan a future study of the mother's role as guardian of her
children in the writings of the early fourteenth-century jurist Petrus Jacobi.

22. Agnes de Bossones, widow of Petrus, money changer, figures frequently in A.
M. II 1, J. Grimaudi, in these roles.

23. I will draw the general context for this study from two works, a book,
*Business, Banking and Finance in Medieval Montpellier* (Toronto: Pontifical Institute of
Mediaeval Studies, 1985), and a long article, "Land, Houses and Real Estate Investment in Montpellier: A Study of the Notarial Property Transactions, 1293–1348,"
in *Studies in Medieval and Renaissance History* 6 (Old Series, vol. 16) (1983): 37–
112.

24. See "Land, Houses and Real Estate Investment," note 27, for a detailed
discussion of the selection of these social categories.

25. These roles are sometimes subsumed under the label "breeder-feeder." See
Elise Boulding, "The Historical Roots of Occupational Segregation. Familial Constraints on Women's Work Roles," *Signs* 1 (1976) supplement: 95–117.

26. As an example, consider A. D. II E 95/371, J. Holanie, f. 109r: "Johanna,
uxor quondam Bernardi Senareti ortolani Montispessulani."

27. Consider "Alazacia, filia Bertrandi de Alamanha, habitatrix Montispessulani" in A. D. II E 95/369, J. Holanie, f. 81v. The name occurs in the dative in the
act itself as Alazacia was owed money in a loan.

28. An exception can be found in A. D. II E 95/369, J. Holanie, f. 4r, "Rixenda
Ganterius, pistrix" (baker), with the name again in the dative in the act as she was
owed money in a loan. On the notarial naming practices in general, see my article
"Patterns of Population Attraction and Mobility: The Case of Montpellier, 1293–
1348," *Viator* 10 (1979): 266.

29. André Gouron, *La réglementation des métiers en Languedoc au moyen âge* (Geneva: Librairie E. Droz, 1958), pp. 245–46.

30. Ibid. One can contrast the Montpellier situation with that of northern Eu-

rope. See E. Dixon, "Craftswomen in the *Livre des Metiers*," *Economic Journal* 5 (1895): 209–28, and Annie Abram, "Women Traders in Medieval London," *Economic Journal* 26 (1916): 276–85. On women in medieval London, see also Sylvia L. Thrupp, *The Merchant Class of Medieval London* (1948; reprint, Ann Arbor: The University of Michigan Press, 1962, 1968), pp. 169–74.

31. See my article "Patterns of Population," p. 267, for a breakdown of all apprenticeship contracts by year and geographic origin of apprentices.

32. On the absence of a cloth industry, see my article "Le rôle de Montpellier dans le commerce des draps de laine avant 1350," *Annales du Midi* 94 (1982): 17–40.

33. "Patterns of Population," pp. 271–72. Recall the baker's trade of the *fournier* ordinances. The term here is *pistor, pistrix*.

34. Ibid., pp. 272–74.

35. Compare Eileen Power, *Medieval Women*, ed. M. M. Postan (Cambridge: Cambridge University Press, 1975), p. 58.

36. E.g., a brother apprenticing his sister: A. D. II E 95/368, J. Holanie, f. 32v.

37. E.g., the apprenticeship of a son of a first marriage by a wife of a merchant and a cousin: A. D. II E 95/368, J. Holanie, f. 127v.

38. "Patterns of Population," p. 272, note 77.

39. A. D. II E 95/368, J. Holanie, f. 135v. The term for gilder is *deaurator;* an alternative translation might be goldsmith. I am currently collaborating on an article with Faye Powe on medieval metalwork, in which she hopes to determine a better rendition of *deaurator.*

40. A. D. II E 95/368, J. Holanie, f. 56v. See *Business, Banking and Finance,* Appendix II, "Monetary Problems," for a discussion of currencies in the Montpellier notarial registers. *D.t.* = *deniers tournois, s.t.* = *sous tournois, l.t.* = *livres tournois.* All sums have been converted to the good silver standard of April 1330.

41. A. D. II E 95/368, J. Holanie, f. 131v.

42. Women of the Mediterranean world were often involved in such activities. See William N. Bonds, "Genoese Noblewomen and Gold Thread Manufacturing," *Medievalia et Humanistica*, fasc. 19 (1966): 79–81. On the importance of women in the silk industry elsewhere in Europe, see Marian K. Dale, "The London Silkwomen of the Fifteenth Century," *Economic History Review* 4 (1933): 324–35, and Dixon, pp. 218–21.

43. A. D. II E 95/377, B. Egidii, f. 227 r.

44. A. D. II E 95/368, J. Holanie, f. 37r: tailoring; II E 95/371, J. Holanie, f. 38v: tailoring; II E 95/368, J. Holanie, f. 136r: linen corduroy; A. M. II 1, J. Grimaudi, f. 80v: silk corduroy.

45. A. D. II E 95/369, J. Holanie, f. 13v: mercery. The statutes of the mercers are found in A. M., *fonds du Grand Chartrier*, Arm. C, Cass. 1, Louvet no. 1117. Mercery as a trade encompasses a broad range of activities in Montpellier, from silk-cloth sales to what we would today term "notions": ribbons, thread, decorative accessories.

46. On the involvement of Montpellier with silks, see my article "Medieval Silks in Montpellier: The Silk Market ca. 1250–ca. 1350," *The Journal of European Economic History* 11 (1982): 117–40.

47. Ibid. See below.

48. A. D. II E 95/368, J. Holanie, f. 50r: basket weaving; II E 95/377, B. Egidii, f. 28r: painting; II E 95/368, J. Holanie, f. 30r: old clothes; II E 95/369, J. Holanie, f. 38r.

49. A. D. II E 95/371, J. Holanie, f. 50r: *ancilla*, or servant.

50. A. D. II E 95/368, J. Holanie, f. 136r.

51. Ibid., f. 37r.

52. Ibid., f. 135v. It should be noted that sons followed their fathers' trade infrequently according to the extant apprenticeship evidence.

53. Chapter 2, "Credit in the Market Place," in *Business, Banking and Finance*, deals in general with the luxury trade and the commodities market.

54. Ibid., for a discussion of credit mechanisms in Montpellier trade.

55. An earlier version of the table "Kinship in Business" was first presented in a paper entitled "Kinship in Business: The Case of Medieval Montpellier," given at the Eighteenth International Congress of Medieval Studies, Western Michigan University, Kalamazoo, Michigan, May 1983.

56. See "Medieval Silks," p. 128.

57. A. D. II E 95/374, G. Nogareti, f. 38r. Another widow of Toulouse dealt through a procurator in Montpellier to purchase mercery of Lucca. See ff. 30r and 38r.

58. The tables of total participants in the grape and grain trades are published in Chapter 2, "Credit in the Market Place," in *Business, Banking and Finance*.

59. On agricultural problems of the south of France, see Marie-Josèphe Larenaudie, "Les famines en Languedoc au XIVe siècle," *Annales du Midi* 64 (1952): 27–39. See also "Commerce and Society in Montpellier," 1: 212–24.

60. See note 58 above.

61. On grape cultivation in the region of Montpellier, see Gaston Galtier, "Le vignoble et le vin dans le Languedoc oriental de la fin du XIe siècle à la Guerre de Cent Ans," in *Etudes médiévales offertes à M. le Doyen Fliche de l'Institut* (Montpellier: Faculté des Lettres et Sciences Humaines, 1952), p. 9.

62. For a synopsis of transport contracts, see "Commerce and Society in Montpellier," 2: 261–67.

63. For a detailed discussion of partnership in Montpellier, see Chapter 1, "Investment in Business Partnerships," in *Business, Banking and Finance*. Tables of total participants are found in this chapter. It should be noted that *comanda* is the local spelling of *commenda*.

64. Table 3 of "Investment in Business Partnerships" lists two women since only the major investing partners were tallied.

65. A. M. II 2, J. Grimaudi, f. 14r.

66. A. D. II E 95/372, J. Holanie et al., f. 13r.

67. A. D. II E 95/369, J. Holanie, f. 45v. On modest investors in maritime *commenda* contracts in other Mediterranean towns, see Hilmar Krueger, "Genoese Merchants, Their Partnerships and Investments, 1155–1164," in *Studi in Onore di Armando Sapori* (Milan, 1957) 1:259–71, and Rosalind Berlow, "The Sailing of the 'Saint-Esprit'," *The Journal of Economic History* 39 (1979): 345–62.

68. A. D. II E 95/368, J. Holanie, f. 36v.

69. A. D. II E 95/372, J. Holanie et al., f. 48v.

70. See Table 4 and A. D. II E 95/376, J. Laurentii, f. 5r.

71. See Table 3.

72. A. D. II E 95/374, G. Nogareti, f. 18rR.

73. Ibid., f. 12vR.

74. A. D. II E 95/372, J. Holanie et al., f. 38r.

75. A. D. II E 95/369, J. Holanie, f. 52r and 95v; II E 95/371, J. Holanie, f. 22r.

76. See note 65 above, and A. D. II E 95/368, J. Holanie, f. 59r.

77. On moneyed dowries, see Hilaire, pp. 98–100. They became increasingly common after the mid-fourteenth century.

78. A. D. II E 95/369, J. Holanie, f. 43r.

79. There were, of course, female vagabonds who coped with such dangers as best they could. See the comments of Boulding, p. 109.

80. Claude Carrère, *Barcelone: centre économique, 1380–1462*, 2 vols. (Paris: Mouton, 1967), found this to be true for merchants of Barcelona. Diane Hughes, "Urban Growth and Family Structure in Medieval Genoa," *Past and Present* 66 (1975): 25, suggested the opposite to be characteristic of Genoese merchants, who married while still in their teens.

81. The notarial registers, the *Grand Chartrier*, and the *fonds de la Commune Clôture* of the Archives Municipales all contain marriage contracts.

82. See note 15 above.

83. See Chapter 5, "Foreign Exchange," in *Business, Banking and Finance* for general background.

84. For a synopsis of foreign-exchange contracts, see "Commerce and Society in Montpellier," 2:269–78.

85. See Chapter 3, "Loans," in *Business, Banking and Finance* for the tables involving total participants and women participants mentioned below.

86. On usury in Montpellier, see my article "Les opérations de crédit dans la coutume et dans la vie des affaires à Montpellier au moyen âge: le problème de l'usure," in *Diritto comune et diritti locali nella storia dell'Europe* (Milan: Guiffrè, 1980), pp. 189–209.

87. On loans by Jews of Montpellier, see R. W. Emery, *The Jews of Perpignan in the Thirteenth Century* (New York: Columbia University Press, 1959), pp. 131–33, Appendix 3.

88. The muncipal chronicle of Montpellier stated in the year 1333 that famine raged, young men were weakened by a diet of raw herbs, and people were dying in the streets. See "La chronique romane," in *Le Petit Thalamus de Montpellier*, ed. F. Pégat, E. Thomas, and Desmazes (Montpellier, 1840), p. 347.

89. See note 17 above.

90. A. M. II 1, J. Grimaudi, f. 37r.

91. A. M. II 2, J. Grimaudi, f. 53v. For a further example, see A. D. II E 95/375, P. de Pena, f. 119r.

92. A. D. II E 95/372, J. Holanie et al., f. 36r.

93. See the comments in Chapter 5, "Deposit Banking and the Recovery of Debts," in *Business, Banking and Finance*. Robert Favreaux, "Les changeurs du royaume de France sous le règne de Louis XI," *Bibliothèque de l'Ecole des Chartres* 122 (1964): 216–51, found evidence of women changers in a slightly later period. Raymond de Roover, *Money, Banking and Credit in Medieval Bruges; Italian Merchant-Bankers, Lombards and Money-Changers* (Cambridge, Mass.: Mediaeval Academy of America, 1948), pp. 173–74, stated that money changing was open to women.

94. See note 22 above. Women may have enjoyed a more generous fate as debtors than did men, thus benefiting from somewhat greater protection under the law. There is a suggestion in the statutes of 29 June 1221 (Teulet, pp. 519–20) that male debtors were subject to a harsher regime of punishment than females. Debtors specifically identified as male could be turned over to the mercy of their creditors, who, if the debtors did not have the means of nourishing themselves, would feed them according to the decisions of the court of Montpellier.

95. My article "Land, Houses and Real Estate Investment" provides tables of

overall real estate participation and women's participation in property transactions. The comments below regarding real estate are drawn from this study.

96. On general fourteenth-century problems, see Elisabeth Carpentier, "Autour de la peste noire: famines et épidémies dans l'histoire du XIVe siècle," *Annales: Economies, Sociétés, Civilisations* 18 (1962): 1062–92. See also Edouard Perroy, "A l'origine d'une économie contractée: les crises du XIVe siècle," *Annales: E. S. C.* 4(1949): 167–82.

97. E.g., A. D. II E 95/369, J. Holanie, f. 75r. Women at times named their husbands procurator to sell their property. See II E 95/369, J. Holanie, f. 68v.

98. See "Land, Houses and Real Estate Investment" for a discussion of these operations.

99. Herlihy, "Land, Family, and Women," pp. 27–30, found a high incidence of land ownership by women in southern France in the early Middle Ages. In urban Montpellier, such a tradition appears to have been perpetuated.

100. There was, however, no *retrait lignager*, in principle, in Montpellier. On the general problem, see P. Ourliac and J. de Malafosse, *Histoire du droit privé, 2; Les biens*, 2d ed. (Paris: Presses Universitaires de France, 1971), p. 167.

101. On the demography of Montpellier, see Josiah Cox Russell, "L'Evolution démographique de Montpellier au moyen âge," *Annales du Midi* 74 (1962): 345–60, and my suggested modifications of this view in "Patterns of Population," p. 257, note 2.

102. On economic trends in southern France, see Archibald R. Lewis, "Patterns of Economic Development in Southern France, 1050–1271 A.D.," *Studies in Medieval and Renaissance History* n.s. 3(1980): 57–83. Lewis (pp. 79–80) maintained that Montpellier continued active after the era of expansion was over. My own work suggests that there was indeed resilience interspersed with crises.

103. See "Patterns of Population."

104. On these problems, see Jean Combes, "Finances municipales et oppositions sociales à Montpellier au commencement du XIVe siècle," *Fédération historique du Languedoc méditerranéen et du Roussillon* 44 (1972): 99–120. See also the study by Jan Rogozinski, *Power, Caste, and Law. Social Conflict in Fourteenth-Century Montpellier* (Cambridge, Mass.: The Medieval Academy of America, 1982).

105. A prominent role for widows was noted by Jean Verdon, "Notes sur la femme en Limousin vers 1300." in *Etudes d'histoire médiévale. Hommage à Philippe Wolff* (Toulouse: Edouard Privat, 1978), pp. 320–29.

106. See note 81 above.

107. For a discussion of Montpellier's population composition, see "Patterns of Population."

108. On the Black Death in Montpellier, see my article "Changes in Testamentary Practice at Montpellier on the Eve of the Black Death," *Church History* 47 (1978): 253–69.

109. David Herlihy, "Mapping Households in Medieval Italy," *The Catholic Historical Review* 58 (1972): 13, speaks of a "proliferation within the city of small, truncated, and incomplete households," in the case of Florence.

110. The influence of kinship may have been subtly active in Montpellier, as it was in Genoa. See Hughes, p. 16.

*Maryanne Kowaleski* 8

# Women's Work in a Market Town: Exeter in the Late Fourteenth Century

Well over fifty years ago, Annie Abram and Eileen Power both noted the active role women played in the commercial life of medieval English towns.[1] Focusing for the most part on larger towns such as London, they distinguished the types of occupations women held and discussed the relatively privileged position of townswomen engaged in trade compared to medieval women of other classes. But in the intervening decades, no historians have really examined all the different types of work medieval townswomen performed, nor have they explored female employment and work status in the hundreds of provincial market towns in medieval England. In this essay I would like to continue the investigation Abram and Power initiated and analyze the various kinds of work women did for wage or for profit and the basic characteristics of women's work in one medieval English town in the late fourteenth century.

The focus of this study is Exeter, a market town of Devonshire in southwestern England. Possessing a population of around 3000 in 1377, Exeter lacked the stature of such national and international market centers as York and London. But the town did function as an important regional exchange center for the southwestern peninsula, largely through its geographic position at the head of a river estuary and through its control of the seaport four miles to the south.[2] Exeter was also an important administrative center. The bishop of the diocese had his seat there; Benedictine, Dominican, and Franciscan religious houses were located in the town; and the king's itinerant justices held court sessions in the local castle. The town's main industries—cloth manufacture and leather and skin crafts—while not highly developed, were, nonetheless, well established and benefited from a steady and cheap source of raw materials from the city's predominantly pastoral hinterland.

Medieval Exeter had no craft guilds.[3] Instead, an exclusive political and

145

economic organization called the "freedom," whose membership was deliberately restricted to the wealthier men in town, controlled trade and politics. In 1377, only 21 percent of all the Exeter heads of household (about 4
percent of the total population) belonged to this elite group, whose members profited from numerous economic and legal privileges, chief among
them the right to trade at retail.[4] Freedom members also enjoyed lucrative
monopolies in such commodities as wool and cloth, and were the only ones
eligible to vote or run for high political office. Entry into the freedom was
generally obtained by patrimony, redemption, and, from the mid-fourteenth
century, by apprenticeship. Women were not allowed to enter the
freedom.[5]

Although the freedom's dominance of the town's political and economic
structure restricted women's opportunities in Exeter commerce and industry,
women did gain access to economic opportunities and resources in other
ways. Women (along with the majority of men, who never gained entry
into the freedom) could engage in the processing and retailing of such
commodities as food, cloth, and hides upon payment of an annual fine or
licensing fee.[6] Moreover, Exeter's favorable inheritance laws allowed
women to inherit equally with men, regardless of marital status. The Exeter
courts also confirmed the widow's right to control property and chattels
whose common title she had shared with her husband. A married daughter
could thus inherit part of her father's estate, and a widow not infrequently
continued to manage her husband's business.[7] On occasion, widows of politically prominent merchants who continued their husbands' trade were
able to enjoy the privileges of the deceased husbands' freedom membership
until they remarried.[8]

The conjuncture of commercial and common law somewhat confused the
legal status of economically active women. Under law merchant or commercial law, a married woman could maintain independent status and plead as a
*"femme sole"* (or single woman) if she traded separately from her husband.[9]
The Exeter courts upheld this juristic distinction; several husbands success-
fully declined legal responsibility for their wives' trading debts.[10] Under
common law, by contrast, women were mere adjuncts of their husbands.[11]
Thus, Exeter husbands generally brought suit on behalf of their wives,
especially in cases of assault or unpaid salaries. In several instances, married
women who sued on their own in the Exeter courts were accused of failing
to appear with their husbands.[12] Many problems also arose over debts
women contracted before marriage (or remarriage), although husbands reluctant to take on their wives' debts were more than happy to pursue their
wives' debtors.[13] Because the husband of a widow could acquire the debtors
of her deceased husband, marriage to such widows could prove immediately
enriching. Thomas Smalecombe, for example, was allowed to enter the

freedom in place of all debts the city owed his new wife's deceased husband, John Bozoun.[14] Marriage to a wealthy widow often prompted access to the ruling merchant elite as well. Philip Seys, John Holm, and Richard Kenrigg all attained entry to the freedom the same year they married wealthy widows of the Exeter oligarchy, and all went on to obtain the highest offices in town government within only a few more years.[15] A woman's economic position in medieval Exeter, therefore, was mixed. She could practice a trade on her own or enjoy an inheritance that made her a significant landowner or business partner, but more often than not she practiced a trade or continued to practice a trade her husband had initiated, and her inheritance more obviously benefited her husband's economic and political position than her own.

It is necessary, however, to go beyond the theoretical and legal position of medieval urban women and look at the realities of their work for wage or for profit. The evidence presented here consists of two analyses of the voluminous and detailed Exeter records from the late fourteenth century. The first is an analysis of 4,526 debt cases in the Exeter courts over a ten-year period from 1378 to 1388.[16] This analysis makes it possible to measure the nature and extent of female and male commercial activity. Second, occupational information drawn from a wide range of sources, including local market courts, customs accounts, wills, and crown and civil pleas was collated for a twenty-year period from 1373 to 1393 to obtain 435 documented cases of Exeter women who worked for wage or profit.[17] While this latter analysis has some problems—for example, common law too often obscured the role of wives who worked in a trade with their husbands so that wives are underrepresented in this study—it nevertheless offers a valuable source of information on the types of independent work women did in medieval towns and the nature of their participation in work for wage or profit.

Women's work in medieval Exeter falls into five general occupational groups. Keeping in mind that wives who worked are underrepresented, the 435 cases of working women breaks down as shown in Table 1. I will first consider those women most actively engaged in commerce, the retailers and merchants. Most of the 99 women who actively participated in Exeter's commercial life during this period functioned as petty retailers. Only a very few oligarchic widows, who were continuing the business interests of their husbands, traded wholesale or overseas and could thus be classified as merchants. Compared with men, women were disproportionately active as retailers. A breakdown of the types of debts contracted in Exeter shows that 66 percent of female litigants were involved in debts concerning sales, in contrast to 48 percent of the male litigants.[18] An even more striking difference between female and male commercial activity can be found in the

TABLE 1

**Exeter Working Women by Occupational Group, 1373–93**

| Occupational Group | No. in Group | % of Women in Group (N = 435) | No. in Other Occupations | % |
|---|---|---|---|---|
| Servants | 160 | 37% | 26 | 16% |
| Brewers, Tapsters | 150 | 34% | 65 | 43% |
| Retailers, Merchants | 99 | 23% | 58 | 59% |
| Prostitutes | 55 |  | 24 | 44% |
| Brothel Keepers | 17 | 17% | 17 | 100% |
| Artisans | 51 | 12% | 30 | 59% |
| Total | 532 | 123%* |  |  |

SOURCE: See note 17.
*The total adds up to 123% because 79 of the 435 women (18%) practiced in more than one occupational group; 16 of these women were engaged in three occupations and one in four occupations.

commodities they traded. Almost three-quarters of the female debts (including both creditors and debtors) involved food and drink, compared with less than one-half of the male debts.[19]

Market court fines also indicate the predilection women had for the victual trade. As shown in Table 2, except for the occasional processing and retailing of cloth and the purchase of hides and wool-fells, all female market activity involved food and drink. Most of these women retailed poultry, dairy products such as eggs, butter, and cheese, or staples such as oats, salt, and flour. Moreover, women did most of the brewing and selling of ale. Food retailing was probably a favorite female occupation because (1) freedom membership was not a prerequisite for retailing food on Exeter market days; (2) it did not require a large amount of capital and equipment; and (3) the skill and time commitments needed were minimal. Men, however, controlled the sale of higher-priced, imported products (spices and wine), victuals in scarce supply (grains), or foods that required a great deal of skilled processing (bread and meat).

The high profile of women in food retailing does not appear to have enhanced their image in society. Small-time retail traders, especially women, were commonly called "hucksters" or "regrators," both terms with pejorative connotations.[20] Hucksters were so poor they hawked wares in the street, while regrators bought up goods in the market and sold them later in the day when scarcity drove the price up. Neither practice endeared such women to consumers, who felt these female traders raised the prices of scarce food items, or to merchants, who frequently resented the intrusion of

## TABLE 2
### Market Fines in Exeter's Mayor's Tourn from 1373 to 1393

| Activity | Women Fined | Total Fined | Female % of Total Fined |
|---|---|---|---|
| Forestalled and regrated dairy products | 88 | 355 | 25% |
| Sold reheated foods | 10 | 82 | 12% |
| Forestalled and regrated poultry | 9 | 81 | 11% |
| Cut and retailed cloth | 40 | 404 | 10% |
| Sold oats, salt, flour in false measures | 105 | 1079 | 10% |
| Brewed against the Assize of Ale | 728 | 8158 | 9% |
| Bought hides and wool-fells improperly | 38 | 1137 | 3% |

Note: In most instances, the market "fines" were little more than a type of licensing fee paid every year by those engaged in these retail activities.

such petty middlemen in their trades. The bias against female regrators is clearly seen in William Langland's *Piers Plowman*, where Avarice boasted that his wife, Rose the regrator, commonly cheated her customers by using false weights and selling thinned ale by the cupful to poor people for the price of better-made ale.[21] John Gower in his *Mirour de l'Omme* had an equally poor view of women in trade. Although he decried the practices of the male regrator, Gower saved his most severe condemnation for female regrators, whom he believed most greedy and deceitful.[22]

Women's lack of commercial privilege and status inhibited not only the range of their marketing activities but also the quality of their participation in commerce. Only 32 percent of the women who appeared in the Exeter debt cases from 1378 to 1388 were creditors, compared with 51 percent of the men. Their disadvantage also shows up in a comparison of the average amount of the debts men and women contracted. As illustrated in Table 3, women's debts involved far lower sums of money than did men's. Among creditors, women's debts averaged 7½s. while male debts were almost 14s. on the average. Among debtors, the difference between the average value of debts of men and women was even greater. Women who appeared on their own, without the benefit of a husband as cocreditor or codebtor, possessed the lowest value debts of all. Indeed, even unenfranchised men who never held any civic office (and who, like women, did not enjoy freedom membership, lacked political power, and possessed little personal wealth) had an average debt rate of 7s. 11d. as debtors, compared with the

## TABLE 3

### Average Amount of Female and Male Debts in Exeter, 1378–88

| Litigants | Creditors' Debt Average | (N) | Debtors' Debt Average | (N) |
|---|---|---|---|---|
| Men | 13s. 10d. | (1815) | 14s. | (1803) |
| Women | 7s. 6d. | (84) | 6s. 4d. | (135) |
| Single Women | 5s. 9d. | (66) | 4s. 6d. | (96) |
| Wives* | 14s. 11d. | (18) | 10s. 1d. | (39) |

SOURCE: M.C.R. and P.C.R. debt cases, 1378–88.
*Women who appeared in the debt case with their husbands.

## TABLE 4

### Outcome of Exeter Debt Cases According to Sex, 1378–88

| | Creditors | | Debtors | |
| Outcome | Women (N = 170) | Men (N = 3668) | Women (N = 367) | Men (N = 3585) |
|---|---|---|---|---|
| In Mercy | 27% | 27% | 21% | 26% |
| Case Not Pursued | 32% | 29% | 32% | 39% |
| License of Concord | 9% | 15% | 14% | 12% |
| False Query | 16% | 6% | 9% | 5% |
| Failure to Wage Law | 4% | 3% | 4% | 3% |
| No Information | 12% | 20% | 20% | 15% |
| Total | 100% | 100% | 100% | 100% |

SOURCE: M.C.R. and P.C.R. debt cases, 1378–88.

4s. 6d. average for single female debtors. Obviously, the mere fact of being female placed women at a disadvantage in local markets. Further disadvantages accrued to female traders because of their lower incomes,[23] inability to join the freedom, and their emphasis on petty retailing rather than the more lucrative wholesale trade or the production of manufactured goods.

Women also faced the court's prejudice when appearing as plaintiffs or defendants in debt suits (see Table 4). In most cases, male litigants received more favorable verdicts than did female litigants. For example, when women initiated debt suits as creditors in the courts, they were almost three times more likely to be fined for pursuing a false complaint than male creditors. Similarly, male debtors were 7 percent more likely than female debtors to have the complaint against them dropped by their creditors. The exception to this general trend involved male debtors who received outright guilty verdicts more often than female debtors (by 5 percent). Historians of crime have found similar patterns among English women indicted for crimes in the fourteenth century. In one study, Barbara Hanawalt noted that only 12 percent of indicted women were convicted, compared with almost 23 percent of the men indicted.[24] The courts appear to have been prejudiced against women who initiated law suits, but favorably disposed toward women who found themselves the victims of prosecution. The courts' attitude also surfaces in their inclination to condone the fines of women and to excuse women's amercements.[25] But whether this was done out of sympathy or because women were often less financially well-off than men is open to argument.

In addition to retailing, brewing and selling ale was a popular female occupation. The vast majority of the 150 women in this occupational group (see Table 1) brewed and sold their own ale; only a small percentage appear to have functioned solely as tapsters or sellers of ale. Of 8,158 brewing fines (actually licenses) in the Exeter market court from 1373 to 1393, women accounted for 9 percent of all fines (see Table 2). But this figure really represents only widows and unmarried women who brewed, since the local court listed brewing fines under the name of the head of household regardless of who did the actual brewing. Although the full extent of female participation in this trade is thus obscured, other evidence clearly shows that women supervised much of Exeter's commercial brewing. In fact, there was only one professional male brewer in Exeter during this period.[26] But the most telling evidence is the sudden appearance of widows paying brewing fines in the years immediately following their husbands' deaths. They, rather than their husbands who had previously been listed as the household brewer, must have been brewing all along. Almost one-third of all the female brewers surveyed in this period fell into this category.[27] Furthermore, even though women ostensibly accounted for only 9 percent of all brewing fines, they were involved in 39 percent of all debts concerning drink (mostly ale) in a similar period.[28] In this respect, Exeter was not unusual; research on other medieval English communities also points to vigorous female involvement in the brewing industry.[29] In most fourteenth-century English towns and villages, women oversaw the production of ale both for domestic use and commercial sale. The majority of female brewers were in their middle married years, and most were aided to some degree by servants or family members.[30] Such activities no doubt supplemented the family income and, in the case of poorer women (who probably acted more frequently as tapsters), may have contributed a significant amount to the household budget.

Besides retailing and brewing, industry or craft work also employed many women, albeit on a smaller scale (see Table 1). Female artisans in Exeter generally worked in three crafts: candle making, leather working, and cloth manufacture. Female candle makers usually also functioned as retailers or victuallers, although at least one, Isabella Candeler, appears to have pursued only the trade of candle making.[31] Women active in the leather crafts exhibited a similar work pattern; only five of the twenty identified women in this craft from 1373 to 1393 practiced the trade with any regularity, and three of the five were employed in other occupations as well.[32] Moreover, at least three of the female leather-craft artisans had husbands working in the same craft.[33] Clearly female participation in leather-finishing crafts, an important industry in the local economy, was quite limited; indeed, only 2 percent of the 1031 fines assessed on those involved in the hide and skin trade in Exeter from 1378 to 1388 were directed at women.[34] A variety of factors may explain women's low level of activity in this industry; for one, freedom membership was desirable in purchasing necessary raw materials (hides, skins, and unfinished leather). Second, a sizable capital outlay was needed not only for raw materials but also for requisite tools, tanning agents, and a workshop.[35] Third, the time commitment, in terms of both the training demanded and the slowness of the leather process, was more substantial than most married women or mothers could afford. The medieval Exeter women's lack of civic economic privilege and access to capital and training opportunities effectively barred her from anything more than minimal participation in one of the town's most vital industries.

By far the most numerous group of female artisans in Exeter worked in the town's thriving cloth industry. After debts involving food and drink, for example, cloth commodities made up the second largest group found in female debts.[36] The records of market licensing fines for women also indicate that cloth working ranked second only to victual retailing (see Table 2). Similarly, the cloth trade was the second most popular occupation for women in a study of female debt litigants in Exeter.[37] Women in the cloth trade also represented the greatest range of female participation and success of any one occupational group. The most successful high-status female merchants in Exeter all sold cloth and may have supervised some of the cloth-finishing process as well. But the three female cloth merchants identified in this period were all widows who were continuing trades their husbands had begun.[38] Unfortunately, the Exeter records generally remain silent on the contribution of the wife to her husband's trade during his lifetime. But evidence from other towns indicates that wives commonly worked side-by-side with their husbands, especially in the cloth trade.[39] Indeed, since the basic unit of production in the medieval economy was the household, and since the workplace and the family home were often one and the same in medieval towns, it is not surprising that the medieval sexual division of labor was not as fully developed as it was to become in later centuries.

Besides the three successful cloth merchants, a number of Exeter women also worked as weavers, tailors, hosiers, and dressmakers—occupations that called for training and skill and were potentially profitable. Emma Taillor, also called Emma Hosiere, made stockings for a living, and her 1377 tax rate (12d.) as a head of household attests to her status in the artisan "middle class."[40] While some craftswomen like Emma Hosiere controlled their own businesses, many others worked as employees or on a piecework basis. Typical of these women workers was Joan Shippestere (a pattern cutter or dressmaker), who habitually received fines for ten years in Exeter market court for cutting up and retailing cloth without freedom membership.[41] Walter atte Wode of the ruling oligarchy, one of Joan's employers, accused her of stealing linen and wool cloth, as well as wool, over a period of three years. Several years later, John Stobbe leveled a similar charge against her. Obviously Joan was not as financially secure or as commercially successful as the merchants' widows or Emma Hosiere.

Joan Shippestere probably had more in common with the great number of women who worked at low-status, menial tasks in the textile trade such as combing, washing, and spinning. Most women engaged in the Exeter textile trades assumed the lower-status jobs within the industry. Women with their own occupational surnames, for instance, usually possessed names that indicated typically female, low-status tasks; Isolda Spynnestere, Magota Spynster alias Lavender, Joan and Cecilia Kemestere (wool combers), Katherine Broudestere, and Agnes, Joan, and Julia Shippestere all worked in the local cloth trade.[42] Without the privileges of freedom membership and adequate capital, women could not hope to advance to prominent positions within the cloth industry.

Servants represented the largest number of women who worked for wage or for profit in medieval Exeter (37 percent of the sample; see Table 1). Also included in this category are wet nurses, midwives, and healers, who offered their services on a part-time basis.[43] But the vast majority of female servants did domestic work, and most were young, unmarried girls, many of whom were probably recent immigrants to town.[44] The low status of this occupation is evident in the manner in which the 160 female servants were identified in the 1373–93 records: 74 percent were designated only by their first name and their employer's name; 6 percent were recorded under the name of a husband or a father; and only 20 percent were called by their own full names. Moreover, wages were low and turnover in employment was rapid.

While the length of contract varied, most servants, in this period of high demand for labor, agreed to work for only one year at a time. Indeed, female servants undoubtedly found themselves in an advantageous bargaining position following the Black Death, which reduced the population of England by as much as one-third to one-half.[45] Exeter, like other areas, experienced labor shortages and took steps to regulate servants through local commissions to enforce the Statute of Laborers and renewed efforts to enroll labor contracts and prosecute labor disputes in the local courts.[46] Employers regularly sued in the city's courts to recover servants enticed away by other employers with promises of better pay or more amenable working conditions.[47] Servants who wanted to break their service contract normally advanced one of two complaints to show just cause: either their employer's failure to pay their salary or physical abuse. Female servants in particular suffered from the latter practice.[48] Employers frequently sued servants for withdrawal of their services before their term had expired, or for leaving "without reasonable cause." Other employers complained about dishonest servants who robbed their masters or cheated them over a period of years.[49] Not all employer-employee relationships, however, were acrimonious. Faithful servants, such as Margaret Bryan and Thomasia, servant of Nicholas Bynnecote, were well rewarded in their employers' wills.[50] Employers also acted as pledges for their servants and aided them in times of distress. But still other employers involved female servants in less savory activities. For example, Walter Radeslo, the most notorious brothel keeper in Exeter at this time, had several female servants who not only worked as prostitutes for him, but also were accused of receiving stolen goods with him on several occasions.[51] Indeed, prostitution was the most common alternative "occupation" for female servants.[52]

Although women were severely underrepresented in the Exeter courts in commercial transactions (accounting for only 6 percent of all creditors and debtors from 1378 to 1388), they were well represented as receivers of stolen goods, petty criminals, and brothel proprietors (32 percent of the brothel keepers were women).[53] Many women plainly fell into these "occupations" because of limits put on their commercial activities, most notably their inability to join the freedom and their lack of legal rights under common law. A profile of women prosecuted as prostitutes in Exeter courts shows them to be poor, unmarried, and immigrants. All fifty-five prostitutes recorded between 1373 and 1393 came from poor backgrounds, and only 15 percent were married. Moreover, based on rough surname evidence, at least 20 percent of these women had no family in Exeter, compared with 9 percent of all other female workers (except servants).[54] Single women such as Emma Northercote, who possessed no apparent family ties in Exeter, received yearly fines for prostitution. At the same time she worked as a servant for the oligarch, Philip Seys, probably in a domestic capacity.[55] The majority of her clients were priests, and one, John Gonlok, maintained a relationship with her for over four years. Interestingly, although a woman of limited means, Emma appealed to the Exeter courts as a creditor at least nine times; three of her debtors were priests, presumably delinquent in payment for services rendered. Women such as Emma, born into a poor family or a recent immigrant from the countryside, had few employment options open to them besides low-paying servant jobs. Without husbands, training in a craft, or some small capital for retailing, they could gain additional income only through petty crime and prostitution.

Regardless of the type of work women performed, five basic characteristics distinguished female employment in late fourteenth-century Exeter. First, women rarely benefited from formal training in the workplace. Since women were not allowed to enter the freedom, they were not allowed to serve as apprentices. This lack of formal training is reflected in the type of work women did; domestic servants, prostitutes, retailers, and brewers required little in the way of long-term detailed instruction. Indeed, the vast majority of women who worked did so in occupations that demanded skills they learned informally within the family. Typically "female" skills such as nurturing, housework, food preparation, child rearing, and clothing production were marketable in occupations like servantry, food retailing, brewing, cloth manufacture, the nursing of children, and even prostitution. In Exeter, women almost never practiced trades that required a long apprenticeship such as metal work, construction work, or mill work. Nevertheless, a few women did pursue other trades that demanded some skilled direction. While a few of these women (for example, weavers) appear to have been trained by employers,[56] many more seem to have received more informal training from family members engaged in the same trade. This situation is most obvious when a widow continued to run her husband's business or when a daughter practiced her father's (or mother's) trade. For example, Joan Strengher brewed and sold ale, retailed eggs, butter, and cheese, and ran a tavern and a brothel—all activities her parents, Agnes and John Strengher, had also pursued.[57]

Second, even when women did receive some skilled training, they still tended to hold low-status marginal positions within individual trades. Women engaged in the cloth industry, for instance, usually functioned as spinners, washers, carders, pattern cutters, and sewers. Even women who worked as weavers always did so as employees in a male-run workshop. Although there were no apparent laws that prohibited women from certain occupational positions in Exeter, their exclusion from the freedom effectively blocked any chance of obtaining real commercial success. The only exceptions were three wealthy widows, Alice Nymet, Magota Golde, and Elizabeth Wilford, all of whom continued their dead husbands' mercantile businesses, thereby enjoying some of the benefits of freedom membership.[58] But all three husbands had held high civic office (in fact, Nymet and Wilford had served as mayor) and were among the wealthiest merchants in Exeter. The success of their widows obviously resulted in large part from the continuing prosperity of a business that had previously been headed by a politically and commercially prominent husband.

The reliance of these three widows on the commercial and political reputation of dead husbands points to a third characteristic of female employment in medieval Exeter. Marital status and position within the household frequently dictated the type and nature of women's involvement in work. Married women and daughters often helped their husbands and fathers in their trades.[59] But this type of female work activity is often hard to trace in medieval documents, since society regarded such labor as a contribution to the household income rather than an individual effort. Wives and daughters who did work autonomously tended to earn a wage in low-status and low-paying jobs such as servantry and prostitution, to retail food staples or dairy products, or to brew ale at home for profit. Retailing food staples and dairy products was clearly not a full-time occupation, for men never relied wholly on this activity for income. Instead, it was the type of part-time, low-investment, household-related trade particularly suited for women juggling the demands on their time of household and family. Brewing was evidently considered part of a woman's contribution to the home economy, since brewing fines were always entered under the name of the male head of household, regardless of who actually did the brewing. The lack of legal recognition of women's work was due to the vagaries of common law, which dictated that a wife was one with her husband under the law. As a result, medieval legal records fail to make the wife's contribution to family business or family income clear. Many women, especially those whose husbands were petty retailers, victuallers, or innkeepers, obviously worked alongside their husbands in trade. Indeed, 42 percent of the Exeter debt litigation from 1378–88 involving women listed wives as cocreditors or codebtors with their husbands. But the nature of the wife's contribution only becomes apparent when the husband died and his widow continued to carry on the same trade. Indeed, it was probably easy for a widow to assume responsibility for her husband's trade after his death because she was his partner in trade during his lifetime.

Since common law allowed widows greater freedom than married women, widows who worked represent the most noticeable group of working women in medieval records. Widows were probably more likely to carry on a full-time trade than were wives because of either (1) their greater freedom under law, (2) their need to support themselves or their household (indeed, according to Exeter tax records, female heads of household who worked had lower average incomes than did female heads of household who did not work but depended on property rents for income),[60] or (3) the usually lighter family responsibilities of widows, which allowed them to devote more time to work for wage or profit.

In fact, older widows and single women were the two groups of women who most closely approached the consistent work patterns of men. The

majority of working women (including many widows) exhibited an incon-
stant pattern of work. Thus the fourth characteristic of female employment
was its intermittent nature. Only a few women in Exeter paid licensing fees
in the market courts year after year to practice a particular trade. Men, on
the other hand, were much more likely to pay an uninterrupted series of
yearly fees, indicating steady pursuit of a trade or craft. In addition, the
types of work women performed were well suited to an interrupted work
career. Servantry, brewing, food retailing, and prostitution did not require a
full-time commitment over several successive years. Indeed, the intermittent nature of women's work may well have contributed to women's low
status within individual trades. Although there is little direct evidence in
the Exeter records, the sporadic female work pattern was probably related to
the demands of family and household, in terms of both time and income.
But indirect evidence, that older widows and single women exhibited work
patterns similar to those of men, suggests that women with fewer family and
household demands were more likely to work full-time for a wage or profit.

The fifth and last characteristic of female employment in medieval Exeter
was the tendency for women to practice in more than one trade. As illustrated in Table 1, at least 18 percent of the identified working women in
Exeter were engaged in more than one occupation. Within particular occupational groups, the percentage of women working in another occupation
was amazingly high. All the female brothel proprietors, for example, worked
for wage or profit in other occupations too, as did over half of the artisans
and retailers. This work pattern differs from that displayed by men.[61] In
fact, national legislation restricted craftsmen to one trade but permitted
women, as the "eternal amateurs," in the words of L. F. Salzman, to follow
more than one occupation.[62] Since women were often not well established
in one trade for any length of time, and since they were excluded from the
more profitable trades because of their lack of freedom membership (or full
guild privileges in other towns), they were not perceived as a threat to male
job security. But even women who appear to have concentrated on one
trade often engaged in supplementary commercial activities as well. The
comfortably established Emma Hosiere, for example, not only made stockings but at the same time retailed dairy products periodically and purchased
and fashioned leather.[63] Even more typical of Exeter working women may
have been Matilda Monioun, who as a head of household paid 4d. in
murage tax in 1377. She brewed and sold ale for at least sixteen years in a
row, retailed eggs, butter, and cheese and sometimes fish, as well as making
woollen cloth. Her textile activities appear to have been a bit on the shady
side since the courts several times accused her of using weavers' leftover
strands of wool thread for her cloth, in addition to receiving stolen wool,
thread, and other goods.[64]

158 *Maryanne Kowaleski*

Clearly the varied commercial and industrial activities Matilda Monioun pursued offered her little in the way of either social prestige or stable income if she so regularly sought to supplement her earnings through petty crime. Indeed, this pattern of multiple occupations that Exeter women exhibited reflects not their varied talents and high work profile but their general inability to secure anything more than marginal, low-paying positions within any one trade. Women had to settle for less remuneration because their work was relatively unskilled, sporadic, unstable, and oriented toward the needs of family and home rather than the single woman. The only women who rose to powerful commercial positions did so as widows of prosperous merchants. But since the work activities of women were so frequently linked to those of their husbands or fathers, women had a weak work identity and failed to participate in existing guilds or to organize themselves. Despite the occasional benefits bestowed on the *femme sole* under law merchant, the limits placed on economic activities of these medieval townswomen through common law and local customary law were far more severe. Denied entry to the town's elite economic and political organization of the freedom and laboring under legal and domestic handicaps, it is not surprising that many women were forced into extralegal alternative "occupations" such as receiving stolen goods, keeping a brothel, or prostitution.

## Notes

Unless noted otherwise, all documents cited here may be found in the Devon County Record Office. Abbreviations employed here are: M.T.—Mayor's Tourn; M.C.R.—Mayor's Court Roll; P.C.R.—Provosts' Court Roll; P.C.A.—Exeter Port Customs Accounts; C.R.A.—City Receiver's Accounts.

1. Annie Abram, "Women Traders in Medieval London," *Economic Journal* 26 (1916): 276–85. Eileen Power, "The Position of Women," in *The Legacy of the Middle Ages*, ed. C. G. Crump and E. F. Jacob (Oxford, 1926), pp. 401–34, reprinted with her other essays in Eileen Power, *Medieval Women*, ed. M. M. Postan (Cambridge, 1975); see especially "The Working Woman in Town and Country," pp. 53–69. Sylvia Thrupp also drew attention to the commercial activity of some London women in *The Merchant Class of Medieval London (1300–1500)* (Ann Arbor, 1948), pp. 169–74. See also Marian K. Dale, "The London Silkwomen of the Fifteenth Century," *Economic History Review*, 1st ser. 4 (1932): 324–35.

2. A more detailed picture of Exeter's commerce and industry may be found in Maryanne Kowaleski, "Local Markets and Merchants in Late Fourteenth-Century Exeter" (Ph.D. diss. University of Toronto, 1982).

3. Craft guilds did not appear in Exeter until the mid-fifteenth century; see Joyce A. Youings, *Tuckers' Hall Exeter: The History of a Provincial City Company Through Five Centuries* (Exeter, 1968), pp. 9–13. Even when the guilds were estab-

lished, however, the freedom continued to exercise considerable political and economic influence; see M. M. Rowe and Andrew Jackson, "Introduction," in *Exeter Freemen, 1266–1967*, Devon and Cornwall Record Society extra series, 1 (Exeter, 1973), pp. xx–xxv.

4. See J. W. Schopp, ed., *The Anglo-Norman Custumal of Exeter* (Oxford, 1925), for the earliest statement of the privileges of freedom members. For more on the political and economic power of the freedom, see Maryanne Kowaleski, "The Commercial Dominance of a Medieval Provincial Oligarchy: Exeter in the Late Fourteenth Century," *Mediaeval Studies* 46 (1984): 355–84, and Rowe and Jackson, "Introduction," pp. xi–xx.

5. There was one exception to this rule; in 1335 Joan, widow of the wealthy merchant Thomas le Spicere, was allowed to enter the freedom at the request of two men, but only for the duration of her widowhood; see *Exeter Freemen*, p. 21. Three other Exeter widows of wealthy merchants, Alice Nymet, Magota Golde, and Elizabeth Wilford, appear to have enjoyed similar privileges, although they were never formally enrolled in the freedom; see note 58 below. Other town freedoms, such as that of York, did admit women, although the majority were widows; see R. B. Dobson, "Admissions to the Freedom of the City of York in the Later Middle Ages," *Economic History Review*, 2d ser. 26 (1973): 13–14. In York, married women had first to obtain entry to the freedom if they wished to practice a trade independently of their husbands; see Francis Collins, ed., *Register of the Freemen of the City of York, 1272–1558*, Vol. I, Surtees Society, 96 (Durham, 1897), p. xiii.

6. These fines were enrolled in the local market court, called the Mayor's Tourn, which met once a year in each of the four quarters of the city (N.Q., S.Q., E.Q., W.Q.).

7. See M.C.R. 16 March 1377, 13 Jan 1382. See also Duryard Court Roll, 19 May 1386, for the inheritance of a bastard daughter from her natural mother. For the chattel and property rights of women in other English towns, see Mary Bateson, ed., *Borough Customs*, vol. II, Selden Society, 21 (London, 1906), pp. ci–cxv.

8. Alice Nymet, Magota Golde, and Elizabeth Wilford sold and exported cloth, appearing, as their husbands before them, in the aulnage and port customs accounts. They also imported wine, dyestuffs, and a wide variety of other goods and paid no custom duties, a privilege reserved for freedom members; see P.C.A. 1391/92 to 1402/03; E. 101 338/11, mm. 8, 9, 11, and E. 122 40/23 in the Public Record Office (P.R.O.).

9. Abram, "Women Traders in Medieval London," pp. 280–81; Power, "Working Women," p. 59; Bateson, *Borough Customs*, II, pp. cxii–cxiii; see also Mary Bateson, ed., *Borough Customs*, vol. I, Selden Society, 18 (London, 1904), pp. 226–27.

10. P.C.R. 30 Aug. 1386; M.C.R. 14 March 1390, 2 May 1390.

11. Frederick Pollock and Frederic William Maitland, *The History of English Law*, 2d. ed. (Cambridge, 1898; reissued, 1968), pp. 399–436.

12. See, for example, P.C.R. 28 April 1379; M.C.R. 27 Jan. 1388, 14 March 1390. For husband and wife liability in other English towns, see Bateson, *Borough Customs*, I, pp. 222–27; II, pp. cxi–cxv.

13. See, for example, M.C.R. 9 Jan. 1391, 23 Jan. 1391. In the Exeter M.C.R. and P.C.R. debt cases, 1378–88, ninety-nine administrators and executors of estates (usually a widow and her new husband) sued for debt recovery, but only forty-six such cases were to be found among the debtors.

14. *Exeter Freemen*, p. 35; C.R.A. 1379/80.

15. *Exeter Freemen*, pp. 34–35; M.C.R. election returns 1378–90; P.C.R. 14 Oct. 1378; M.C.R. 14 July 1382, 12 Jan. 1383. Seys married Gonilda, widow of Nicholas Boghewode, Holm married Christina, widow of Walter Fouke, and Kenrigg married Helewisia, widow of Robert Noble. Boghewode, Fouke, and Nobel had all served in the highest civic offices during their lifetimes.

16. M.C.R. and P.C.R. 29 September 1378 to 29 September 1388; courts for the period 29 Sept. 1383 to 29 Sept. 1384 were missing. About 70 percent of the debts involved purely commercial matters such as credit purchases, loans, custom payments, and cash transactions. Roughly 10 percent of the disputes concerned salaries, slightly over 10 percent centered on unpaid rent or relief, and the remaining 10 percent of the cases involved unpaid amercements, damages, or pledging arrangements. There were a total of 537 female litigants and 8,794 male litigants. For more information on this analysis, see Kowaleski, "Local Markets," pp. 407–32.

17. The main sources used for this analysis were the Mayor's Tourn, Mayor's Court Rolls, Provosts' Court Rolls, City Receiver's Accounts, Port Customs Accounts, Exeter City Deeds, Exebridge Wardens' Accounts, Duryard Manorial Accounts and Court Rolls—all located in the Devon Record Office. Also employed were the St. Sidwell's Fee Court Rolls and the City Accounts of the Dean and Chapter and Vicars Choral in the Exeter Cathedral Library, as well as K.R. Customs Accounts (E. 122), K.R. Accounts Various (E. 101), L.T.R. Enrolled Accounts Miscellaneous (E. 358), and Gaol Delivery Rolls (JUST. 3) in the P.R.O.

18. M.C.R. and P.C.R. debt cases, 1378–88; the nature of the debt case was specified for 106 female litigants and 1,189 male litigants.

19. M.C.R. and P.C.R. debt cases, 1378–88; the commodity involved in the debt case was specified for 72 of the female debts and 323 of the male debts.

20. L. F. Salzman, *English Trade in the Middle Ages* (Oxford, 1931), pp. 75–80. Michael Prestwich, *York Civic Ordinances, 1301.* Borthwick Papers, no. 49 (York, 1976), pp. 11–12, 27–28. See also R. H. Hilton, "Lords, Burgesses and Hucksters," *Past and Present* 97 (1982): 3–15.

21. William Langland, *The Vision of William Concerning Piers the Plowman.* ed. Walter W. Skeat (Oxford, 1886), I, pp. 148–49.

22. *The Complete Works of John Gower*, ed. G. C. Macaulty (London, 1899), I, pp. 291–92.

23. In the 1377 Exeter murage tax, Miscellaneous Roll 72, the average household tax was 13*d.*; but the twenty-three households headed by women paid only 7*d.* on the average.

24. Barbara Hanawalt, *Crime and Conflict in English Communities, 1300–1348* (Cambridge, Mass., 1979), p. 54.

25. See, for example, the fines in the Mayor's Tourn. Frequently the scribe noted that these fines were condoned because the woman was a "pauper"; see also Exebridge Wardens' Accounts, 1395/96.

26. John Scarlet, brewer; see E.Q.M.T. 1373–93; M.C.R. 29 Oct. 1380.

27. M.T. 1373–93; 42 of the 150 female brewers noted in this period first appeared in the M.T. brewing lists the year their husbands died; all 42 husbands had been enrolled as brewers the year before they died. Many of these men were active in the town's local markets and government; it seems implausible that some of Exeter's busiest merchants and craftsmen actually took the (considerable) time to brew ale and to retail it.

28. M.C.R. and P.C.R. debt cases, 1378–88; women were involved in twenty-nine out of a total seventy-five cases concerning drink.

29. For English towns, see Annette Koren, "Ely in the Late Middle Ages" (Ph.D. diss., Indiana University, 1977), pp. 235–36; Henry Wood, *Medieval Tamworth* (Tamworth, 1972), p. 56; Thrupp, *Merchant Class of London*, p. 170; William Hudson, ed., *Leet Jurisdiction in the City of Norwich During the Thirteenth and Fourteenth Century*, Selden Society, 5 (London, 1892), pp. xxxviii–xxxix, 51. For English rural communities, see Judith M. Bennett, "The Village Ale-Wife: Women and Brewing in Fourteenth-Century England," chap. 2 of this volume.

30. See, for example, the comments of Margery Kempe of Lynn concerning her brewing efforts and the help rendered by her servants; *The Book of Margery Kempe*, ed. S. B. Meech and H. E. Allen, Early English Text Society, no. 212 (London, 1940), pp. 9–10. For more on the age and marital status of female brewers, see Bennett, "The Village Ale-Wife."

31. There were at least five women engaged in candle making in Exeter from 1373 to 1393. For Isabella Candeler, see N.Q.M.T. 1392; M.C.R. 18 March 1392.

32. Regularity of trade was measured by appearance in the Mayor's Tourn annual lists of those selling, buying, or working leather without freedom membership or outside the appropriate marketplace; see M.T. 1373–93. Only five women (Emma Knyght, Claricia Crewys, Isabella Tanner, Claricia Wolbeter, and Emma Hosiere) were fined at least three years in a row.

33. Joan, wife of John Boggebrook, cordwainer; N.Q.M.T. 1384; Alice, widow of Robert Frank, cordwainer: S.Q.M.T. 1374–79, M.C.R. 1 May 1385; and Claricia Wolbeter, probably widow of Richard Wolbeter, who had also worked the leather trade: W.Q.M.T. 1373, 1379–82.

34. M.T. 1378–88; these fines were usually assessed only on those without freedom membership, so the level of male participation in the trade is actually underestimated.

35. See Robert Delort, *Le commerce des fourrures en occident à la fin du moyen âge (vers 1300–vers 1450)* (Rome, 1978), pp. 708–49. L. F. Salzman, *English Industries in the Middle Ages*, 2d ed. (Oxford, 1923), pp. 245–57.

36. M.C.R. and P.C.R. debt cases, 1378–88; 18 percent of a total 72 female debts involving specified commodities concerned cloth, clothing, wool, or dyestuffs, compared with 14 percent of a total 323 male debts for which the commodity was identified.

37. M.C.R. and P.C.R. debt cases, 1378–88; of a total 68 known female occupations, 54 percent were merchants, retailers, or victuallers, 24 percent were textile workers, and 22 percent were servants. Moreover, most of the female merchants sold cloth.

38. See note 58 below.

39. E. Lipson, *The Economic History of England*. Vol. I: *The Middle Ages*, 12th ed. (London, 1959), pp. 359–63; see also Abram, "Women Traders," and Power, "The Working Woman," pp. 53–67.

40. W.Q.M.T. 1373–83; Miscellaneous Roll 72; 420 heads of household were taxed. The mean tax was 13*d.*, the mode was 6*d.*, and the median was 6*d.*

41. See W.Q.M.T. 1378, 1388; M.C.R. 22 June 1377; P.C.R. 11 Jan. 1382 for this and the following.

42. W.Q.M.T. 1378–88; S.Q.M.T. 1376; E.Q.M.T. 1385, 1390; P.C.R. 30 Oct. 1380, 28 Feb. 1381, 28 June 1386; M.C.R. 22 June 1377; C.R.A. 1376/77, 1397/98; all of these women appear to have been unmarried or widows; none had the same surname as her husband. In general, the female occupational surname evidence for Exeter is not plentiful and indicates few female occupations outside the cloth trade or victualling ("Huckstere," "Tappistere"). See above, note 31, for an

Isabella Candeler and note 32 for an Isabella Tanner. Eileen Power was a bit more optimistic about female occupational surnames based on her research on the late fourteenth-century poll tax returns for the West Riding in Yorkshire; see "The Working Woman," p. 65.

43. Unfortunately, the extant records of Exeter and other English towns reveal little about this form of female employment, largely because midwives, wet nurses, and healers worked part-time, did not receive formal training or organize into guilds, and were not regulated by civic laws. We catch only occasional glimpses of women who worked in this capacity. In 1364, for example, six Exeter midwives were summoned to the city jail to verify a female inmate's claim that she was pregnant (pregnant women received stays of execution so that the unborn child would not be killed); see JUST. 3 221/6 in the P.R.O. In 1384, Joan Burnard and her husband, Robert, sued a man for payment of medicine they had sold him, P.C.R. 21 May 1384. For women in these occupations in other towns, see Shulamith Shahar, *The Fourth Estate*, trans. Chaya Galai (London, 1983), pp. 201–205, and Merry Wiesner, "Early Modern Midwifery: A Case Study," chap. 6, this volume.

44. Other historians have also noted the high proportion of female immigrants to towns. R. H. Hilton estimates that perhaps three-quarters of the immigrants to Halesowen between 1272 and 1350 were women; see "Lords, Burgesses and Hucksters" p. 10.

45. John Hatcher, *Plague, Population and the English Economy 1348–1530* (London, 1977), pp. 21–26.

46. *Calendar of Patent Rolls*, Edw. III. vol. X (London, 1910), p. 494; M.C.R. 5 March 1380; see also Miscellaneous Roll 2 as cited in *The Records of the City of Exeter*, Royal Commission on Historical Manuscripts, Reports, 73 (London, 1916), p. 384. See the M.C.R. of the 1350s and 1360s for the increased number of contracts enrolled and the labor disputes. Many of these cases were tried as proceedings under the Statute of Laborers; in 1353 alone there were at least eight such proceedings, M.C.R. 21 Jan., 28 Jan., 18 Feb., 1 April., 29 July, 5 Aug., 12 Aug., and 9 Sept. 1353. For labor shortages elsewhere, see Nora Kenyon, "Labour Conditions in Essex in the Reign of Richard II," *Economic History Review* 4 (1934): 429–51.

47. See, for example, M.C.R. 17 Jan. 1379, 25 Nov. 1381, 29 Nov. 1378, 7 Oct. 1392, 19 Aug. 1381; *Calendar of Patent Rolls*, Henry IV, vol. III (London, 1907), p. 338.

48. See, for example, P.C.R. 27 April 1381, 28 Feb. 1381; M.C.R. 27 May 1392, 3 March 1393.

49. See, for example, P.C.R. 30 Jan. 1380, 6 March 1382, 7 Nov. 1381.

50. M.C.R. 27 Oct. 1382, 16 Feb. 1400.

51. M.C.R. 20 Jan. 1388, 24 Feb. 1388, 15 March 1389, 12 April 1389, 18 Oct. 1389, 31 Jan. 1390, 15 Jan. 1392, 12 Aug. 1392, 21 July 1393; W.Q.M.T. 1391; N.Q.M.T. 1391; S.Q.M.T. 1390.

52. At least 9 percent of the 160 servants were presented in court as prostitutes, 3 percent were brewers, 3 percent retailed foodstuffs, and 1 percent worked in the cloth trade.

53. There were a total of 9,331 creditors and debtors; see M.C.R. and P.C.R. debt cases, 1378–88. Brothel keepers were identified by fines assessed on them in M.C.R. and M.T. 1373–93; there were twenty-seven male and seventeen female proprietors; four of the women were listed and fined along with their husbands.

54. These figures actually underestimate the number of women without family in

Exeter since only women who possessed a surname held by no other Exeter residents were counted; many more women obviously just happened to have surnames similar to Exeter residents even though they were not related by blood. It is impossible, however, to tell what proportion of servants were recent immigrants to Exeter and without family ties there, since three-quarters of them were identified only by their first name and their employer's name (a good indication in itself of either their youth, recent arrival in town, or the low status of their occupation).

55. See P.C.R. 25 Aug. 1384, 27 June 1385, 28 June 1386; M.C.R. 2 July 1386, 6 May 1387, 27 Jan. 1388, 17 Feb. 1388, 31 Aug. 1388, 18 Oct. 1389, 31 Jan. 1390, 29 Aug. 1390.

56. For the anomalous status of women in this position, see the reference to Joan Blakhay as the "servant and apprentice" of William Wymark, a weaver; M.C.R. 26 Nov. 1380. She was the only woman ever referred to as an apprentice, however, in the Exeter records. Alice Greneweye worked as a weaver for Walter Floit but was called a servant; see M.C.R. 16 Feb. 1383, 24 Aug. 1388. In some English towns women did receive formal training as apprentices; see Levi Fox, "The Coventry Guilds and Trading Companies with Special Reference to the Position of Women," in *Essays in Honour of Philip B. Chatwin* (Oxford, 1962), pp. 13–26. But few women received such formal training and even if accepted into guilds, they rarely enjoyed the full privileges of guild membership; see Power, "Working Woman," pp. 58–61.

For the more prominent position of women in Parisian guilds and their greater opportunities for formal training, see E. Dixon, "Craftswomen in the 'Livre des Métiers'," *Economic Journal* 5 (1895): 209–28. Craftswomen in medieval Danish towns, however, appear to have suffered real disadvantages in their access to guilds, formal training, and the free exercise of their trade; see Eva Trein Nielson, "Une contribution au débat concernant le statut de la femme dans les villes du Danemark au Moyen-Age," in *Aspects of Female Existence: Proceedings from the St. Gertrud Symposium 'Women in the Middle Ages', 1978*, ed. Birte Carte et al. (Copenhagen, 1980), pp. 73–75. Natalie Zemon Davis also remarks on women's lack of formal training in the workplace in sixteenth-century Lyon, although some women did serve as apprentices or received work training in schools for poor girls; see "Women in the Crafts in Sixteenth-Century Lyon," chap. 9, this volume.

57. For Joan, see M.C.R. 11 Feb. 1387, 18 Oct. 1389; S.Q.M.T. 1388–91; E.Q.M.T. 1392–93. For Agnes and John, see M.C.R. 2 March 1377, 29 Aug. 1379, 16 Dec. 1381, 14 Jan. 1387, 24 Feb. 1388, 28 Feb. 1390, 30 May 1390, 13 June 1390; P.C.R. 8 Feb. 1379, 3 July 1382; S.Q.M.T. 1378–90; N.Q.M.T. 1382–84; E.Q.M.T. 1374–76, 1384–88.

58. Alice Nymet: *Exeter Freemen*, p. 38; ED/M/527; C.R.A. 1395/96, 1397/98; P.C.A. 1391/92 to 1402/03; Cathedral Fabric Roll 2654 in Exeter Cathedral Library; E. 101 338/11, ms. 8,9,11 in P.R.O.; Alice was the widow of John Nymet, a wealthy merchant who served as mayor of Exeter. Magota Golde was the widow of Adam Golde, another wealthy merchant of the oligarchy; see his will in M.C.R. 14 Aug. 1396. His only son, Roger, did not enter the freedom until 1407; *Exeter Freemen*, p. 39. For Magota's commercial activities, see P.C.A. 1397/98, 1399/1400, 1402/03; E. 101 338/11, ms. 8,9,11 and E. 122 40/23 in the P.R.O. Elizabeth Wilford was the widow of Robert Wilford, the richest man in 1377 Exeter; Miscellaneous Roll 72. See his will in M.C.R. 8 Jan 1397; his son William entered the freedom in 1396; *Exeter Freemen*, p. 37. But Elizabeth continued to conduct Robert's business interests into the first decade of the 1400s; see P.C.A. 1397/98, 1398/99; E. 101 338/11, ms. 8,9,11 in the P.R.O.

59. See, for example, P.C.R. 27 April 1381, where Robert Carbure successfully asked for damages from an Exeter couple because they had injured his daughter Joan to such an extent that Robert lost her service. Married women frequently worked alongside their husbands in business in Exeter and in other English medieval towns; see J. S. Furley, *Town Life in the Fourteenth Century as Seen in the Court Rolls of Winchester City* (Winchester, 1947), pp. 98–100; Thrupp, *Merchant Class of Medieval London*, pp. 169–74; Power, "Working Woman," pp. 55–57. Indeed, labor legislation passed in several English towns restricted the use of cheap female labor but made an exception for wives or daughters who worked in the business of their husbands and fathers; see Power, "Working Woman," p. 60, and Salzman, *English Industries in the Middle Ages*, pp. 339–40.

60. Miscellaneous Roll 72; excluding brewing (as an intermittent household-related activity), the eleven women who worked paid on the average 5½d. murage tax while the other twelve women paid 8d. on the average.

61. Male artisans also engaged in retail trade (notably victualling) from time to time, but their extra-craft participation did not match that of women; see Kowaleski, "Local Markets," pp. 170–72.

62. This act was promulgated in 1363; *The Statutes of the Realm*, ed. A. Luders et al. (London 1810), I, p. 380. For Salzman's comment, see *English Industries in the Middle Ages*, pp. 328–29.

63. W.Q.M.T. 1373–83.

64. Miscellaneous Roll 72; W.Q.M.T. 1378–93; P.C.R. 6 March 1382, 8 Jan. 1383, 30 Aug. 1386.

# PART V

## *Is There a Decline in Women's Economic Position in the Sixteenth Century?*

Urban women in the later Middle Ages, and early modern period appear to have very similar lives to those women of the fourteenth century. They are still fitting their crafts into their life cycle and the structure of their family's needs. They do tedious but nimble work such as spinning gold and silk thread, operating either within a family establishment or as wage earners. The women of Lyon, Leiden, and Cologne take their housewifely skills into victualing and innkeeping, just as they did in Montpellier and Exeter. The pattern of widows of craftsmen and merchants being the only women to achieve substantial independence in the marketplace again emerges. In the later period as in the earlier one, legal restrictions against women fully participating in the marketplace and the traditional social taboos against women traveling limit the extent to which even these women can assume an equal footing with men. In spite of the similarities of women's work and participation in the marketplace, however, both Natalie Zemon Davis and Martha C. Howell look upon this later period as one of marked decline in the role of women in work and business.

We have met earlier with the effect on women's wages and employment of the increased population during the sixteenth century and the general decline in living standards. Christiane Klapisch-Zuber noted that female servants became less common in the sixteenth century than they had been in the fifteenth century and that their real wages declined. Leah Otis observed that the pay for wet nurses in sixteenth-century Montpellier was the same as it was in the fifteenth century and yet the demand for wet nurses increased because the population had increased. Women accepted these set wages even though their buying power had decreased because, with the general impoverishment of the population, they were desperate for extra income. Of the essays presented in this collection, only the Nuremberg midwives appear to have done well with the growing population of the sixteenth century.

Alice Clark, as Davis observes in her essay, attributed the decline of women's economic position to the onset of capitalism and others have attributed it to the stranglehold of the guilds. But Davis, who also observed a decline in women's independent voice in the marketplace, attributes the change to an enhancing of the patriarchal character of the society. Both city fathers and the growing state emphasized the male head of household as "The Artisan" and restricted women from becoming entrepreneurs on their own. Women's work became contained within the family or sunk to the lower levels of craft production.

Howell observed a more formal move toward the elimination of women from high-status work in Leiden and Cologne. When access to market production was chiefly through the family craft, women had more access to high-status positions, but as trades became more closely associated with political institutions, women could not belong because of the legal limitations on women in official functions. Thus in Leiden when the crafts were officially organized, women were automatically excluded from production because it had acquired a political role. In Cologne, where women had their own guilds, they were excluded from representing them in the city government and the power structure of the guild came to rest in male hands. Furthermore, as the cities moved to regulate crafts by establishing production rules and hours of work, women found that they could not accommodate their own familial obligations to the new rules. The rules, therefore, tended to erode the old family-based unit of production and women became relegated to low-status occupations. Even those traditional trades for women, victualing and beer making, gave way to male-organized production and distribution of these products, leaving women to produce small quantities of often "inferior" quality.

The essays in the volume document the work of women very well, but do not provide a final answer to the question of the status and pay for women's work in preindustrial Europe. That women worked within the constraints of their life cycle and the needs of their family is well established and so too is the value of their additional income for the family economy. Some women also successfully carried on businesses of their own, particularly widows. While these observations on women's work do not add up to a golden age for women in the Middle Ages, many of the authors have observed that women's economic opportunities were greater in the Middle Ages than in the sixteenth and seventeenth centuries.

*Natalie Zemon Davis* 9

# Women in the Crafts in Sixteenth-Century Lyon

> And being of the female sex did not turn me
> from the enterprise of publishing, nor the fact
> that it be more a manly office: . . . It is not
> new or unheard of for women to have such a
> trade, and one can find many of us who
> exercise not only the typographical art, but
> others more difficult and arduous, and who
> obtain thereby the highest of praise.
>
> Jeanne Giunta,
> book publisher of Lyon, 1579

Among the words of praise bestowed on Lyon in the sixteenth century for its economic achievement, one can find little mention of the female sex. "Commercial office for the whole world," said one local observer of the city; "very rich in manufacturers," said another; "in few towns in Europe can the Artisans find it easier to make their profit." There the poet Peletier sang of "the merchant's display / His fine silk, oriental pearl / And fashioned gold," while Joachim Du Bellay marveled "to see pass so many messengers / So many bankers, printers, armorers / Thicker than the flowers in the fields." The women who brought glory to Lyon were either beauteous "Damoiselles and Dames" or the poets Louise Labé and Pernette du Guillet, "two spirits, noble and virtuous." When Lyon presented itself to King Henri II and his court in the Entry parade of 1548, no female walked among the hundreds of costumed dyers, silkweavers, butchers, carpenters, and other artisans; the only women to delight the king's eyes were the daughters of six notable townsmen, dressed variously as Diana, Immortality, Virtue, and the like.[1]

Unrecognized as it might be on occasions of public celebration, women's work had, nevertheless, an important and complex role to play in the economy of the sixteenth-century French city. Over eighty years ago, Henri Hauser wrote suggestive pages on the subject, in which he pointed out the

167

difference between all-female trades (such as linen making in Paris) and "mixed trades," and between female labor in towns with guilds and in towns with open industrial organization. Since his day, studies on individual trades and occupations, such as textile manufacture, prostitution, wet-nursing, and domestic service, have supported Hauser's speculations about the low ratio of female wages to male wages and have gone on to demonstrate the special vulnerability of the female to hard times. But we still need to develop an overall, systematic approach to women's work in the sixteenth century, a period of population increase, economic expansion, and religious change. We still need for sixteenth-century France an equivalent to Alice Clark's *Working Life of Women in the Seventeenth Century* and the studies of Olwen Hufton, Louise Tilly and Joan Scott, and Keith Snell on the eighteenth century and after.[2]

This essay will look at only one aspect of the question, the role of women in the crafts, in the *arts mécaniques* in sixteenth-century Lyon. I will examine both the nonmarket and the market sectors of the economy; it is partly by ignoring the former that a historian has recently been led to say of Florence that "the urban wife and child made little substantial contribution to the productivity of their household and to the wealth of the city."[3] The framework will be the woman's life cycle, for the character of her activity within the family economy was likely to change as she moved from stage to stage. To account for the distribution of females among the crafts and their relation to movements of economic resistance, I will consider not only calculations of profit and loss, but also cultural norms and taboos. And finally, I shall comment on the sources of the gradual limitation on female independence in the crafts in the early modern period. Some historians have blamed it on the narrow spirit of the masters who ran the guilds. The Fabian socialist Alice Clark thought rather it was the encroachments of capitalism which reduced women's roles as mistresses in the crafts and left them only in ill-paid toil.[4] Are either of these theories adequate to the Lyon case, or must one draw on other features of sixteenth-century society, such as a growing attachment to private property?

Lyon is a particularly interesting place for such an exploration. After Paris, it was the second or third largest city in France. Within its walls were both traditional trades and those with the most advanced technology, such as printing, silk, and metallurgy. Its artisans produced both for neighbors down the street and for merchants who came from across France and Europe to the city's fairs, which were held four times a year. A few of its crafts were organized into sworn guilds (goldsmiths, locksmiths, barber-surgeons, and after 1588 apothecaries),[5] but the rest were in principle open to anyone who could afford to set up shop, with no requirement of masterpiece, residence, or fee. A period of rapid population growth and relative prosperity in the first part of the century was followed by contraction after the economic troubles, war, and plague of the 1560s.[6] It may be possible, then, to sort out what circumstances allowed the most scope for female activity and which ones provided the most constraints.

Women's production in the crafts was of two kinds: that which they did as unpaid helpers to a father, a husband, or a son; and that which they did for wages or fees paid directly to themselves. In both cases, their strictly occupational identity was thinner than that of the men in their milieu, the women's energies available to be shifted into other work channels if the situation demanded it. (By the widely held humoral theory of sexual temperament, men were hot and dry, and therefore firm and stable, while women were cold and wet, and therefore changeable and slippery. Our artisan women have some cold and wet characteristics.) Much of the time, female work was seen as a necessary complement to male work; but on occasion, it could be perceived as dangerous, if not to the woman's own kin, then at least to the established masters in a threatened trade. I will try to see what, if any, consciousness women developed of themselves as actors under these conditions.

## Training

The imprecise work identity of females was in part a result of their training in girlhood. The ordinary training for a boy destined for a craft was apprenticeship, either carried on informally with his own father or stepfather, or arranged by contract with another master, if the lad were entering a new trade or if his mother were widowed. The number of years so spent might vary from trade to trade and even within a trade (for dressmakers and shoemakers the median was three years; for printers, four years; for velvetmakers and goldsmiths, five years), and the cost of apprenticeship varied also; but even modest peasants in the Lyonnais, the Dauphiné, and Savoie were willing to scrape together savings or lumber or hemp or wine so that a Lyon master would take on their son.[7] If the family were too poor, the boy would go into domestic service in hopes that his wages and a legacy from his master would make possible an apprenticeship when he was older.[8]

In contrast, most girls were taught whatever skills they would need as an adult either by their parents or in the course of domestic service. Only a small percentage of them were formally apprenticed. Of 204 apprenticeship contracts remaining in the Lyon archives for the years 1553 through 1560, only 18 (9 percent) were females. The same pattern is found among the orphans at the municipal hospitals of La Chana and Saint Catherine's. During 1557, for instance, while 7 orphan boys were apprenticed out to velvet makers, typecasters, and so forth, 18 orphan girls were hired out, 8 as chambermaids (*chambrieres*), 7 as chambermaids who would also prepare silk thread, and 3 as simple silkwinders.[9]

The little band of female apprentices have some interesting characteristics, if I may comment on only these eighteen cases and not another eight from nearby years. They do range in background: a notary's daughter was learning to make wimples, a goldsmith's daughter to make silk ribbons, a shoemaker's daughter to make pins, a carder's daughter to make gloves, and a packer's daughter to make buttons. But many more of them than the male apprentices had been born in Lyon, and a few more of them were fatherless. Some of the girls had lost their mothers as well and were being apprenticed by guardians; one was the illegitimate daughter of a notary, who could not make a home for her. (Unfortunately, the contracts, though they do mention whether a mother apprenticing her child is a widow, do not mention whether a father apprenticing his child is a widower. The characteristic thing about these female apprentices may be that so many of them were motherless.) Unlike the males, the female apprentices were clustered in the textile and clothing trades, in small metal work, and provisioning. No contract was made for more than seven years, while for the males contracts went up to ten years, and the apprenticeship fees for the girls were lower on the whole. Thirteen of the girls were apprentices to women and thirteen to masters, including one to her own uncle, and all the males were apprentices to persons of their own sex.[10] In short, a family disruption may often have preceded the unusual decision to give formal apprenticeship to a girl; she was as likely to be sent nearby to a skilled woman in her household as to a master in his shop; and she learned skills that did not require much equipment and could be easily adjusted to whatever work her future husband might do.

But there were other ways besides apprenticeship that a girl could acquire knowledge of the crafts. One was the sewing or spinning school for poor girls. If the schoolmasters who taught boys to read, write, and compute outnumbered the schoolmistresses in Lyon tenfold,[11] the "vocational school" seems to have been pioneered for females. We see them first sponsored by the new municipal welfare organization, the Aumône Générale, in the 1530s, although they may have had medieval precedents. The mistress in charge of the orphans at Saint Catherine's Hospital was to teach the girls not only their credo and housekeeping, but also how to spin and sew, as their mothers might. Once the silk industry was established in Lyon, a Dame Lucresse from Italy was hired to show the orphan girls how to unwind silk from cocoons, prepare a thread, and wind it onto a bobbin. Then silk-winding centers were set up in different parts of town by entrepreneurs with subsidies from the Aumône Générale—in the Saint George quarter, where the boatmen lived, near La Chana Hospital on the Saône side, and over at the Rhône Bridge Hospital—and there women from Lucca or nearby Saint Chamond taught their skills to poor girls in the neighborhood. A few years later, cotton spinning was introduced into the city; orphan girls were sent out from Saint Catherine's to learn the work, and the Aumône went on to hire an Italian widow, Bartholomée la Piedmontese, to instruct the girls right at the hospital. When the rectors realized how easy the technique was, they fired Dame Bartholomée and let the experienced girls teach the new ones. All of these centers were, of course, productive units as well, providing small wages for the trained girls and cheap labor for the manufacturers.[12]

Similar training establishments were set up by individual women on a smaller scale. So in 1567, we see Marie Darmère, wife of a royal sergeant, taking in a button-maker's daughter and "other poor girls" to teach them to make lace and giving them modest wages along with room and board while they worked for her. Dame Marie de La Camelle, who had been brought to Lyon as a girl by her father, a Florentine silk weaver, opened a school in the parish of Saint Romain to instruct poor girls in "sewing and good morals." In 1592, then sixty-three years old, Dame Marie was still keeping girls *en sa puissance* ("in her power"), as she said in the course of a hearing to legitimate one of them who was born out of wedlock.[13]

These institutions come the closest to providing girls the kind of work experience with people their own age that boys had when apprenticed in a medium-sized or large shop. But while the boy's training might be marked off at its beginning by a contribution to a craft confraternity, and at its ending by a banquet required by the journeymen, or other such rituals,[14] the girls had no parallel events to validate a precise work identity. Indeed, these training centers were reminders of their unfortunate lot: they were "poor girls," unable to follow the usual paths for females growing up among the *menu peuple.*

Girls could also familiarize themselves with craft techniques in the course of domestic service in the artisanal family. Apart from the orphans from Saint Catherine's, it was mostly young women from villages in the Lyonnais, the Dauphiné, and Savoie who were chambermaids and domestics in the city: of the thirty-three servant girls making marriage contracts in 1558–59, twenty-eight were not natives of Lyon. Some of them worked in wealthy households; but with domestic wages as low as they were—at midcentury they ranged from five *livres* down to two *livres* per year, plus room and board—the families of coopers, saddlers, locksmiths, velvet makers, printers, and other artisans were often able to keep a chambermaid.[15] Then if the atelier were part of the household, the serving-girl could observe the rhythms and processes of craft life, and might well be called upon to help. So Claudine Plantin, a servant for the pewterer Claude de Longueville and his wife in the 1540s, was occasionally involved in preparing alloys and was dispatched to pick up merchandise for her master. When Pernette Carra, servant to the wife of a tripe seller, married a tripe seller in 1559; when Claudine Bourriquant, servant of a maker of printer's ink, married a printer, then we can assume that they brought to their husbands usable craft skills, along with a dowry based partly on their own earnings.[16]

As for the daughters of tradesmen and master craftsmen established in Lyon, most of them seem to have stayed with their families until the time of their marriage. Here they would not only learn spinning and other skills at the side of their mother (or stepmother), but they might also receive training in the shop. This could be in the form of "helping": Agathe Minot did errands for her father's inn, such as going out to purchase wine; the daughters of master printers might hang up printed paper to dry. But sometimes fathers and older brothers gave more systematic instruction to the girls. So accepted was this practice among master silk weavers, wimple makers, and button makers that an agreement among them in 1561 simply assumed that "father can show [his art] to his daughter and the brother to his sister."[17]

Such training surely bore fruit for the welfare of the family, for it meant a few years of unpaid labor from the girls before they left home. And because it was instruction at the hands of a person with a public work identity— someone who paraded before the king in the colors of his trade, who marched under the banners of his craft confraternity, whose occupation was announced after his name in public documents and proclaimed by a trade-mark or a sign at the door—the daughter or sister may have prized it more than instruction at the accustomed, intimate hands of the mother. What the implications of this training were for the girl's later life, however, is another matter. Of the daughters of Lyon artisans and tradesmen contract-ing marriage for the first time in the years 1553–60, about 84 percent married artisans among the menu peuple, but only one-quarter of them wedded men in the same occupations as their fathers (or stepfathers). If we include closely allied trades such as a shoemaker's daughter marrying a saddler, the percentage rises only to one-third.[18] Perhaps the wife might carry on the work patterns she had grown up with, but more likely she shifted them to fit into those acquired by her husband.

## The Married Woman as Unpaid Artisan

When a young woman of the menu peuple changed her status from "the daughter of so-and-so" to "the wife of so-and-so," she ordinarily left the household of her family, or the family she had served, to move into rooms or a part of a house with her husband. Other arrangements were possible, of course: Odette de Luire, daughter of a whitewasher, married the printer's journeyman, Jean de Tournes, and they lived in the house of Odette's widowed mother. Years later, in 1545, their daughter Nicole married Guillaume Gazeau, and the newlyweds stayed on in the same house, where Jean, then a proud master (and considered today one of France's finest printers), printed with his son-in-law. Only in 1551 did Jean move into an establishment of his own on the nearby rue Raisin, leaving Nicole mistress of the house that once belonged to her maternal grandmother.[19]

Although the varieties of work that the wife did in her new household—child rearing, marketing, cooking, washing, and helping her husband—were not paid, the notion that they could be assigned a rough cash value was not wholly foreign to the cultural assumptions of the *menu peuple* in the sixteenth century. Husbands making large testamentary bequests to wives—that is, beyond the return of the dowry and the *augmentation de dot* ("increase in the dowry") agreed on in the marriage contract—would sometimes use the formula "And this for the good and agreeable services which she has done for him during their marriage." Families accounting their household and workshop expenses together could conceive of the *idea* of a salary for wives, even if it were not used. Thus in 1559, two silk merchants set up both a partnership and a joint household, to be run by their wives, and agreed that the women would take "no salary," but would be supported at the expense of the partnership.[20]

The wife's ability to help her husband in his craft was a function of several things: location and character of the work; social life and customs in the atelier; and physical state of the wife and the amount of time she had free from other tasks. As for the location, work regularly performed on sites away from the house, as in the building or transport trades, rarely seems to have involved wives as "helpers." (When women have jobs in these areas, they are usually employed on their own.) The wives of journeymen would not be in a position to help their husbands at work either.

As for the character of the work, the crafts of the weaponmaker, of the smith and the caster, which by cultural definition had a marked masculine quality about them, probably drew little on wifely aid for the technical processes. Such artisans may not have agreed with the judgment of the town lawyer Claude de Rubys, who (citing Aristotle) called them "vile, sordid and dishonest," but they may well have followed the view of a current metallurgical manual that the "fire arts" (hot and dry!) were not for those with a "gentle spirit." Here the craftsmen had to be very strong; here they looked brutish, with their faces full of powder and half-burned; here they were plagued with worries till the work was done, "by reason of which they are called Fantasmes."[21]

The nature of social relationships and mores in the atelier might also set limits to the wife's assistance. Imagine a printing shop with an apprentice or two and a few journeymen. If the master's wife tried to order the men about, they might resent this violation of nature's order or at least of their contract, which bound them only to serve their master in his art. So in 1549 in Geneva, the proofreader Guillaume Guéroult, soon to be working in the Lyon shop of Balthazar Arnoullet, complained bitterly of his master's wife: she refused to comply with her husband's rulings, would not unlock the cabinet for his *vin de compagnon* ("journeyman's wine") when he started proofreading at 2 A.M., and in fact "she would rather the printing house be ruined so that she could live better according to her voluptuous tastes." And then, what of the sexual excitement that a wife could cause in the shop? Anne de Noyer, the spouse of printer Claude de Huchin, was said to have committed lewd acts with her husband's tall apprentice René and to have been unduly familiar with his journeyman Gabriel Challiot. Challiot had to admit "that he would like to have a wife as beautiful as she."[22]

Finally, the wife's participation in the work of the atelier was affected by how much time she had free, even with the help of the inevitable servant, from other household tasks (including preparing food for journeymen and apprentices), and from childbirth and nursing. In Catholic artisanal families, the "state of pollution" which clung to a new mother may have kept her out of the shop until she had her churching ceremony, the *relevailles*, lest her glance bring everybody bad luck. And popular beliefs about the dangers of menstruating women to technical and natural processes, which we know were current in the sixteenth century, may have barred the wife from some workshops at certain times of the month, lest she rust iron and brass, dull cutting instruments, jeopardize the already hazardous process of casting, and so forth.[23]

Wifely help, then, was bound to be periodic, affected by custom, and more readily drawn upon by some crafts than by others. But it was needed for the survival of the family and could sometimes involve the woman so much that she took on a joint work identity with her husband. The evidence we have on this comes primarily from the provisioning and textile trades, with some interesting examples from barber-surgery and printing.

Among the provisioning trades, the households of butchers, hotelkeepers, and tavernkeepers show much joint work by husband and wife. For instance, Benoîte Penet, a butcher's daughter and herself the mother of four girls, aided her husband at his trade, and after he died in the 1540s, went on selling meat to hostelers and private individuals. Presumably her husband bought the cattle over at the Croix de Colle market on the Fourvière Hill and did the slaughtering with his journeymen, while Benoîte Penet helped with preparing the meat and with sales. One of her clients was the nearby Bear Inn, a hotel catering to Germans at the northern end of the peninsula. It was kept by Michel Hiberlin and his wife, Katherine Fichet, natives of Nimburg in Breisgau, who together sought letters of naturalization from the king in 1536. Several years later, Hiberlin married a local woman for his second wife, and she bought meat and took out small loans from Benoîte Penet. Meanwhile, the keeper of the Popinjay Inn was so grateful to his wife "for all the trouble she had taken to help him earn and amass his goods" that he donated one-half of them to her.[24]

Among the textile trades, silk making emerges as a family enterprise, even when apprentices and journeymen were also in the shop. Certain tasks assisting at the loom were ordinarily done by girls, either a daughter or a hired worker. The wife of a silk thrower, a taffeta maker, or a velvet maker might specialize in unwinding the cocoons and preparing the thread for bobbins, so we learn from the records of the orphan girls farmed out by the Aumône Général: indeed, Estienette Léonarde, wife of a silk thrower on the rue Grôlée, took on six girls for unwinding during a nine-month period in 1557. If these were to be characteristically female tasks until the nineteenth century, in the sixteenth century we can also find wives who spelled their husbands weaving at the looms. The 1561 agreement among the male silk manufacturers and silk weavers took it as a matter of course that the wives of masters were working the looms if they knew how. Sometimes this is even given recognition in notarized acts, as in 1561 when Etienne Buffin and his wife, Gabrielle Fourestz, involved in a donation, are both described as "silk weavers (*tissotiers*), inhabitants of Lyon."[25]

Joint activity can be found in trades like pin making, where we know women were apprenticed, but it is perhaps more surprising to find it among printers and barbers, where the formally trained and hired labor force was exclusively male. Barber-surgery was, in addition, one of the sworn trades in Lyon, and that meant that the masters of the guild were especially vigilant lest "incapable persons" set up shop and practice. Yet in 1537, King François I granted "letters of mastership in barbering" both to Benoit Fanilhon and to his wife, Anne Casset. (The young couple may well have gone over the heads of the local sworn masters and purchased these letters without examination.) It is significant that approval seems to have been given only for the simple tasks of barbering—shaving, bleeding, and similar jobs—rather than for surgery, which Fanilhon was to add himself later on. His wife helped him over the years, although she remained unlettered, signing her daughters' marriage contracts only with an X. The number of widows of barber-surgeons who tried to run a practice with the aid of journeymen after their husband's death suggests that if Anne Casset's royal letters were unusual, her working experience was not.[26]

In printing shops, pulling the press was "men's work," and only a small percentage of artisanal women could read well enough to help with typesetting and proofreading. But there are, nonetheless, a few examples of wives who went beyond the occasional tasks to associate themselves more directly in running the atelier. One is Louise Giraud, wife of the well-known humanist master Etienne Dolet and a formal partner in a "printing company" with her husband and their backer, the financial officer Hélouin Dulin. Because at least thirteen editions came out under Dolet's name and mark in 1542–44, while he was in prison on charges of heresy or in hiding, Louise Giraud must have had considerable familiarity with the business and good relations with the journeymen at the shop at the Sign of the Hatchet.[27]

Another example is Mie Roybet, wife of Barthélemy Frein, alias Rapallus, journeyman printer and one of the leaders of the workers' Company of the Griffarins (as they called their secret union) during and after the strike of 1539, keeper of a small tavern which was a favorite journeymen's haunt, and finally master printer from 1545 until his death in October 1556. Mie Roybet helped with the tavern, but must also have had a full knowledge of the shop, if we may judge by the printing activity into which she was plunged right after her husband's demise. By August 1557, she was in the royal prisons in Lyon together with Michel Chastillon, "governor of the printing house," for having printed "certain books in the French language touching matters of the Christian Religion, without privilege and permission of the Faculty of Theology of Paris." Chastillon was, of course, the brother of the liberal Protestant of Basel, Sébastien Castellion, early advocate of religious tolerance. Roybet was literate enough to write her brother-in-law letters in French and surely knew what she and Chastillon had been printing. Hearing about the arrests, Pastor Theodore Beza was to say from Geneva, "Castellion's brother has been seized at Lyon and thrown into prison with an abominable libel by his brother on predestination, which he has just printed there." Beza did not bother to mention Mie Roybet, but without her collaboration, Castellion's plea for the liberty of the will would not have seen the light of day.[28]

Released from prison, Roybet and Chastillon married in September, and then he died a few months later. Roybet immediately married another printer and kept on as she had been, helping with printing and running her first husband's little tavern.[29] Many women in Lyon did not have this continuity in their work lives. Of all the widows contracting marriage in an artisanal milieu in the years 1553–60, only 25 percent married men in the same trade as their first husbands. If we add marriages to men in allied trades (such as a clockmaker's widow marrying a goldsmith), the number rises to only 34 percent.[30] Some wives may then have carried on a trade of their own. Some may have tried to influence the course of their new husband's career through the money, equipment, contacts, and skills they brought from the past. But for most it was a matter, as it had been when they first married, of accommodating their work abilities and energies to a new family setting.

## The Woman as Wage-earning Artisan

At whatever stage of her life cycle, a Lyon woman who hired herself out for wage labor in a craft was likely to be poor and needy. In the years between their first "training" and marriage, most girls of the *menu peuple* were either in domestic service or helping father, mother, or brother with a craft in the household. If a girl had no such resources—her parents were themselves wage-earners or were dead or widowed—then she provided for herself as best she could. She might try prostitution in rooms in the Saint George quarter, near the Rhône Bridge Hospital, on the rue Mercière, or elsewhere.[31] But if she had some craft skill, she might look for a mistress with whom she could make lace, wimples, buttons, cords, hats, or gloves; with whom she could unwind silk from cocoons or weave linen cloth. She might find a tavern-keeper who would take her on to serve the customers. She might find a master silkworker who would hire her to pull the cords for the large looms that made the fanciest silks. Indeed, in 1561 the master silk weavers were still talking about *compaignonnes,* as well as *compaignons,* in their shops, which means that some trained females were weaving for wages.[32]

Married women who fell upon hard times or widows with children might leap into any kind of short-term paid work to support themselves and their families. The wife of an urban gardener helps a shoemaker's wife travel to Romans in Dauphiné; the wife of a printer's journeyman leaves her own daughter at home to take care of a surgeon's daughter during her illness; the wife of an unskilled day laborer wet-nurses the triplets of a weaver's wife; over at the cathedral a woman comes in from time to time to change the straw for the choirboy's pallets. Some adult women unwound cocoons together with the girls at the silk centers; and adults were evidently the main source of semiskilled female labor at construction sites, doing road repair and other building along with the male hod carriers. So the royal architect Philibert Delorme, the son of a Lyon mason, asked, "can anything be found which can employ and busy more people of either sex than building? . . . poor people, who otherwise would have to go beg for their bread?"[33] On the other hand, I have found no sign of Lyon women at this stage of life farming themselves out for a year or two to a master or mistress in a craft, an arrangement probably incompatible with their family responsibilities. Rather than live in such dependence, some of the women would try to get inscribed on the rolls of the welfare organization for a weekly handout of bread and cash, or even try to keep out of sight of the beadles of the Aumône and beg for a few hours each day.

What about the wages of female workers in the crafts? The evidence is very scanty, but it confirms the usual picture of lower compensation for females than for males. Of the masons working for the *ingénieur* Olivier Roland widening a street up near the Church of Saint Vincent in 1562, masters were paid five *sous* a day, and journeymen and hod carriers were paid variously at four, three, and two *sous*, and one *sou* and six *deniers* per day. The women were clustered at two *sous* and at one *sou* and six *deniers*, although it should be noted that some men were remunerated at this low level as well.[34] In 1567, Marie Darmère paid a young woman making lace for her three *livres* a year, together with room and board, while in 1557 the wages of the girls hired out by the Aumône Générale to unwind cocoons ranged from one *livre* and ten *sous* to four *livres* and two *sous* per year. Although we have no exactly comparable wages for males (unwinding silk was a female task, as we have seen), the lowest salary for a male in silk manufacture that I have found for this decade is ten *livres* per year *avec bouche, couche et chausse* ("with board, room, and pants")—and this for a young velvet maker from Avignon early in his work career. To find male wages approximating those of women, we have to look over to the poorer leather trades, where shoemakers' journeymen in 1555 were being paid as little as three *livres* per year with board, room, and pants, and in 1560–63 they were paid four *livres* and sixteen *sous* per year, with room and board.[35]

When male workers were unhappy with their wages, they sometimes organized to get higher ones. Over decades, the consulate complained of "the monopolies of the masons, carpenters, hod carriers and mortar-mixers, who every day raise the price of their day's work," "who make themselves be paid more for their day's work than is customary." The dyers' journeymen had a company and a captain; insisted that hiring take place only on Mondays in front of the Church of Saint Nizier, where they appeared armed and made "resolutions pernicious to the good of the dyers' estate"; and maintained a "jurisdiction" over the apprentices so as to keep down the labor supply. The printers' journeymen had a *compagnonnage*, a full-fledged journeymen's organization, with rites of initiation and techniques for work stoppages, for punishing Forfants (as they called those not in their Company of the Griffarins), and for bringing suits against their masters.[36]

Now there is no sign whatsoever of women workers in sixteenth-century Lyon participating in such activities. The men made no effort to include them in the brotherhood of their "assemblies" and organizations, where rowdy banquets were held, lascivious songs sung, and secret oaths were sworn over daggers. Indeed, one wonders how *compagnonnes* and serving-girls fit into the predominantly male culture of the mixed shop: What was it like when the men collected grumbling at 4:30 A.M. (as they did in dyeing); when they argued every noon with the mistress about whether their customary "journeyman's wine" was of the same quality and amount as that drunk by the master? Interestingly enough, despite the low wages of the women, the journeymen did not seek "jurisdiction" over them as they did over apprentices and over journeymen coming in from other towns, nor did they use sanctions against them as they did against Forfants, willing "to work for beggar's pay."[37] Relatively few in number, less highly skilled in their own vocational niche, the women did not appear a threat. How could they carry on work at the construction site if the men walked off?

But even in the all-female shops and larger centers for unwinding silk, the girls do not seem to have organized protests. This is not because the modesty of their sex prevented them from ever being disobedient: the individual serving-girl was sometimes saucy and recalcitrant; wives and mothers were prominent actors in the Grande Rebeine, the grain riot of 1529, and their voices were to be heard again in the streets during the religious struggles of midcentury.[38] Rather, it was because the sphere of work, unlike that of food and religious protection for their families, was one in which most women—and especially young women—did not believe they had primary rights. With little to bolster their work identity, who were they to argue, as the journeymen did, for the "ancient customs" of their craft?[39] And with little active involvement in organizational structures, like confraternities, who were they to institute secret societies and clandestine rituals? By the mid-sixteenth century, stories of witches' sabbaths were arousing fear on all sides. Although no group trials took place in Lyon, individual women among the *menu peuple* were being accused by their neighbors of sorcery and maleficent harm. Under these circumstances, a female *compagnonnage* might look like a witches' coven and bring down upon itself much more wrath than the Company of the Griffarins.[40]

The girls unwinding cocoons for Dame Lucresse and Dame Estiennette Léonarde, making lace for Marie Darmère, and making gloves and wimples or pins for other mistresses must have had customs and a shop culture of their own, however. From the glimpses we can get of them from early texts, such as *The Gospels of the Distaffs (Les Evangiles des Quenouilles)*, they connected female work and its timing with love, magic, and Christian practice. The events of a spinning day could be used to foretell the future: a broken thread meant a quarrel; a man crossing a thread stretched at the doorsill (it must be the first thread spun that day) bore the same name as one's future husband. A good day's work could be helped by spinning a thread first thing in the morning, before praying and with unwashed hands (still part of the magic of the night), and throwing it over one's shoulders. Washing one's thread, one must not say to one's gossip, "Ha, commère, the water's boiling," but rather "the water's laughing," or else the thread would turn to straw. The women's workplace was itself open to fairies. At best they came when everyone was asleep and finished the spinning. More often they were mischievous, and would take a spindle as their right if all the week's thread had not been properly wound on the reel on Saturday. Saturday was, however, an unlucky day to work. A Franciscan in Lyon condemned those "women who don't want to spin on Saturday out of superstition and who apply themselves instead to other vain activities," while he approved "the devotion of the good dames who on Saturday after [mid-day] dinner turn aside from spinning, sewing or other mechanical work in honor of the Virgin Mary, to whom Saturday is voluntarily dedicated."[41]

What we seem to have here is a domestic work culture, hidden from the streets, eliciting comment not from city councils, but from storytellers. It drew on certain general features of a woman's life, as adaptable to spinning as to any other setting where women were working together, in contrast to "ancient customs," connected with the technology of a particular craft, which one might find in a shop dominated by men. The domestic work culture provided a kind of vertical identity between mistress and female worker, which could sometimes be used by the former to hurry along the work process and sometimes by the latter to slow it down. It was available to any woman—at least to any Catholic woman—who wanted to impose a rhythm on her work life.

*The Woman as Independent Artisan*

Unlike mere wage earners, independent women artisans in Lyon elicited respect and even apprehension and could sometimes defend openly their economic turf. They were ordinarily married women or widows and were likely to have (or have had) husbands also prospering in a craft. And they appear in quite a variety of trades—at least as many as Epistémon told Pantagruel he saw being performed in Hell by Melusine, Cleopatra, Dido, and other classical ladies. If we know of no "verdigris grater" at Lyon—one of the amusing female trades Rabelais refers to in this episode—we do hear about "les bastelieres de Lyon" ("the boatwomen of Lyon"), of whom Epistémon was reminded when he saw the knights of the Round Table rowing devils across the Styx. As the student Felix Platter reported during his visit to the city in 1552, "there are always small boats in the charge of women along the length of the quay, ready to transport you to the other shore [of the Saône]." There was no shyness about them: his boatwoman threatened to throw him in the river unless he paid his fare immediately, and then refused to give him change. The young man got his revenge by throwing stones at her from a safe distance.[42]

In the building and construction trades, there were few, if any, women carpenters or fully trained masons, but we do find Catherine Fromment, "cabinetmaker," in the local prison for some kind of crime in 1548. Similarly, in the metal trades, only pin making had women operating on their own. Thoine Riniere and a certain Jehanne, *espinglières de Lyon*, were among the poor sick at the Rhône Bridge Hospital in 1560. More successful in their trade were the widows of two pin makers, carrying on the craft in their own right after their husbands died: Dame Ysabeau de Seure worked with her son, but was also able to hire a journeyman in 1565, while the next year, Jehanne Tutilly was buying 170 *livres* worth of brass wire for her pins from German merchants. Dame Anne Durtin made gold thread with at least one female apprentice at her side, while her husband busied himself with gold objects.[43]

Many more women had independent artisanal status in the textile and clothing trades. Languishing at the hospital in 1560 were Thoine Baton, the cord-maker, Claude Cousande, the hat maker, and Marie Odet, a dressmaker from the Saint George quarter. Monette, the glove maker, headed a household on the rue Mercière in 1557 and was expected to provide a man for the urban militia. Wimple making by females was common enough for the ordinances of the trade to envisage "maistresses" as well as "maistres." Such a one was Pernette Morilier, a goldsmith's wife, who took on a female apprentice for a goodly fee in 1564 (clearly a busy household, for her husband accepted a male apprentice the same month). Lacing makers also had their mistresses, appropriate perhaps, because the witch who knotted trouser lacing to make bridegrooms impotent (*nouer l'aiguillette*) was characteristically a female. In weaving linen, women were a familiar sight, and pattern books printed in Lyon had pictures of them at work. In silk making, in addition to the women running shops for unwinding cocoons, we can find Françoise la Regnarde, a silk thrower, and Germaine Clément, a silk weaver, both taxed in their own right in 1571.[44] In fact, the independence of *maîtresses* like Clément had begun to trouble the *maîtres tissotiers*, as we will see.

On the other hand, the enthusiasm of Benoîte Larchier for the linen trade did not worry her husband, the merchant-shoemaker Jean Pierre, alias Pichier. He had come to Lyon as a young man from the Piedmont, had married Larchier around 1536, and received the astonishingly high dowry of 1,000 *livres*. For twenty-five years, they pursued their trades "separately," he with his shoes, she in "linen making and commerce in linen cloth." So great had been her profits, Pierre admitted in 1561, that they had paid for most of his purchases of real estate. In recognition of this, he changed the initial arrangements of their marriage contract to a community of goods, so as to reward her more amply if he predeceased her. Possibly the husband of the linen maker Barbe de Valle had similar reasons to be grateful to his wife. She appears on the tax rolls in her own name, assessed "for her movables and craft." Indeed, on a 1567 list of Huguenots reconverted to Catholicism, he is characterized simply as "le mary de La Barbe, lingere" ("the husband of La Barbe, linen maker"), without any name of his own.[45]

The provisioning trades also afforded scope for female economic activity. Among millers and bakers, we find only the occasional widow continuing on her own ("La vefve de Champaignon" is the sole member of her sex on a list of forty-eight bakers compiled by the consulate in 1564). There were several other fishmongers like Michelette Godet, a boatman's wife, and especially there were females running butcher shops. Some *bouchières* were poor, such as Monde Bazare, who entered the hospital in 1560 having "nothing," and some "marchandes-bouchières" were well off, such as widow Estiennette Moyne, official purveyor of meat to the hospital a few years later. Quarrels among women in the craft even came to the attention of the courts: in 1549 three butcher-women, all married and at least one the mother of six or seven little children, were accused of hurling a duck in the face of a fourth woman, perhaps a case of economic rivalry. One might have expected the missile to be a piece of liver, for selling *la triperie* ("innards") seems to have had special attraction for members of the so-called weaker sex.[46]

As for the world of the tavern and the inn, the role of the female was so pronounced that a book for the traveling merchant, published in Lyon around 1515, promised in its title to teach what to do "to speak to the hostess to ask how much one has spent." A few years later, Erasmus's *Colloquy on Inns* maintained that guests stayed extra days at Lyon because of the graciousness of the *hôtesses* and their daughters. They might be simple women like "La Loyse," at whose inn a fight broke out in 1531, or like Jane, hostess at the Sign of the Broken Lupine on the rue Grôlée, whose last name could not be remembered by a neighboring widow when she left her a bequest of ten *livres*.[47] The women might come from more substantial families: Catherine Berthaud, daughter of a paper manufacturer and widow of a pewterer, hostess in 1573 at the Sign of Our Lady, rue de Bourgneuf; Claudine Dumas, daughter of a notary, hostess at the Golden Chariot at the Fossés de la Lanterne.

Dumas was one of the most interesting women of her day in the city. In the 1520s she had married the proprietor of the Golden Chariot, Pierre Peraton, who was also a merchant and financial officer. By 1551 he had died, and she continued to administer the inn and went on to buy properties in the Dauphiné and Lyonnais. And La Dame du Chariot, as she was called, had connections. As a young bride she had served as a godmother to the sons of the learned Cornelius Agrippa of Nettesheim, then living in Lyon (and author of a book on *The Nobility of the Female Sex*). She was also kin to Hélouin Dulin, financier of the evangelical publications of the ill-fated printer Etienne Dolet and his wife, Louise, and of the vernacu-lar Bibles of publisher Guillaume Rouillé. In her mature years, La Dame du Chariot was to let her inn be used as a place of Protestant worship. [48]

Finally, one can even find independent artisanal women in unusual trades like the manufacture of tennis rackets. Such a woman was Widow Estien-nette Gonter, who assured her labor supply by marrying off her orphaned goddaughter to a racket maker. The young couple would live with her; she would give them board if "they would obey her," and Gilles would make rackets for her at forty *sous* a racket, "as she was accustomed to pay other workers in the said craft." [49]

What can we say of the work identity—as perceived by themselves and by others—of La Loyse; La Dame du Chariot; Widow Estiennette, the tennis-racket maker; Monette, the glove maker; and Dame Anne Durtin? It did not grow out of the experience and rituals of apprenticeship, for, as we have seen, female training was often informal, and some of these women struck out on their own only as widows. It was hardly buttressed by organizational struc-tures and formal public or political recognition in Lyon. The females did not march in their craft's parades; the few sworn guilds had no women as officers or in any significant role; the city council never selected women to be *maîtres de métier*, that is, the two persons from each craft who ratified the new consuls and attended meetings of notables. Mistresses were expected to pay dues to a painters' confraternity in 1496 and to a confraternity of lacing makers in 1580, but they were never officers of any craft confraternity, played no part in confraternity drama, and may not always have been invited to the banquets. In any case, confraternities were much weakened during the years 1550–65 by the Reformed movement, and no self-respecting Protestant woman would even have sought such recognition. Only on certain limited occasions might the artisanal status of a female be recognized by notary or political officer: when she was making a contract specifically related to her work (in other contracts she would be "Pernette Morilier, wife of Jean Yvard the goldsmith"); when she was responsible as a widow for taxes or a militia-man from her household; and when the consulate wanted to summon her and others in her trade, perhaps to tell them the fixed price of meat or bread. [50]

The sense of craft for an independent artisanal woman probably arose, then, from the esteem in which she was held by those in her immediate environs: her husband and kin, her neighbors—and especially her female neighbors—and her clients. It was marked in small ways: the feminization of her last name (the silk mistress Estiennette Léonard became Estiennette Léonarde; the tavernkeeper Estiennette Cappin became Estiennette Cap-pine); the attribution of nicknames (La chevauchée de Rohanne, the Cav-alcade of Rohanne, for Jeanne Seiglevielle, hostess of the Ecu de France de Rohanne); and especially by addressing her as Dame, a worthy title not often accorded women of artisanal status. Her position was indicated by her frequent role as godmother, bringing with it influence over the gossip networks in the quarter; by the petty loans she made to kin and neighbors, listed and sometimes forgiven in her will; and by gifts of her clothing and money, bestowed on less fortunate women for whom she felt responsible.[51] Some men played a similar role, but the master's prestige drew more heavily upon his excellence in his métier, and his connections and reputation stretched out through his craft beyond his street and beyond his parish. The Dames among the *menu peuple* were noted for a cluster of womanly achievements, of which work skill was only one, and they were primarily rooted in their neighborhood.

The one exception was in the printing trade, where the names of eight females in Lyon were carried far and wide on the title pages or in the colophons of books. Or rather, in most cases their names were listed as widows of printers or booksellers whose trade they were continuing—"La vefve de Balthazar Arnoullet," "La vefve de Gabriel Cotier." Some of the women may have been content to entrust the "governance" of the atelier wholly to a senior journeyman or a male relative; but not a woman like Antoinette Peronet, who outlived two husbands, the first a printer, the second a bookseller, to marry a publisher younger than herself in 1555. Gabriel Cotier's publishing business was financed by her dowry of 2,080 *livres* in books, tools, money, and rents, from which she carefully reserved dowries for her daughters and income "for her small pleasures and wishes." After Cotier's death in 1565, she maintained the publishing house at the Sign of Milan for eleven years, using his mark, reissuing some of his editions, and accepting the services of a scholarly translator who had worked with the firm earlier. But she also addressed herself to a new printer and brought out some fresh works, obtaining a royal privilege to protect them against being pirated. In one of these, a French translation of a work by Marcus Aurelius Antoninus, she wrote a dedicatory letter to the governor of the Lyonnais, taking credit for initiating the edition, so important for teaching how to conduct oneself happily and to govern. Although she spoke conventionally of her "smallness," praising the governor as "the true asylum for poor widows charged with orphans," she signed herself firmly with her own name, "Antoynette Peronnet.'[52]

And what of Jeanne Giunta, whose praise of women in the crafts we heard in the opening of this essay? She published under her own name, as did Sibille de La Porte, because they were carrying on their father's house. Indeed, both women were somewhat at odds with their spouses: Giunta sued for separation of her goods and return of her dowry in 1572 because of her husband's poor management of the business (he died the next year). La Porte, as a new widow, left Calvinist Geneva, where her publisher husband had taken refuge, to return to Lyon and ultimately to Catholicism. Neither woman was an artisan, of course; by birth and marriage they were part of the rich Consular elite of Lyon, and their publishing houses were great commercial enterprises. Neither woman was educated or experienced enough to be involved in the daily administration of firms publishing religious, legal, and scholarly texts in Latin; this they left to their sons, to editors, and male employees. Yet Giunta frequently intervened to keep the business going in the wake of religious turmoil and family quarreling; she presented herself in a 1579 dedication (presumably dictated in French to a Latin translator) as devoted to the typographical art, lest the honor that her father and Florentine ancestors had won thereby be lost. And La Porte may have helped compose the letter from the Bibliopola to the Benevolent Reader, which insists on the correctness of her 1591 edition of the Commentaries on Aristotle's *De Anima* by the Jesuit François Tolet.[53] At any rate, these two women are the closest we come in sixteenth-century Lyon to the high-level female entrepreneur. It is perhaps no accident that it is a merchant-publisher who raises a lone female voice in that city to celebrate woman's work.

No one perceived these widows as dangerous competition to other printers and publishers; there were too few of them, and, in any case, they were maintaining family firms, not creating new ones. In some trades, however, the independent female artisan was eyed with suspicion as a slippery opening (cold and wet?) for interlopers. (Already, royal edicts were trying to curb the use of property by widows who remarried and to constrain married women to make contracts only with their husbands' consent.)[54]

The unbridled female could be a matter of concern even in a free trade, where supposedly anyone could set up shop without hindrance. A 1554 ruling for silk manufacture had made no effort to limit access to the craft. But in 1561, the market began to look uncertain, and about 158 merchants and masters engaged in various kinds of silk making met before a notary to set up "good order" among them, prevent "ruin," and "obviate disturbance, debates and disputes." The number of male apprentices in silk weaving was limited to two per master, with a duration of four to five years. *Apprentisses* ("female apprentices") were to be eliminated from the trade entirely, except for the daughters and sisters of masters. All masters were to send away their *apprentisses* within the month under penalty of twenty-five *livres* to the Aumône Générale, and this because of the "great prejudice and danger" they offered to the craft, especially because some of them were married to men in other arts. *Compagnonnes* ("journeywomen") who had already done an apprenticeship could be hired for wages, but were not to be supplied with work they could do "apart" in their rooms, unless they were married to men in the trade. Wives and widows of master silk makers could work on the looms, but could take no apprentices, male or female, except their own children. In short, mastership was to go from male to male and not pass through the female line.[55]

In fact, these provisions were not fully realized. A 1583 ruling for the master silk makers was still trying to limit male apprentices to two per master, but in regard to females it now prescribed that there could be no *apprentisses* except girls taken from Saint Catherine's orphan hospital or "poor orphan girls" begging in the master's quarter.[56] Nevertheless, in both cases we see fearful action against the independent female artisan, generated by hard times in an industry under the control of commercial capitalism.

Among the barber-surgeons, the quarrel broke out in prosperous times and was connected with the attempt of the sworn guildmasters to control the quality of practice in their art. Already in the fall of 1540, the Parlement of Paris was judging a case between thirteen sworn masters of Lyon on the one hand, and five *varlets* ("journeymen"), barber-surgeons, and three widows on the other hand. The journeymen were ordered to close their *boutiques*, and the widows were told they could keep shops open only for shaving beards and simple wounds (penalty for violation—1,000 *livres parisis*). In 1548–52, there were more cases before the Sénéchausée of Lyon. Now the masters would no longer tolerate journeymen who gave shaves and minor care from time to time in their own rooms. Now the widows would have to be constrained "because of the masterships and shops that they are renting out day after day to journeymen barbers, incapable and ignorant, leading to accidents and misfortunes." The letters of *maîtrise* must be turned in, and the women would be compensated with the small sum of nine *livres* per year.[57]

As with the widows of master printers and booksellers, some of these widows may have participated little in the shops they rented out. But Dame Marguerite Roybet was actually called a *barbière* in the 1550s after the death of her husband, a master barber-surgeon. And we can find a few other women so described, perhaps widows, perhaps females carrying on their art in defiance of the sworn masters. At any rate, the renting out of shops by widows continued unabated. From 1552 to 1565, Master Simon Guy was trying to put a stop to such activity; in 1571 his widow, Claudine Cazot, was renting out his kerchiefs and other barber's equipment. Perhaps these women obeyed their husbands while they were still alive, but when they were dead it was another matter.[58]

One last group of women should be mentioned among practitioners of the medical art: the midwives. In sixteenth-century Lyon, they were not yet experiencing the competition with male midwives that the royal midwife Louise Bourgeois was to complain of in Paris in 1609. And the physicians of Lyon, eager though they were to have some kind of control over the surgeons and apothecaries, were not yet interested in the *sages-femmes*, as the midwives were called. The latter went about their business freely on their street or at the Rhône Bridge Hospital: Etiennette Jay, widow of a printer and of a collar maker; Françoise Ru, a currier's wife; Anne Beauroy, godmother to an illegitimate child she had delivered in the parish of Saint Nizier; and others. These were Dames par excellence, pride in their manual skills merging with the sense of their importance at critical moments in a woman's life. Perhaps, too, they enjoyed the devotion from their female neighbors that Louise Bourgeois described in Paris in the old days: "When their midwives died, the women went into deep mourning and prayed God not to send them children any longer."[59]

## Conclusions

Women's work was important in this sixteenth-century city for the products created and sold and the services performed, and also for the flexibility it introduced into the craft economy and the economy of the family. That flexibility was prepared for by the girls' relatively informal training and was maintained by some of the other features of female life we have considered: weak connection with organizational structures in shop and craft, relatively weak work identity, and high identity as a member of a family and neighborhood. In good times and in bad times, the female adapted her skills and work energies to the stages of her life cycle and to the states of her body; to the needs of the families of which she was a part successively as a daughter, wife, mother, and if she lived long enough, as widow and second wife. A craft as a whole could expand on semiskilled female labor, could respond to busy periods by adding low-paid or unpaid female labor, could allow some vertical mobility through shops run by females, and could contract by shedding or curbing female work.

Male artisans could also display such flexibility on occasion. The painter Mathieu Charrier married and decided to go into innkeeping with his wife's brother; musician Hélie Gachoix took up glove making during a slack season. At the construction site, most of the mason's helpers were male, not female; in a large shop, young semiskilled males as well as females could be found in peripheral jobs. Through thick and thin, however, the male artisan held on to his work identity: Gachoix was called *musicien* even when he was buying his calf leather and paying his hired glover; Jacques Lescuyer, alias *Le Boiteux* ("The Limper"), changed his abode "to earn his living" as a printer rather than remain in Lyon and do something different. The female, in contrast, stayed put and improvised, patched together what work she could to fit her family requirements. In her availability for multiple uses, she prefigures the casual worker in industrial society.[60]

Finally, we return to those features of Lyon life which may account for the scope of female work and for efforts to limit female autonomy in the crafts. Neither the guild nor capitalism were to blame by themselves. On the one hand, the complex economy of a large city offered a wide range of jobs for both sexes and included many textile shops and taverns in which female work was welcome. On the other hand, the craft economy was unsteady, social inequality in the city had much increased since the days of the medieval commune, and the interest of the city dwellers in private property—in maintaining, increasing, and passing on the family's private property—was intensifying.[61] These factors usually acted to enhance the patriarchal character of institutions and values inherited from the past and to give a patriarchal twist to new ones; the wives went along with conventions which represented the husband as The Artisan in a métier to which the whole household had in fact contributed. Therefore, the guild, which in principle could be (and in some cities sometimes was) an apparatus available for mistresses in a trade, served in Lyon as a means for sworn master surgeons to limit female activity, along with that of journeymen competitors. So entrepreneurs and masters in the "free" trade of silk making tried to achieve the same goals by informal combination.

The regime of "free work" was a mixed blessing for women as it was for poor journeymen. It encouraged the establishment of new industries in Lyon and of work unwinding cocoons, embroidery with gold thread, and so forth. It made it easier for women to use their ingenuity to get around economic restrictions aimed at them, their husbands, and other male accomplices. But it also facilitated the capitalist organization of wholesale manufacture, and important female entrepreneurs were almost as rare as mistress masons and much rarer than mistress butchers. Lyon tradeswomen had enough credit and cash to take out and make small loans, but patriarchal society did not entrust the weaker and slippery sex with the control of large amounts of capital or with the direction of a major industrial enterprise. Compare the genteel, all-female shops of silk makers in medieval Paris or London, limited in output, with the female and mixed shops of Lyon's busy export industry, their few mistresses and many masters dominated by entrepreneurs. By the eighteenth century, the women would be clustered at the bottom of the trade.

Still other factors shaped the character of day-to-day work in the shop. The politics of the property-oriented family, supported by the politics of the slowly building state, was gradually concentrating decisions for everyone's good in the husband's hands. This could compromise the authority of the female, both in dealing with male workers and in working in the trade at large. Then, too, the strongly held attitudes which sorted out the technical work appropriate to each sex seemed to be favoring the male. Either sex could now make silk, with only the watery process of unwinding cocoons left to females; but manual operations at the printing press, the forge, and the foundry were to be confined to males. Men could also dominate the mixed atelier by their articulated and public associational life: the magical culture of female work had less bite to it, especially when one had to be wary of witchcraft accusations.

For a time, the Protestant movement may have assigned more sanctity to women's work as it did to all lay vocations ("You can even say sacramental words in the kitchen, washing the dishes," said a male proselytizer), and the Dames among the *menu peuple* were often converts to the new religion. Merchant-shoemaker Jean Pierre, who acknowledged the contribution of his linen-making wife to the family's profits, was an elder of the Reformed Consistory. In the longer run, the Reformation strengthened the hand of the father and energetically proscribed fairies and devotions to the Virgin from the workshop. Artisanal woman in seventeenth-century Geneva were to have no more scope than those in Catholic Lyon.[62]

Within all these constraints, women worked however and wherever they could, helping husbands and making anything from pins to gloves. "The highest of praise" they may have received for the exercise of their craft, as Jeanne Giunta said, but it usually remained within the world of their street, their gossip network, their tavern, their kin—unpublished and unsung.

## Notes

This chapter is reprinted from *Feminist Studies* 8, no. 1 (1982): 47–80, by permission of the publisher, FEMINIST STUDIES, Inc., c/o Women's Studies Program, University of Maryland, College Park, MD 20742. It is a revised and extended version of an essay that first appeared in *Lyon et l'Europe. Hommes et sociétés. Mélanges d'histoire offerts à Richard Gascon* (Lyon: Presses universitaires de Lyon, 1980), pp. 139–67. The author is grateful to the University of California, Berkeley, and to Princeton University for grants aiding this research, and to the editorial board of *Feminist Studies* for suggestions for revision.

The following abbreviations will be used in this article: AN—Archives nationales, ADR—Archives départementales du Rhône, AML—Archives municipales de Lyon, AChl.—Archives de la Charité de Lyon, ADHL—Archives de l'Hôtel-Dieu de Lyon, and AEG—Archives d'Etat de Genève. In those cases where the standard published inventory for a given archive has been used, it will be indicated by adding the letter I before the abbreviation.

1. Guillaume Paradin, *Mémoires de l'histoire de Lyon* (Lyon: Antoine Gryphius, 1573). pp. 1, 355; Antoine Du Pinet, *Plantz, Pourtraitz et Descriptions de Plusieurs Villes* (Lyon: Jean d'Ogerolles. 1564), p. 31; Jacques Peletier, *L'Art Poetique* (Lyon: Jean de Tournes, 1555), pp. 108–109; Joachim Du Bellay, "A Louise Labé, Lion-

noese"; *Les regrets* (Paris: F. Morel, 1568), poem no. 137; and G. Guigue, ed., *La Magnificence de la superbe et triumphante entree de la noble et antique Cite de Lyon faicte au Treschrestien Roy de France Henry deuxiesme de ce Nom . . . le XXIII de Septembre M.D. XLVIII* (Lyon: Société des bibliophiles lyonnais, 1927), pp. 37, 65, 325–26.

2.   Henri Hauser, *Ouvriers du temps passe*, 5th ed. (Paris: Librairie Félix Alcan, 1927), chap. 8; Hauser's book first appeared in 1899. See also G. Fagniez, *La femme et la société française dans la première moitié du dix-septième siècle* (Paris: J. Gamber, 1929), chap. 3; E. Le Roy Ladurie, *Les payans de Languedoc*, 2 vols. (Paris: SEVPEN, 1966), 1: 276–80; Pierre Goubert, *Beauvais et le Beauvaisis de 1600 à 1730* 2 vols. (Paris: SEVPEN, 1960), 2: 293–304; Jean-Pierre Gutton, *La société et les pauvres. L'exemple de la généralité de Lyon, 1534–1789* (Paris: Société d'édition "Les Belles Lettres," 1971), pp. 61–83; Jacques Rossiaud, "Prostitution, jeunesse et société dans les villes du sud-est à la fin du Moyen Age," *Annales. Economies. Sociétés. Civilisations*, 31 (1976): 284–325; B. Geremek, *Les marginaux parisiens aux XIVe et XVe siècles*, trans. D. Beauvois (Paris: Flammarion, 1976), chap. 7, "La prostitution"; and Alice Clark, *Working Life of Women in the Seventeenth Century* (London: Routledge and Sons, 1919). For the eighteenth century, see L. Abensour, *La femme et le féminisme en France avant la Révolution* (Paris: Editions Ernest Leron, 1923), pt. 1, chap. 6; Maurice Garden, *Lyon et les lyonnais au XVIIIe siècle* (Paris: Société d'édition "Les Belles Lettres," 1970), pt. 2; Olwen H. Hufton, "Women and the Family Economy in Eighteenth-Century France," *French Historical Studies* 9 (1975): 1–22; Olwen H. Hufton, *The Poor of Eighteenth-Century France* (Oxford: Oxford University Press, 1974); and Louise A. Tilly and Joan W. Scott, *Women, Work, and Family* (New York: Holt, Rinehart and Winston, 1978), pt. 1.

Recent and forthcoming studies on women in urban economic life in the sixteenth century are Judith C. Brown and Jordan Goodman's "Women and Industry in Florence," *Journal of Economic History* 40 (1980): 73–80; Liliane Mottu-Weber, "Les femmes dans la vie économique de Genève," *Bulletin de la société d'histoire et d'archéologie de Genève* 16 (1979): 381–401; E. William Monter, "Women in Calvinist Geneva; 1550–1800," *Signs* 6, no. 2 (Winter 1980): 189–209; and Merry Wiesner Wood, "Paltry Peddlers or Essential Merchants: Women in the Distributive Trades in Early Modern Nuremberg," *Sixteenth Century Journal* 12 (Summer 1981): 3–14. Keith Snell has important data on the seventeenth to early nineteenth century in England in "The Apprenticeship of Women," forthcoming in his *Essays on Social Change and Agrarian England, 1660–1900.*

Among recent cross-cultural examinations of the question are Ester Boserup, *Woman's Role in Economic Development* (London: Allen and Unwin, 1970); Sidney Mintz, "Men, Women and Trade," *Comparative Studies in Society and History* 13 (1971): 247–69; and *Signs* Special Issue on Women and National Development 3, no. 1 (Autumn 1977).

3.   David Herlihy, "Deaths, Marriages, Births, and the Tuscan Economy," in *Population Patterns in the Past,* ed. Ronald D. Lee (New York: Academic Press, 1977), pp. 162–63. Herlihy did call for further study of this matter, however, and the article by Brown and Goodman, cited in note 2, has already given fresh evidence on the participation of Florentine women in wool and especially silk manufacture.

4.   Clark, *Working Life of Women,* chaps. 1, 5, 7.

5.   Claude de Rubys, *Les privileges, franchises et immunitez octroyees par les roys treschrestiens, aux consuls, eschevins, manans et habitans de la ville de Lyon* (Lyon: Antoine Gryphius, 1574), pp. 48–49; Natalis Rondot, *L'ancien régime du travail à Lyon* (Lyon: Alexandre Rey, 1897), p. 42; and Hauser, *Ouvriers,* pp. 111–12, 133.

6. On the economy of sixteenth-century Lyon, see Richard Gascon, *Grand commerce et vie urbaine au XVIe siècle. Lyon et ses marchands*, 2 vols. (Paris: Ecole pratique des hautes études, 1971).

7. Material on apprenticeship based on all the apprenticeship contracts remaining in the archives for the years 1553–60 (see note 9) and numerous contracts from ADR for other years. For duration of apprenticeship: *couturiers* (1535–67)—twenty contracts, one to five years, median, three; *cordonniers* (1534–62)—thirteen contracts, one and one-half to six years, median, three; *imprimeurs* (1539–73)—fourteen contracts, two to seven years, median four; *veloutiers* (1549–71)—thirty-seven contracts, two to eight years, median, five; and *orfèvres* (1539–66)—fourteen contracts, one to ten years, median, five. Examples of range in fees paid by the apprentice to the master in the years 1553–60: *cordonniers*—three *livres* and seven *sous* per year to twelve *livres* per year; *veloutiers*—twelve *sous* per year to twelve *livres* per year. Payment of fees in wood, hemp, grain, and so forth, in ADR, 3E7176, 30 October 1559, 27 December 1559, 28 February 1559–60; 3E367, 6 March 1548–49. (Unless otherwise indicated, all money value is given by the weight scale known as "tournois.") Hauser found that apprentices in dyeing in Paris frequently started at age twelve (Hauser, *Ouvriers*, p. 22). Two Lyon wills give fifteen for the age at which sons or nephews should be apprentices (ADR, 3E7195, 2 June 1562, 25 February 1562–63).

8. ADR, B. Insinuations, vol. A (1565–66), 58$^v$–60$^v$: Jean Bezines leaves thirty *livres* for his *serviteur* Jean-Baptiste to learn a trade.

9. All notarial registers remaining for the years running from Easter 1553 to Easter 1561 (that is, 1553–60 by the old style of reckoning), were searched. Female apprenticeships were found in ADR, 3E7172, 7173, 7174, 7175, 7176, 7177, 3E3228, 3E371, 372, 3E562. The Archives de la Charité de Lyon were examined for a nine-month period in 1557 (AChL, E8, E9). Mottu-Weber found that female apprenticeships in Geneva in the years 1570 to 1629 were concentrated in textiles and pin making and represented only "a weak proportion" of all apprenticeship contracts (Mottu-Weber, "Les femmes," p. 392). See also her "Apprentissages et économie genevoise au début de XVIIIe siècle," *Revue suisse d'histoire* 20 (1970): 340–41. Keith Snell has found in Southampton and east Suffolk in the seventeenth century that the percentage of girls among all children apprenticed through parish poor relief was 20 to 22 percent and that they were trained in a wide variety of trades; the percentage of girls apprenticed *through their families* in several counties in the early eighteenth century was 3 to 7 percent, and more of them were concentrated in genteel needle trades (Snell, "Apprenticeship of Women").

10. In addition to the eighteen female apprenticeships found in 1553–60, eight more examples from AChL, E4, 29$^v$; ADR, 3E367, 3 December 1548; 3E4062, August 1571; 3E7180, 707$^v$, 988$^v$–989$^r$; 3E8030, 5 November 1565; AEG, Jovenon, 1, 412$^v$–413$^r$ (contracts made in Lyon).

11. Natalie Zemon Davis, *Society and Culture in Early Modern France: Eight Essays* (Stanford: Stanford University Press, 1975), p. 73.

12. *La Police de l'Aulmosne de Lyon* (Lyon: Sébastien Gryphius, 1539), p. 39; Paradin, *Mémoires*, pp. 291–92; AChL, E5, pp. 182, 192; E5, pp. 272, 332, 368; E7, pp. 374, 385. Gutton, *La Société et les pauvres*, p. 278; Gascon, *Grand commerce et vie urbaine*, p. 319; and Davis, *Society and Culture*, p. 43.

13. ADR, 3E8031, 8 September 1567; BP1881, 20 November 1592. AN, jj263$^B$, 44$^r$.

14. For example, for rituals surrounding the apprentices in the dyeing trade, see AMI, BB102, 52$^r$–53$^r$.

15. All marriage contracts remaining in the ADR were examined for the eight years going from Easter 1553 to Easter 1561, that is, 1553–1560 by the old reckoning (see note 18). Of the 324 women marrying in the two years 1558–59, 33 could be identified as servants. For servants in craft families and their wages, see ADR, 3E3908, 38ᵛ–40ᵛ, 54ᵛ–57ʳ, 114ᵛ–117ʳ, 155ᵛ–157ᵛ, 222ʳ–223ʳ, 286ᵛ–290ᵛ; AChL, E8 and E9 *passim*. I studied all the marriage contracts from Easter of 1553 to Easter of 1561, and all the quantitative data in this article are based on those eight years—except the information about the servant girls, which is based only on 1558–59.

Maurice Garden found a similar distribution in the geographical origin of female servants in eighteenth-century Lyon: few natives of the city, most from nearby regions, a few from more distant places—probably more in the eighteenth century from far away than in the sixteenth century (Garden, *Lyon et les lyonnais* pp. 250–51).

16. ADR, B. Sénéchaussée, Sentences, 1543–45, 114ʳ (suit of Claudine Plantin for back wages); and ADR, 3E7184, 393ᵛ, 408ᵛ. Other examples: Jane Chardonyer, a domestic servant to a carter's household marries a carter; Marguerite Jacquet, a servant to a boatman's household, marries a boatman; Francoise Serpillet, a servant to a butcher's household, marries a butcher (ADR, 3E366, 1ʳ, 3E345, 135ᵛ, 3E536, 263ʳ). Sometimes servants marry men in trades very different from that of their master: Claudine Nimoyre, a daughter of a peasant and servant to a blacksmith, contracts marriage with a journeyman shoemaker in 1558 (3E538, 153ʳ).

17. AN, JJ246, 24ᵛ–25ʳ (letters of pardon, October 1531); and ADR, 3E7170, 4ʳ–19ʳ.

18. Marriage contracts were searched in the ADR for the years Easter 1553 to Easter 1561 (again, 1553–60 by the old reckoning); all registers were covered in 3E and B, Insinuations. A total of 1,067 contracts was found, which may represent only one-fourth of all marriages made in Lyon in those years, but they came nevertheless in substantial number from the *menu peuple*. Of those brides marrying for the first time, 277 of them were the daughters of Lyon artisans. Among these 277 women, only 71 married husbands in the same trade as their fathers or stepfathers; in 23 more cases, the husbands were in allied trades.

19. ADR, 3E3765, 105ᵛ–106ʳ, donation of further goods in her house by Michellette Gibollet, widow of Georges de Luire, *blanchisseur de maisons* ("whitewasher"), to Jean de Tournes, *imprimeur* ("printer"), and her daughter, Odette de Luire. Her son, Benoît de Luire, may have been living in part of the house (ADR, 3E3765, 105⁵–106ʳ; document unknown to A. Cartier and E. Vial.); ADR, 3E297, 21 September 1547; AML, EE23, 14ᵛ, 19ᵛ; GG1, 15ᵛ. See A. Cartier, *Bibliographie des Editions des De Tournes, imprimeurs lyonnais*, ed. M. Audin, "Notice biographique," by E. Vial (Paris: Bibliothèque nationale, 1938–39), pp. 8, 124.

Another example of a daughter living in her father's house is Antoinette Servain and her second husband, *imprimeur* Grégoire François. They lived in the same house on the rue Grolée with her widowed father, master printer Claude Servain, and her brother, the printer Etienne Servain, and his wife (AEG, Procès criminels, 1374, testimony of 4 August 1566).

20. ADR, 3E3908, 15ᵛ–18ᵛ; 3E3949, 2ʳ–5ᵛ (31 March 1559; only one of the two silk merchants was married at the time the household was established, but provision was made for a future wife). The jurist Denis Le Brun talked of the husband's gifts to his wife in his testament as a form of "récompense" for her work as "menagère," in Le Brun, *Traité de la communauté entre mari et femme* (Paris: Michel Guignard, 1709), p. 4.

21. De Rubys, *Privileges*, p. 76; and *La Pyrotechnie ou Art du feu . . . Composée par le Seigneur Vanoccio Biringuccio . . . Et traduite . . . par feu maistre Iacques Vincent* (Paris: Guillaume Jullian, 1572), f. 98ᵛ. The many woodcuts illustrating this work contain no women among the artisans.

22. AEG, Procès criminels, 2d series, 794, reprinted in E. Balmas, *Montaigne a Padova e altri studi sulla letteratura francese de cinquencento* (Padua: Liviana Editrice, 1962), pp. 207–208. On the conduct of Anne de Noyer and Gabriel Challiot in Lyon and Geneva, see AEG, Procès criminels, 1308 (August–September 1565); Registres du Consistoire, 11(1556), 92ʳ, 25 (1568), 159ʳ, 165ʳ, 173ʳ.

23. Keith Thomas, *Religion and the Decline of Magic* (London: Weidenfeld and Nicolson, 1971), pp. 38–39; Pierre Viret, *Disputations Chrestiennes* (Geneva: Jean Gerard, 1552), p. 295; Jean-Baptiste Thiers, *Traité des Superstitions qui regardent les Sacremens*, bk. 1, chap. 12 in *Superstitions anciennes et modernes*, 2 vols. (Amsterdam: J.F. Bernard, 1733–36) 2: 34–35; Jean Massé, *L'art veterinaire ou grande marechalerie* (Paris: Charles Perier, 1563), f. 164ᵛ (on the dangers of menstruating women to pregnant animals); *C Plinii Secundi Historiae Mundi Libri Triginta Septem* (Lyon: G. and M. Beringen, 1548), bk. 7, chap. 15 (col. 160: "De menstruis mulierum"), bk. 27, chap. 7 (col. 734: "De remediis mulieribus"); and *L'histoire du monde de C. Pline Second . . . Le tout fait et mis en François par Antoine du Pinet*, 2 vols. (Lyon: Claude Senneton, 1562), 1:262 ("Des fleurs des femmes"), 2:400 ("Des medecines prinses et tirees des femmes").

24. ADR, 3E3908, 219ᵛ–223ʳ; AN, JJ249¹, 10ʳ⁻ᵛ, ADR, BP3891, 82ᵛ–83ʳ. See also ADR, 3E8031, 13 December 1567, Mye Mossier, "citoyenne de Lyon," acting for her husband Etienne Rolin, "hôte du Pin," renting out part of their inn to a pastry cook. See 3E4980, 189ʳ, for a marriage contract in which both the father and mother of the bride are characterized as bakers (1555).

25. AChL, E8, E9: Estiennette Léonarde, wife of silk thrower Claude Julliand, hires Guillemette Coynde for two years to be a chambermaid and to unwind cocoons; Catherine Ranyer and Jane Paulet hired for one year each for *dévidage* ("unwinding cocoons"); and Irene Gay, Marguerite Berthe, and Ancelly Cousturier hired for one year each to be *chambrières* and *dévider la soie* ("to wind silk from cocoons"). See L. Strumbingher, "Les canutes de Lyon (1835–1848)," *Movement social*, 105 (October–December 1978): 60–64; ADR, 3E7170, 4ʳ–9ʳ; B. Insinuations, Donations, 23, 25ʳ. See also ADR, 3E370, 24 October 1553, button maker François Prusseau and "by his authority" his wife, Claudine Crassarde, purchase 350 *livres* of silk thread.

26. AML, BB84, 124ᵛ; ADR, BP3640, 29ᵛ–30ʳ; ADR, 3E3930, 314ᵛ–315ᵛ, 3E3931, 115ʳ–117ᵛ, 3E6942, 315ʳ–316ᵛ, BP3895, 174ʳ.

27. ADR, 3E3765, 179ᵛ, 289ᵛ, 3E3766, 232ᵛ. Richard Copley Christie, *Etienne Dolet. The Martyr of the Renaissance, 1508–1546* (London: Macmillan and Co., 1899), pp. 547–52; and Claude Longeon, *Bibliographie des oeuvres d'Etienne Dolet, ecrivain, editeur et imprimeur* (Geneva: Librairie Droz, 1980), p. xxxvi.

28. On Barthélemy Frein, ADR, Insinuations, Testaments, V 82ᵛ–83ʳ (will of Barthélemy Frein, dated 17 May 1556, registered 18 October 1556); AML, CC281, 71ʳ; H. and J. Baudrier, *Bibliographie lyonnaise*, 12 vols. (Lyon: F. Brossier, 1895–1921), 10: 348–53; and Natalie Zemon Davis, "A Trade Union in Sixteenth-Century France," *Economic History Review* 19 (1966): 57, n. 4. On Mie Roybet, see F. Buisson, *Sébastien Castellion, sa vie et son oeuvre (1515–1563)*, 2 vols. (Paris: Hachette, 1892), 2: 108–109, 434–37; Baudrier, *Bibliographie lyonnaise*, 1:92; and E. Droz, "Castellioniana," in her *Chemins de l'hérésie*, 4 vols.

(Geneva: Librairie E. Droz, 1970–76), 2:355–67. AML, EE23, 23$^r$. See ADR, B, Sénéchausée, Sentences (June 1557–May 1558), sentence of 14 August 1557, describing the arrest of Mie Roybet and Michel Chastillon, and undated and incomplete sentence between 17 August and 23 August 1557. These last two documents, hitherto unknown, support Beza's claim that a new work of Castellion was printed at Lyon, and they contradict Mlle Droz's speculation that the arrests were inspired by journeymen's agitation. (H. Aubert et al., *Correspondence de Théodore de Bèze*, 9 vols. [Geneva: Librairie Droz, 1960–] 2:83).

29. ADR, B, Insinuations, Donations, 12, 111$^v$–112$^v$; 15, 163$^v$–165$^r$; Sénéchaussée, Sentences (April, 1559–January 1560), sentence of 31 October 1559.

30. Out of 1,067 women contracting marriage with men residing in Lyon in 1553–60, 245 were widows (22 percent), of whom 181 had an artisan for their first or second husband (usually both). Of these 181 widows, the occupation of the first and second husband is known in 154 cases: 39 of these 154 widows married men in the same occupation as their first husbands; 14 more married men in allied trades.

31. AN, JJ235, 78$^v$, JJ249, 1$^v$–2$^r$, JJ255 , 30$^r$–$^v$, AML, CC39, 103$^v$; IAML, BB56, BB57, BB58, BB65, BB71.

32. ADR, 3E8031, 8 September 1567; 3E7180, pp. 988$^v$–989$^r$; BP3645, 261$^v$–263$^v$; 3E7174, May 1557; 3E539, 217$^r$, 3E538, 36$^v$, 3E370, 7 January 1553–54; J. Godart, *L'ouvrier en soie* (Lyon: Bernoux & Cumin, 1899), pp. 67, 172–73; and E. Pariset, *Histoire de la Fabrique lyonnaise* (Lyon: Alexandre Rey, 1901), p. 36. On the *tireuse de cordes*, or drawgirl at Lyon, see also Daryl M. Hafter, "The 'Programmed' Brocade Loom and the Decline of the Drawgirl," in *Dynamos and Virgins Revisited: Women and Technological Change in History*, ed. M. M. Trescott (Metuchen, N.J.: Scarecrow Press, 1979); and ADR, 3E7170, 4$^r$–9$^r$.

33. ADR, 3E8029, 27 June 1566; 3E6942, 307$^r$–308$^r$; Jean Tricou, ed.; *La chronique lyonnaise de Jean Guéraud* (Lyon: L'imprimerie Audinienne, 1929), p. 84; ADR, 10G1612, 12$^r$ (November 1552, April 1553); Gascon, *Grand commerce et vie urbaine*, p. 319; Tricou, ed., *Chronique lyonnaise*, p. 76; and Philibert Delorme, *Le premier tome de l'architecture* Paris: F. Morel, 1568), f. a iv$^v$–a v$^r$.

34. ADR, 3E7179, 411$^v$–421$^r$.

35. 3E8031, 8 September 1567; AChL, 9, passim; 3E7176, 30 March 1559–60; 3E7180, 411$^v$–412$^r$; 3E7172, 7 January 1554–55, hiring of Claude Paury, native of a village in Savoie, by a master shoemaker for one year for three *livres*, "vivre, couche et chausse;" 3E7177, hiring of Jehan Jasso, *cordonnier*, native of Saint-Antoine-en-Viennois, for one year for four *livres* and sixteen *sous*, "bouche et couche." On wages in Lyon, see Gascon, *Grand commerce et vie urbaine*, 2: 743–64, 930–36.

36. AML, BB37, 152$^r$, BB55, 127$^r$, 147$^v$; G. Guigue, ed., *La magnificence de la superbe, Entree* (cited in note 1), p. 143; *L'ordre tenu en la chevauchée faicte en la ville de Lyon* (Lyon: Guillaume Testefort, 1566), reprinted in G. Guigue, *Archives historiques et statistiques du départment du Rhône*, 9 (1828): 410–11; AML, BB102, 52$^r$–54$^v$; BB118, 65$^v$–67$^v$; and Davis, "Trade Union."

37. AML, BB102, 53$^v$–54$^r$; and Davis, "Trade Union," pp. 62–63.

38. M.C. Guigue and G. Guigue, *Bibliothèque historique du lyonnais* (Lyon: Vitte & Perrussel, 1886), p. 258; Symphorien Champier, *Cy commerce ung petit livre de lantiquite, origine et nobless de la tresantique cite de Lyon: Ensemble de la rebeine et coniuration ou rebellion de populaire de ladicte ville* (Lyon: n.p., 1529–30), f. xviii$^r$; and Davis, *Society and Culture*, pp. 92, 182–83.

39. AML, BB102, 54$^r$; and Davis, "Trade Union," p. 54.

40. AN, JJ256$^3$, 30$^v$–31$^r$: Jehanne Pasquellet accuses Ysabeau Malefine, washer-

woman of Lyon, of being a sorceress and making her sick (1554). Malefine was allegedly acting at the behest of another woman who was jealous of Pasquellet. AN, JJ261$^{bis}$, 96$^r$–$^v$: Philiberte Guillon, an old woman from Savoie living in Lyon, is accused of doing harm through sorcery to a silk weaver's daughter and to a merchant's son (1552).

41. P. Jannet, ed., *Les Evangiles des Quenouilles* (Paris: P. Jannet, 1855), especially pp. 18, 37, 92–93, 118. Composed in the midst of the fifteenth century, this imagined conversation among spinning women had printed editions at Lyon, Bruges, Paris, and Rouen in the late fifteenth and sixteenth centuries. Paul Sebillot, *Légendes et curiosités des métiers* (Paris: Flammarion [1895]), "Les Fileuses." Also see Jean Benedicti, *La somme des Pechez, et les Remedes d'iceux* (Lyon: Pierre Landry, 1593), bk. 1, chap. 8, par. 47. For an important study of present female work culture, see Yvonne Verdier, *Façons de dire, façons de faire. La laveuse, la couturière, la cuisinière* (Paris: Editions Gallimard, 1979), especially chap. 4.

42. François Rabelais, *Oeuvres*, ed. A. Lefranc et al., 6 vols. (Paris: E. Champion and Geneva: E. Drox, 1912–55), 4:310. "Basteliers" was the word used in the editions of *Pantagruel* printed in Lyon by Francois Juste in 1533 and 1534, but the feminine "bastelières" was used in the edition corrected by Rabelais himself in 1542, and this is accepted in the critical edition. See Felix Platter, *Beloved Son Felix*, trans. S. Jennett (London: F. Muller, 1961), pp. 36–37. AHDL, F 21, 10–17 November 1560: "Tinance, riveran de Vienne, femme de Pierre Roc" received in the Hotel-Dieu: IAML, BB128 (1591): order to the 'Bateliers de Lyon, tant hommes que femmes" ("boatmen of Lyon, both men and women") to take no persons into the city by boat. ADR, 3E370, 18 May 1553: Estiennette Andree bequeaths a small boat, a "besche garni," to Anthoinette Jaqueme.

43. ADR, 1G185, 85$^v$. AHDL, F 21 (7–14 December 1560, 23–24 March 1560–61). ADR, 3E8020, 3 September 1565; 3E8031, 2 July 1566; 3E8030, 5 November 1565.

44. AHDL, F 21 (14–20 April, 15–29 December 1560), AML, EE23, 5$^r$; ADR, 3E7180, 4$^r$, 988$^v$–989$^r$; BP3654, 261$^v$–263$^v$; 15G27, 157$^r$–$^v$; *Livre nouveau dict patrons de lingerie . . . en comprenant lart de broderie et tissuterie* (Lyon: Pierre de Sainct Lucie, n.d., after 1533); IAML, CC151.

45. ADR, B, Insinuations, Donations, 25, 222$^v$–225$^v$; AML, CC44, 21$^v$; GG87, pièce 4. AML, CC150, 8$^v$; GG87, peèce 5. Also, AHD, F21: Jehanne Guline, "Lingere de Lyon," enters the Hotel-Dieu in late 1560; IAML, 947, Simonde de Lorme, "marchande de toiles" ("merchant of linen cloth"), living near the nunnery of Saint Pierre (1541–42).

46. ADR, 3E542, between March and May 1564: of the 48 bakers who owe "des carolus," (a traditional payment), la vefve de Campaignon is the lowest taxed. Jehanne James, widow of miller Etienne Boudron, continued to run his grain mill after his death (ADR, 3E4961, January 1562–63). ADR, 3E370, 17 January 1553–54. AHDL, F 21 (15–22 December 1560), E607, receipts of 24 February 1569, 21 September 1569; ADR, BP2640, 133$^v$–134$^r$, 1G185, 10$^r$, AML, BB82, 32$^r$, BB56,95$^v$.

47. *Sensuyt ung petit Livre pour apprendre a parler Francoys Alemant et Ancloys* [sic]. *Pour apprendre a comter a vendre et acheter pour demander le chemin et le logis et pour parler a l'hostesse pour demander combien on a despendu . . .* (Lyon: Pierre Mareschal, [c. 1515–20]), edition at Beinecke Library, Yale University; not in Baudrier, *Bibliographie lyonnaise*, 11; Erasmus, *Diversoria*, 1523 in *The Colloquies of Erasmus*, trans. Craig Thompson (Chicago: University of Chicago Press, 1965), pp. 147–48; AN,

JJ255^A, 41^v–41^r; ADR, 3E7311, 10 January 1572. Among others: La veufve Loys Guillien, hostesse (AML, EE21, 63^v); Les hostesses du Lyon d'or (EE23, 94^v); Irène, widow of Pierre Chiron, hostesse (CC281, 137^r); Françoise Clappier, widow of Etienne Portallier, hostesse du logis à l'Enseigne des Trois Mores (ADR, B, Insinuations, Donations, 21, 166^v).

48. Baudrier, *Bibliographie lyonnaise*, 5:35, 9:20. ADR, 3E3908, 139^r–140^v; 3E565, testimony of 5 October 1560; 3E7595, 11 May 1537; 3E367, 23 November 1548; 3E343, 148^r; 3E346, 179^v–181^r; 3E370, 24 October and 11 November 1553; 3E5018, 9 June 1562, 15 December 1562; AML, BB82, 52^r; CC1174, 25^r; CC1174, 25^r; EE23, 101^v; EE24, 39^r; EE25, 157^v–161^r; Tricou, ed., *Chronique lyonnaise*, p. 146.

49. ADR, 3E4981, 137^v.

50. Charles Ouin-Lacroix, *Histoire des anciennes corporations d'arts et mètiers et des confréries religieuses . . .* (Rouen: Lecointe, 1850), pp. 741–46; ADR, BP3654, 261^v–263^v; and AML, BB118, 24^v–25^r.

51. ADR, 3E3908, 144^r–146^r; 3E5018, 11 March 1562–63; AML, CC1174, 26^v; ADR, 3E3908, 219^v–222^4–245^r; 3E372, 3 August 1555, 31 October 1555.

52. On Antoinette Peronet, see Baudrier, *Bibliographie lyonnaise*, 4; 64–82; AML, CC281, 49^v; *Institution de la vie humaine, Dressee par Marc Antonin Philosophe, Empereur Romain. Remonstrance d'Agapetus Evesque . . . Elegie de Solon Prince Athenien . . . Le tout Traduit, par Pardoux du Prat, Docteur ès Droits* (A Lyon, A l'Escu de Milan, Par la vefve Gabriel Cotier, 1570), ff. 2^r–5^v. Also, Jeanne de La Saulcée, widow of Barnabé Chaussard (Baudrier, *Bibliographie lyonnaise*, 10:39–71); Claudine Carcan, widow of Claude Nourry (ibid., 3:75); the widow of Jean Crespin (ibid., 1:112); Michelette de Cayre, widow of Jacques Arnoullet (ibid., 10: 27–28); Denise Barbou, widow of Balthazar Arnoullet (ibid., pp. 150–54); and Bonnette Pattrasson, widow of Melchoir Arnoullet (ibid., pp. 158–61). Denise Barbou was fiercely loyal to her father's atelier, carried on by her husband, Balthazar Arnoullet, after his death, and she sustained the shop while Arnoullet was in prison being questioned for his printing of Servetus's *Christianismi Restitutio*. Although editorial decisions about the books she printed as a widow were left to her learned brother-in-law, Guillaume Guéroult, she was probably actively involved in shop administration.

53. On Jeanne Giunta, see Baudrier, *Bibliographie lyonnaise*, 6: 337–84 (her dedication to *Iulii Clari Patritii Alexandri . . . Opera* on p. 374); ADR, B, Sénéchaussée, Sentences (1572) 221^r–223^3 (not in *Bibliographie lyonnaise*); BP3645, 95^r–^v. In an act of 1572, Jeanne Giunta did not sign her name (Baudrier, *Bibliographie lyonnaise*) 6: 245; she may nonetheless have been able to read in French, as women might well learn to read without learning to write. On Sibille de La Porte, ibid., 7:347–58; D. Fr. *Toleti e Societate Iesu, in Tres Libros Aristotelis De Anima Commentarii* (Lugduni, Sumptibus Sib. a Porta, 1591), Lectori Benevolo Bibliopola, dated 3 Ides of December, 1590, f. a 2^r–^v.

54. P.C. Timbal, "L'esprit du droit privé," *XVIIe siècle*, 58–59 (1963): 30–39; A. Rosambert, *La veuve en droit canonique jusqu'au XIVe siècle* (Paris: Dalloz, 1923), p. 145; and P. Bascou-Vance, "La condition des femmes en France et les progès des idées féministes du XVIe au XVIIIe siècle," *L'Information historique* 28, no. 4 (1966): 139–41.

55. F. A. Isambert et al., *Receuil général des anciennes lois françaises depuis l'an 420, jusqu'à la Révolution de 1789*, 29 vols. (Paris: Belin Leprieur, 1822–33), 13: 374–79; ADR, 3E7170, 4^r–19^r (document hitherto unknown); and Pariset, *Histoire de la Fa-*

*brique lyonnaise*, 32–34; Pariset's statements about the open character of the industry until 1596 would have to be modified by the contents of the 1561 document.

56. ADR, BP3646, 242$^r$–243$^v$; and Pariset, *Histoire de la Fabrique lyonnaise*, pp. 36–49.

57. AN, X$^1$ 9215, 51$^{r-v}$, 77$^{r-v}$; and ADR, B. Sénéchausée, Sentences, 15 March 1551–52, 5 April 1551–52, 4 May 1552, 15 May 1552.

58. J. Pointet, *Historiques des propriétés et maisons de la Croix Rousse du XIVe siècle à la Révolution*, 2 vols. (Lyon: Imprimerie des Missions Africaines, 1926), 2:44; ADR, 3E7184, 100$^{r-v}$; B. Insinuations, Donations, 22, 10$^v$–12$^r$; AHDL, F21 30 June–7 July 1560, 26 January–1 February 1560–61; ADR, B. Sénéchausée, Sentences, 1551–52, 14 May 1552; AML, BB84, 124$^v$; ADR, 3E4062, June 1571; and 3E4542, October 1556.

59. Louise Bourgeois, *Observations diverses sur la sterilité, perte de fruict, foecondité, accouchements et maladies des Femmes et Enfants nouveaux naix*, 2d ed. (Rouen: La veufve Thomas Daré, 1626), Livre deuxiesme, pp. 234–35; ADR, 3E6942, 134$^v$, 3E2813, 62$^r$; AML, GG2, 85$^v$; and AHDL, F22, December 1575.

60 . ADR, 3E3764, 91$^v$; 3E8029, 5$^r$–6$^v$; Paul Chaix, *Recherches sur l'imprimerie à Genève de 1550 à 1564* (Geneva: Libraire Droz, 1954), p. 202; and A. Cartier, "Arrêts du Conseil de Genève sur le fait de l'imprimerie et de la librairie de 1541 à 1550," in *Mémoires et documents publiés par la société d'histoire et archéologie de Genève* 3, 2d ser., (1888–94): 459, n. 1. See Hufton's excellent discussion of the female "economy of expedients" in her "Women and the Family Economy."

61. On family and property in sixteenth-century France, see Ralph Giesey, "Rules of Inheritance and Strategies of Mobility in Prerevolutionary France," *American Historical Review* 82 (1977): 271–89; and Natalie Zemon Davis, "Ghosts, Kin and Progeny: Some Features of Family Life in Early Modern France," *Daedalus*, Special Issue on the Family (Spring 1977), pp. 87–114.

62. J.G. Baum, ed., *Procès de Baudichon de La Maisonneuve accusé d'hérésie à Lyon* (Geneva: Imprimerie Jules Fick, 1873), p. 54; AML, GG84, 13 November 1564; Davis, *Society and Culture*, p. 81; Monter, "Women in Calvinist Geneva"; and Mottu-Weber, "Les femmes."

# Women, the Family Economy, and the Structures of Market Production in Cities of Northern Europe during the Late Middle Ages

T he Wife of Bath had such a "bent" in making cloth, Chaucer tells us, that "she bettered those of Ypres and of Ghent," and Langland's Rose the Regrator wove coarse woolen cloth, brewed and sold ale, and practiced "huckstery all her life time."[1] Literary figures such as these alert us to an aspect of ordinary life in the late Middle Ages that scholars have recently begun to explore more seriously: women were regular participants in the market production of this society.

Like Rose the Regrator, these women often sold food and clothing, some of which they had made themselves, or they spun wool and did similar sorts of work requiring very little capital, few skills that could not be learned running a household, and no commitment to a regular schedule. Studies documenting this work and tracing its development indicate that it had a long history. Women, especially urban women, had done work of this sort since the beginnings of market production in medieval Europe, and they continued to do so into the early modern and modern periods, even as other sorts of work dramatically changed with the further development of markets, the emergence of capitalism, and the rise of industrialism.[2]

Some women in the cities of northern Europe, however, women such as the Wife of Bath, did work that required greater capital, skills, and commitment. This work was located in the more formal market economy, where women worked as skilled artisans, owned their own retail shops, or imported and exported commodities, industrial products, and luxury goods.

198

This essay explores the history of that work, showing that it had a different history from the lower-skilled or less specialized work in the less formal market economy, which was more commonly and for a longer period associated with women. The essay begins by distinguishing this more special work in terms of its ability to confer high labor status and focuses on how women gained and lost access to this high-status work.

As the term is used here, labor status refers simply to the degree to which a person's role in economic production grants her or him access to economic resources—those of production, distribution, or consumption. By this definition, high labor status accrues to individuals who, in their occupations, can obtain their own raw materials and supplies (their means of production), and who can control distribution and consumption of the products of their labor.

In the subsistence or near-subsistence economies characteristic of rural and even much of urban society in the Middle Ages, these processes were scarcely separated. In producing dairy products or vegetables intended principally for home use, for example, the medieval household typically made its own production, distribution, and consumption decisions. Its members rarely gained high social or economic status through this work, but the medieval householders clearly enjoyed a higher labor status than their typical early modern successors, who often produced goods or services for sale only under the direct orders of distributors or simply for wages.

The tasks assumed by women who managed this typical medieval household gave them labor status comparable to that of the men who usually headed the household. These women by and large possessed resources such as gardens, animals, malt, and tools. They decided what to make with them and who (the family or local market) should have them. They decided how the family should use its resources, as raw materials for future production or as means of subsistence, and whether their consumption ought to be deferred. Men, although specializing in somewhat different tasks, possessed no greater autonomy and thus had no higher labor status.

Of course, in this traditional economic world, labor status was a fairly uncomplicated matter. In the urban economies of medieval Europe, where a growing share of production was directed toward markets, however, the concept of labor status became more complex. In these situations, some labor was rendered more productive as it was specialized and subdivided or as it was leveraged by technology. Talent, training, and access to capital (for training as well as for raw materials, equipment, and marketing) became more important in determining the degree to which one's occupation gave control over economic resources, and individuals without these advantages fell to the bottom of an increasingly hierarchical pyramid. An urban weaver without specialized skills, for example—a weaver, that is, who

by definition was outside the institutions providing extensive training, good
materials, or sophisticated equipment—would have had lower labor status
than a specialized weaver managing his or her own business, for he or she
would have had less control over the production, distribution, and consumption of the product. Moreover, such weavers would have had difficulty
competing with their specialized counterparts precisely because their access
to materials and markets was more limited, and they would constantly have
been threatened with loss of their shops, on which maintenance of even
relatively impoverished labor status depended.

The meaning of labor status in market production changes in other ways
as well, for in market societies work is related to status of other sorts in a
way it is not in nonmarket societies. This feature of work is, in fact, an
element in the definition of a market society, for only there does one's
occupation determine much about one's place in other status systems. In
market societies, the kind of work done may not only account for economic
status but may also grant political status and establish the degree of honor
an individual is accorded in the society. In nonmarket societies, in contrast,
the connection between labor status and other kinds of status is less frequent and is sometimes even inverse.[3]

There is little doubt that late medieval cities provided women opportunities for high-status work in market production. In late thirteenth-century
Paris, for example, five guilds were staffed by just women, and another
women's guild was founded in 1360.[4] Extensive surveys of craft and guild
regulations from Germany and the Low Countries have also turned up many
instances of women working as full mistresses in trades and enrolled as
apprentices. Women were also regularly mentioned in records as dealers in
both local and long-distance commerce.[5] Historians have demonstrated that
women in England were equally active in crafts, in distributive trades, and
even in long-distance trade.[6]

Information of this sort has led some historians to the conclusion that
women in late medieval cities regularly enjoyed access to prestigious jobs, to
jobs that this essay has called high status. A recent survey of medieval
women, for example, confidently reported that "widows were a universal
element in the city crafts"; "daughters as well as sons served as apprentices";
women "worked side by side with men, usually their husbands" in a "hun-
dred-odd crafts" but also worked alone as independent entrepreneurs in
textiles and in the manufacture and sale of food and beverages. The authors
of this survey also observed that women belonged to guilds.[7]

Despite the evidence used in such surveys and despite widespread agreement about its meaning, however, much about women's place in high-status
work is not yet understood. Most perplexingly, a few studies have shown

that it did not everywhere follow the patterns described above, that, in fact, not every city offered women high-status jobs and no two cities offered the same range of such work. While women apparently organized the production of high-quality wool cloth during the late Middle Ages in Douai, Bruges, and Leiden, they did very little, if any, similar work in Cologne or Hondschoote. While women seem to have regularly made clothes in Leiden, they were barred from most of these crafts in Paris. We hear of women merchants and retailers of substance in London, Lübeck, and Cologne, but we have no hints that they did similar work in Utrecht or Paris. Moreover, we have clear evidence from many places that even where women had once enjoyed high labor status, their position at this level of market production was evidently quite susceptible to erosion; by about 1700, only an occasional woman appears in a high-status job.[8] It is thus evident that women's participation in high-status work in market production in late medieval northern cities had a peculiar history: women had a marginal position in this work during the late Middle Ages, one that was secure in only a small number of particular situations, and during the early modern period, they lost even the apparently secure places.

Undoubtedly, many factors combined to create this pattern, and a great deal of work remains before us if we are to understand them. We can begin the investigation, however, by examining the family economy. It was here, after all, that much, if not most, economic production took place in late medieval cities, and, because late medieval urban women, like women elsewhere, were closely tied to the domestic unit and because their work was therefore part of the family's work, it was likely that women achieved high labor status when the family took a central role in market production and that they lost the status when the family lost its central role.

Although it is clear that economic activity in western Europe before the advent of industrial capitalism was centered on the family, it is equally clear that different forms of the preindustrial family economy existed side by side. One kind produced for subsistence or near-subsistence, another produced goods and services for sale to others, either on direct commission or simply in anticipation of demand, and a third worked for wages in the hire of others. While all of these have been called family economies, they differed in important ways. Only in the first two did workers control the means of production, and it was only workers in these two who could exercise control in their markets. Workers in the third never possessed these attributes.[9]

This essay is hence concerned with families of the second sort—families concentrating on producing for the market. If it was normally through the family that women participated in economic production, then only through family units of this sort would women have achieved high labor status in market production, and it is likely that with the disappearance of this family production unit, as it was replaced by other methods of production, women lost labor status.

Following this reasoning, this essay explores the connections between women's achievement of high labor status and the role of the family in market production in two important centers of late medieval urban market production, Leiden and Cologne. It specifically asks whether women with high labor status were members of family economies, how the family economy functioned, whether the demise of this unit was associated with a decline in women's labor status, and under what circumstances the demise occurred.

Fifteenth- and early sixteenth-century Leiden and fifteenth-century Cologne were two of northern Europe's most important trade and industrial centers in the late Middle Ages. In accord with the hypothesis that women's labor status reflected the place of the family in market production, the research on each city began with an examination of the way market production was organized. The examination included such questions, for example, as whether skilled crafts were organized in corporative guilds with political power or in loose associations established simply to supervise production; whether long-distance trade was handled by formal institutions like Hansas or by individuals acting on their own; whether early forms of capitalism had developed, typically represented by merchants who had entered production and set up putting-out systems with dependent artisans in their employ. Leiden and Cologne differed from each other both in terms of these factors of economic, social, and political structure and in terms of the opportunities they afforded women for high-status work in market production. Thus, they provided a way of investigating the links between these structural conditions, the family economy, and women's labor status.

*(ii)*

Leiden, a city with a highly specialized economy and a somewhat peculiar set of political, social, and economic institutions, provided women few opportunities for high-status work. Having achieved international importance as a manufacturer of heavy wool cloth made of English wool, the famous medieval drapery, by about 1450, the city reached a population of about 15,000 in 1500. The drapery industry, which employed about two-thirds of the city's population, was closely supervised by the city government, which was in turn dominated by Leiden's largest drapers, people who organized the production of cloth. Perhaps because the drapery was so important to Leiden's government, which generated virtually all the records we have of trade and industry, we know little about other economic sectors. Since the drapery held so central a place in the economy, however, we can safely concentrate on this industry when examining the city's economy and women's labor status in it.

Leiden's drapery had some unusual features. Unlike the elites of many other cloth towns of the Low Countries, Leiden's largest drapers were not international merchants. They bought wool used in the drapery at the English Calais Staple and sold most of the cloth made in Leiden to Hansa merchants at regional fairs. Again unlike the elites of the drapery else-where, they did not monopolize production. Instead, they allowed the gov-ernment to make and enforce laws restricting their own production, pro-tecting artisanal economic independence and assuring each Leidener access to wool they brought from Calais. As a consequence, Leiden's large drapers were in business alongside hundreds of small drapers, many of them artisans who produced as few as ten cloths each year. Another consequence was that the city's master craftsmen, both those in textiles and those in the much smaller trades concerned with food, clothing, and shelter, survived with few exceptions as independent entrepreneurs.[10]

While the system left most artisans economically independent, however, it rendered them politically powerless. The municipal authorities blocked artisans' attempts to form guilds and instead established organizations called "crafts."[11] Typically, a "craft" was a formal body, sometimes having a charter and always having clearly defined functions, work rules, and mem-bership requirements. The "crafts" both regulated production and set mem-bership and training requirements, but they did so at the direct orders of and often under the eyes of municipal officers. They were thus quasi-public bodies, almost government agencies, and were not like the more familiar guilds in many late medieval cities that were outgrowths of artisanal soci-eties with strong roots in the family and community and that sometimes shared in government.

The weavers and fullers of the drapery each formed a "craft," as did the drapery finishers after 1508; the linen weavers after 1563 and the makers of coarse woolen and wool-blended textiles after 1562 were in the process of being made "crafts." Other trades, while often subject to the municipal authorities' strict supervision, seem not to have been accorded such institu-tional status. In the textile industry, the dyers may be regarded as a more loosely organized trade of this sort. Most small crafts, especially those not involved in the production or sales of food, seem to have been ignored by the government.

It is hence clear that, although its economic, social, and political system was highly stratified, Leiden was not dominated by merchant-capitalists who sought to end all artisanal autonomy. On the other hand, it was not artisanal organization that insured the survival of the small shop in Leiden, for the artisanal organizations that existed had few independent powers. Rather, it was thanks to a traditional elite that monopolized political power in Leiden that artisans enjoyed economic independence. While the system hardly bred social and economic equality, it halted the process of polarization and promoted political stability.[12]

In this structure women held a narrow and, during the sixteenth century, a diminishing range of high-status jobs. No women worked among the approximately 1,500 skilled weavers and fullers in Leiden's drapery. A few women did, however, work as dyers, and until the early sixteenth century women regularly finished cloth. Until late in the same century they also made linen as well as cheap woolen and wool-blend fabrics. Moreover, until the collapse of the drapery in the 1560s and 1570s, women regularly worked as drapers, that is, as organizers of cloth production. Throughout the period of Leiden's participation in the medieval drapery (some 150 years), women made up about 20 to 25 percent of the drapers. Evidence covering an earlier period, from 1371 to 1419, also shows that women made up about 25 percent of Leiden's retail merchants of good cloth, a job that demanded both capital and expertise.[13]

The Leiden case suggests several specific features about women's high-status labor. Most significant is the inverse correlation between women's access to skilled work in textiles and the designation of the trade as a "craft." For example, while women did not weave or full high-quality drapery jobs that belonged to "crafts,' they did weave, full, and otherwise prepare linen and coarse woolen and wool-blend fabrics until these trades were also so organized. The case of the finishers shows clearly that the organization of a trade into a "craft" drove women from it. The ordinances founding this "craft" in 1508 specifically forbade women to train to become mistresses in the trade: "Henceforth, girls and women may not shear *scepwerck* of any kind; nor may they train to shear, to finish or to help with dry finishing."[14]

This correlation may also explain the perhaps unexpected appearance of women in the even higher status trades of draping and selling cloth, for neither was organized as a "craft." While cloth owned by drapers was subject to rigid inspections designed to insure quality, no special organizations of drapers existed, and governmental supervision was of individuals rather than of a drapers' organization. Hence there were no rules about who could manage cloth production or how drapers should run their business. Cloth sales were equally unstructured. Other than tax legislation covering sales of cloth at Leiden's biennial market, there are virtually no records of any government involvement in cloth retailing. The correlation might also explain why some women worked as dyers; this trade, although subject to extensive quality controls (especially from the end of the fifteenth century, when dyeing became more important in Leiden) and although requiring training schedules, nevertheless had no official designation as a "craft."

The Leiden case also suggests that it was as family members that women achieved high labor status. The information we have about dyers provides an especially clear example. The marital status of most women dyers can be established; all of them were married or widowed, and all, the records leave no doubt, served as full partners with their husbands in household-based shops.[15] Moreover, the records suggest that women had no other means of access to the trade, for there are no records of women having served as apprentices or skilled helpers outside their own homes. It seems clear that women entered the dyeing trade through their position in a family in which the head of household practiced the trade.

Evidence about the marital status of women in other high-status textile trades confirms this pattern. Most of Leiden's women drapers and makers of other textiles were married. For example, of thirty-six female drapers appearing in criminal records, the *Corrextieboeken*, over six sampled periods between 1436 and 1541, twelve can be positively identified as married and fourteen as widows, while only one can be positively identified as single; we know nothing about the marital status of the remaining nine. Another source, one that surveys production in Leiden's suburbs and thus does not include the drapery that was confined to the city proper, mentions ten women producers, weavers, or fullers of lower-quality textiles, all of them married. (The female labor force in the suburbs totaled fifty-three, forty of whom could be identified as married). Like the women dyers, many of the women textile producers, both urban and suburban, seem to have shared the trade they practiced with their husbands, but a significant percentage did not. Of the twelve married women who worked as drapers in the city, we know that three had trades different from their husbands' and that only one practiced her spouse's trade. Of the fourteen urban widows who produced cloth, one took over her late husband's job, but there is no evidence about the remaining thirteen. Of the nine married suburban women in high-status textile work whose husbands' trades are known, five were in the same business as their husbands, but four were in different trades.[16]

The evidence suggests, then, that women in Leiden did high-status textile work as family members, evidently as comanagers of a family production unit (presumably made up as well of children, servants, and resident kin who did lower-status work). While a woman did not always work as her husband's partner or heir in his trade, the majority seem to have done so. Furthermore, when women worked in their own trades, they concentrated on those that could be learned in the family. Either they practiced crafts such as weaving and fulling cheap cloths, the rudiments of which doubtlessly were part of most girls' training, or they took on managerial functions requiring skills any good housewife would have already possessed. Significantly, they did not participate in the few formal apprenticeship programs about which we have information.

If women's access to high-status work was through the family, then women would have lost high-status jobs as the family production unit was undermined. This seems to have occurred, as has been suggested, when a trade was organized as a "craft." Two particular features of "craft" organization in Leiden seem to have weakened the family production unit. As we shall see, these features were not necessarily exclusive to "craft" production, and, when they existed in economic spheres outside of the "crafts," they still functioned to drive women out of market production.

The first feature was the association between "craft" membership and political status. Women in Leiden, it seems, had no place in trades that had links to political bodies, that took organized political action, or that granted access to participation in government. We cannot yet explain this phenomenon, but it is hardly a surprising finding, for women elsewhere in medieval Europe were similarly excluded from politics, that is, from the active exercise of public authority.[17] The "crafts," as emphasized, were quasi-governmental organizations, and their political nature becomes more obvious when we consider how often they took united action. The fullers in particular frequently staged protests for better pay and working conditions and negotiatied as a single body with their employers, the drapers, or the municipal government itself.[18] That the "crafts" were political bodies may help to explain why women were systematically excluded from participation in them, even when, as in the case of the finishers mentioned earlier, they had been members of the trade right up to its incorporation as a "craft."

The inverse association between a trade's political status and women's place in it becomes clearer when we consider that it existed even outside the "crafts." The functions often performed by male drapers but never performed by women drapers were, for example, precisely those requiring political status. Women seem never to have been among Leiden's largest drapers, for, had they produced in quantity, they would have had to assume political functions. Leiden's large drapers, those usually producing upwards of one hundred cloths per year, negotiated at Calais and with other cities concerned with Leiden's cloth trade and held appointments by the government that allowed them to oversee production.[19] Many of them were also members of the municipal government.[20] Another example of women's exclusion from the political aspects of market production is provided from a mid-sixteenth-century document that records the plans of ninety-two drapers to set up a sales office in Amsterdam and to elect six officers to manage it: although thirty-three of the drapers named were women, not one of the association's officers was female.[21]

The second feature of "craft" organization that seems to have infringed upon the family production unit was its establishment of work rules and schedules incompatible with family life. For example, weavers and fullers of the drapery were required to serve one to three years as apprentices and another three as "free" journeymen before being eligible for masterships; weavers were also subject to a daily schedule of work regulated by a clock; fullers labored in fixed teams of one master and two journeymen, who had to deliver a finished product in a fixed time period and who were paid as a team by the job.[22] None of these working arrangements allowed the flexibility needed by someone bound to household rhythms. It thus seems that, while "craft" members often worked in their households, the "craft" rules by which they worked were directed at individuals considered independent of the household.

Records from the 1470s concerning fullers illustrate other ways "craft" formation could undermine the family production unit. One document forbade the master fullers' wives to handle their husbands' accounts along with their own, thus suggesting that women entrepreneurs at one time had not distinguished their own businesses from their husbands', but combined them in a family budget. By requiring wives to separate their work from their husbands', the "craft" thus demolished the unit.[23] Another document contained a complaint by journeymen fullers that the wives of master fullers were infringing on their territory; one of their demands was that fullers' wives no longer remove cloth from the drying frames on which it was stretched and finished, a task the journeymen were presumably claiming for themselves.[24] This demand can also be read as a spearhead of the "craft's" attack upon the family enterprise.

The conduct of business even in unorganized economic sectors may also have weakened the traditional family production unit. Many large drapers in Leiden, for example, traveled much of the time; they made at least one annual trip to Calais, and they regularly visited regional markets in cities such as Bergen op Zoom, Amsterdam, and Bruges. Keeping such a schedule would have been difficult not just for women, who would probably not have found business travel feasible because of cultural norms and safety considerations, but also for any individual bound to the rhythms of a household and care of a family. Thus, women and perhaps some men would have found the demands of producing cloth in quantity too burdensome.

Presumably, men able to keep these schedules could have depended upon wives left at home to manage the local aspects of business: overseeing production, receiving shipments, and dealing with local purchasers. These women would not, however, have shared their husbands' skills, but would have known only the part of the business over which they had only indirect control when their husbands were away. Being only intermittently and partly in charge, they may have been unable to perform as well as necessary, and at some point it might have seemed more efficient for men to form partnerships among themselves, thus creating businesses large enough to support two or more individuals who devoted themselves entirely to the enterprise. This point seems to have been reached in Leiden, where women rarely worked as large drapers, even as the wives or widows of men prominent in the business.

Few records survive concerning the structure of production in nontextile sectors of Leiden's economy. In sampled court records dated between 1436 and 1541, however, scattered references to women can be found: two female bakers among eight male bakers (both worked with their husbands); a peat merchant and an oil presser, neither of whom had a male colleague. In all, the samples taken from these records name seventy-three men in high-status nontextile jobs and eight women.[25] One source surveying Leiden's suburban population in 1540, where virtually no official organization of production existed, names thirty-six men in high-status nontextile jobs and fourteen women, eleven of them married or widowed.[26] Although the information is scarce, it suggests that women who held high-status jobs outside textiles also worked in economic sectors where the family production unit had survived and thus where the degree of organization was low.

(iii)

The evidence from fifteenth-century Cologne, a much larger city of perhaps 40,000 residents with a more complex economy, appears at an initial examination to undermine the hypothesis tentatively confirmed by the study of Leiden. Women in Cologne seem to have been much better positioned in high-status jobs. They belonged to the political-military guilds called *Gaffeln* by virtue of their membership in the craft guilds into which most skilled and some unskilled trades were organized, and there were three guilds and a branch of a fourth that were exclusively female. Women also regularly traded on the Staple, through which almost all import or export trade destined for Cologne or coming from Cologne passed and through which much north-south and east-west European trade necessarily flowed. Moreover, women belonged to some of the long-distance trading ventures that dealt, for example, in English wool and German wine or in Flemish cloth and Bohemian metals. It seems then, that the women of Cologne more often achieved high labor status than the women in Leiden and that they achieved their high labor status in the very sorts of economic institutions—guilds, trading ventures, Staples, etc.—that were closed to women in Leiden.

A closer look at the information in the context of the particular structures of production in Cologne does not, however, bear out this conclusion. Careful scrutiny shows that women's labor status in Cologne, as in Leiden, depended on the survival of the family economy and that processes similar to those described for Leiden weakened the family production unit in Cologne. The reason that women in Cologne more often achieved high labor status is that market production in some of Cologne's most important economic sectors had not yet been subjected to the kinds of political and production organization that would have destroyed the family production unit.

To understand the structure of market production in fifteenth-century Cologne, it is necessary to understand something of the city's history.[27] Cologne's economy had traditionally had two parts. One, devoted to finance and a long-distance carrying trade, had been founded by an elite that had early retired from commerce to devote itself to government. At least by the mid-fourteenth century, its place in commerce had been taken by a new group of long-resident, smaller merchants, by newcomers to Cologne, and by artisans who were beginning to take on merchandising as well as productive functions. Over the centuries, the composition of long-distance trade had changed as well. Some goods, such as English wool, German wine, and spices, had lost importance, and others, such as English cloth, German metalwares, and silk fabrics, had gained new stature. The change in its composition reflected a significant change in the character of long-distance trade as well; merchants no longer normally dealt in large volumes of undifferentiated goods drawn from and destined for markets all over Europe and even beyond, but, instead, tended to specialize in one kind of product or material or in one trade route. By the fifteenth century, many of the merchants were devoted to serving Cologne's expanding export industries in silk, other textiles, metal goods, and leather. Moreover, as suppliers of and merchandisers of industry, members of this new economic elite were increasingly seeking to usurp the entrepreneurial role of artisans producing goods for export. When successful, they made wage workers of entrepreneurs, who then lost control over production or access to markets.

The second part of Cologne's traditional economy was, not unexpectedly, industrial. Artisans in Cologne had originally produced simply for the local markets, but by the thirteenth century some of their products, particularly leathers, metals, and textiles, had entered export markets then controlled by long-distance merchants. Some of the artisans had managed to transform themselves into merchants, thus joining the merchants who were simultaneously entering production during the development of this early form of capitalism. In the same period, new industries producing luxury goods for export were established by people who controlled both merchandising and production. These industries typically moved toward a form of production in which merchant-artisans controlled trade and the most skilled aspects of craft production but farmed out many of the lesser jobs in manufacturing to other, less well established artisans who were thus made pieceworkers. Silk making, probably Cologne's single largest export industry between 1450 and 1500 was the most important of these, but specialists in work with precious metals and luxury textile products also followed in this kind of capitalist development.

The skilled trades in Cologne had a history quite different from Leiden's, and by the fifteenth century their organizations were also very different. As early as the thirteenth century, Cologne's artisans had established guilds of their own and, despite some supervision by the government then in power, had controlled the internal affairs of their organizations.[28] By the late fourteenth century the guild system was firmly established, but the most important of the guilds, without exception those whose members were the producers for export markets, had lost their character as associations of independent craftsmen. Instead they had become hierarchical organizations run by artisan-merchants whose putting-out businesses often employed guild brethren, now, of course, artisan-entrepreneurs in name only.

In 1396 Cologne's new economic elite, made up of merchants and artisan-merchants, took over the city government. Since the group included many men who controlled important guilds, especially wool weavers, goldsmiths, armorers, and leather workers, the government they set up was, understandably, a guild government. It represented twenty-two corporative bodies named *Gaffeln*; eighteen were composed of all the then existing artisanal guilds but the remaining four were continuations of previously existing merchants' associations. These merchant *Gaffeln*, along with the *Gaffeln* controlled by producer-merchants, dominated the new government.

A close look at the places in which women found high-status jobs in this economic, social, and political structure reveals that, as in Leiden, they were in economic sectors that preserved the family production unit and in which no political status was required. This is most evident in craft production, especially in the guilds women staffed.

The one we know most about and by far the most important was the silk-making guild. The mistresses of this guild were, with few exceptions, relatives or wives of merchant capitalists, many of them silk traders and members of Cologne's new political elite.[29] For example, of the 113 mistresses active in the trade between 1437 and 1504, at least 78 were married or widowed. Many more may well have been, for of the most active 68, the group for which we have the most information, all but one were married or widowed. We cannot reliably determine how many of these women were married to merchants and political leaders, for we know little about many women's husbands. But the information we do have strongly suggests that these women were part of families in Cologne's new economic and political elite. Of the 157 women registered as mistresses between 1437 and 1504 (not all of them active), at least 41 were married to merchants, an additional 15 were themselves also active in trade, and another 4 had fathers active in trade; at least 39 of the 157 are known to have been daughters or wives of members of the city Council (Cologne's governing body). We can thus conclude that women in the silk-making guild were part of the family business, often part of businesses in which both family members were actively engaged.

The evidence further demonstrates that women's status in the guild was that of family members, and, indeed, they were viewed as subordinates to men, who possessed the full status associated with guild membership. Men ran the guild itself. Although the board had two women as well as two men, men controlled the political and administrative functions, leaving women only the technical job of inspecting the silk-making process. Rather than a true artisanal guild, this was an organization created to serve the capitalist interests of families who divided productive and commercial tasks according to gender but reserved political power for males.

Guilds of gold spinners and yarn makers also had male directorships and were of similar socioeconomic composition.[30] Like silk making, these trades served luxury export markets, required expensive imported raw materials, and were made up of husband-and-wife teams who strictly divided production and trade. The last all-female guild, the silk spinners, was made up of unskilled pieceworkers in the pay of silk makers and exploited by them.[31] This guild was thus composed neither of artisans, as would have been the case in a traditional guild, nor of merchant-artisans, as was the case for other women's guilds, but of unskilled wage workers to whom the high labor status normally associated with guild membership cannot be attributed.

While it seems incontestable that the three women's guilds providing high-status work were in fact special kinds of organizations that accommodated what might be called a capitalist family production unit, it is less clear how or why this symbiotic relationship worked. The evidence reviewed does, however, point to some possible explanations. The chief method of adapting guild structure to the family production unit, and thus to women, was by reserving the political aspects of guild membership for men. The men who sat on the governing boards of these guilds did not share political power with women, but held it exclusively. These guilds in turn had no share in government. They sent no representatives to the Council, and, although the yarn makers and the gold spinners were organized in guilds when the corporative government was set up, they were not even listed among the guilds to be assigned to *Gaffeln*.[32]

Why were women not simply forced out of guilds as they apparently were in Leiden? And why, in fact, were the trades women practiced organized at all? Two complementary explanations can help answer the second question. The government set up in 1396 was defined as a body representing all people active in market production, whose interests were to be expressed and addressed through the corporation, the guild, to which she or he belonged. To exclude one trade from guild organization, especially an important one like silk making in which, it must be recalled, men had important direct interests, was to undermine the guild system that underlay the *Gaffeln*. Surely it made better political sense to incorporate all skilled trades, as well as a few unskilled trades, and to exempt those with strong female representation from political activity than to leave even a few trades unorganized. Moreover, from the point of view of the trades themselves, guild status must have seemed necessary, for the only trades recognized as having control over markets, production, and membership were those organized as guilds.

The explanation of why women were not forced out of these guilds may lie in the history of the trades themselves. The skills involved in making decorative yarn or gold thread and in working with silk had long been the preserve of women from "good" families, those which alone could afford the expensive raw materials and had access to long-distance markets. These women could have expanded their roles and become production agents for their husbands as these luxury crafts took on growing importance in long-distance trade. Moreover, it would have been to the advantage of these families to keep this craft within the guild structure, for it could reserve the highly skilled and lucrative aspects of luxury-goods manufacturing for them.

The remaining craft guilds in fifteenth-century Cologne seem to have begun, like the guilds of many medieval cities, as artisans' associations rooted in the family and devoted to meeting the religious and social as well as the economic needs of their members. By the late fourteenth century most had moved a considerable distance from these origins, having become hierarchical organizations with political and economic interests.[33] Most, however, bore vestiges of their origins in the way they organized production and in the way they defined their membership. Typically, their regulations envisaged a small shop run by a master and his wife with apprentices at various stages of training. The leather workers' (*Riemenschneider*) regulations issued in 1398, for example, described a family business to which widows could accede as full mistresses with apprentices in training as long as they kept a journeyman.[34]

The erosion of the familial roots of Cologne's guilds and women's dependence on them for inclusion in a craft can be further appreciated when we consider the nature of the brotherhoods there. Unlike many cities where brotherhoods were the predecessors of guilds and were generally superseded by them, the brotherhoods in Cologne were sometimes offshoots of guilds, first formed in the fourteenth and fifteenth centuries as auxiliary organizations to the guilds, which were then taking on more political functions. These brotherhoods were presumably intended to preserve the social and religious aspects of craft association that could not survive in the guilds.[35] What is interesting for this investigation is that, just as women were losing their place in these changing guilds, they retained places in brotherhoods. The brotherhood of the belt makers, for example, listed fifty-four male members in 1500 along with thirty-six female members, twenty-nine of them wives of masters and seven their widows. In the guild itself, however, female members were rare, and we may presume that most were masters' widows.[36]

In almost every case, a particular guild's disposition toward women seems to have directly reflected the degree to which the original guild functions had been superseded. While we can seldom observe the entire process by which a guild was transformed from an association of family shops into a political organization made up of individual male artisans (by late fourteenth century when good records first become available, the process was already far advanced), we can witness its end. By the fifteenth century, we find no references at all to women in the records of nine of the existing forty-two guilds, and we find that six others had already strictly limited widow's rights and provided women no other access to the trade. Eighteen of the remaining guilds still allowed widows' rights, and in them a few widows seem to have vigorously carried on their husbands' trades.[37] In some cases, however, we luckily can trace the process by which even the rights of wives and widows were restricted. The hat makers, for example, in 1378 forbade wives, daughters, and female servants to help in the trade; the cloth retailers in 1397 forbade wives to help their husbands to cut cloth; in 1484, the Council forbade the widow of a sword maker to assume her husband's craft.[38]

In sum, all but six of the forty-two guilds seem by the fifteenth century to have become virtually male preserves, either so restricting women's participation, typically by restricting widows' rights, or numbering so few mistresses among their members that they cannot really be considered mixed guilds. That these six alone—needle making, baking, belt making, linen weaving, beer brewing, and silk embroidery—should have retained female mistresses seems unsurprising, for all but needle making and belt making involved skills in the traditional preserve of the women household managers. Since they had probably originated as trades exclusively in the province of women, it is understandable that they were slower than others to close women out, although they were developing into guilds with public status. The cases of the needle makers and belt makers are more difficult to explain, but also reflect the nature of the skills they required. Not only were these guilds members of the same *Gaffel* (in fact the belt makers' *Gaffel*), but they both also used metal raw materials and involved fine handwork with metallic fibers; these skills may well traditionally have been in women's preserve. In apparent confirmation of this supposition, both trades employed females when, in the fifteenth century, they began to use wage workers.[39] Of the six, only the belt makers, who counted among its members some of Cologne's merchant-artisans, sent representatives to the Council; of course, none was a woman.[40]

Women's position in the high-status jobs in commerce, most of them linked to export-import trade, depended on the same kinds of structures. Most women merchants were married, and all seem to have owed their access to commerce to a family business. Significantly, none that we know of belonged to the merchant *Gaffeln* which existed in fifteenth-century Cologne, and all seem to have depended upon the fact that commerce, even long-distance commerce, in Cologne had by and large remained part of family businesses and had not been absorbed by public organizations.

The major source of our information about such trade derives from government records of taxes or fees collected on Cologne's Staple or from merchants selling imported products, in this case wool cloth and wine.[41] Most women dealing on the Staple as wholesalers were widows carrying on their late husbands' trades, and they usually worked for only a few years at a reduced scale. Seldom did the business of all these women together account for more than 5 to 10 percent of imports. There were also a few women trading on the Staple who were single or, more often, who acted independently of their husbands. But these women did not manage a significant portion of sales and arguably owed their access to this kind of trade to the fact that wives and widows were already so common a sight on the market.

A somewhat higher percentage of merchants buying for retail distribution or for use in family shops, rather than for wholesale, were women who were quite often single or widowed. But those dealing in industrial products such as metals or leathers were, it seems, commercial agents for their artisan husbands.

Women who wholesaled wool cloth or wine in Cologne seem also to have been part of family businesses. While this did not always mean they were insignificant factors in their businesses—one cloth merchant, for example, carried on her husband's business for about twenty years and she had 20 to 30 percent of the market—it does imply that women's place in trade was dependent both on the continued identification of the family and the business and on the low incidence of political organization among merchants.

*(iv)*

While the situations in which women achieved high labor status in Leiden and Cologne were by no means identical, fundamental similarities suggest some answers to the problems with which this essay began. The hypothesis toward which this research leads can be briefly summarized. Women, we can surmise, first entered market production via the family production unit, where market production often began. They were thus naturally most active in those sectors of market production which grew out of tasks connected with their roles in the traditional household economy— textile and clothing production, food production, and retail sales. But they also had a more limited place in male-dominated trades simply because, as wives, they were often partners and always heirs of their husbands.

But both routes to high labor status were closed when the family production unit was destroyed as the market economy further developed. Both Leiden and Cologne provide examples of the manner in which the process occurred. They can be summarized in two points. First, women were denied a place in high-status work when the job came to involve tasks requiring political status, because a trade's direct association with political institutions automatically substituted adult males for families as the unit of concern. This process occurred in Leiden when women were forced out of official "crafts" and when women were excluded from the kind of drapery production that required political roles. It also occurred in Cologne, for women there had no power to represent their own guilds or to decide policy for them and were, often visibly, being edged out of all other guilds with corporative power. Second, the decline of the family production unit also occurred when city governments imposed formal work rules on craft production or trade that conflicted with women's obligations to their families. Thus, when fixed work or training schedules were adopted in organized trades or when frequent long-distance journeys became necessary for commerce, women could no longer participate.

Once high-status work was removed from the family production unit, married women, who were still bound to the household in law, ideology, and fact, had little choice but to leave market production. If they could not afford this option, they had to accept the few jobs still accessible to women. In developed market economies, these jobs were almost invariably of low status.

To be sure, some of the jobs held by married women, such as ale brewing, cheese and butter manufacture and sales, or seamstressing, were in many ways unchanged from the jobs that once had granted high labor status. But, increasingly, women participating in them were moved to the periphery of the market economy as more specialized labor, costlier materials, and more sophisticated equipment moved into these trades.[42] For example, female ale brewers became small producers with a brew "inferior" in quality and price to the better tasting and longer lasting beer sold by market producers with the capital for storing inventories, importing supplies, and reaching markets. In short, "women's" market production, even if done by independent businesswomen, was now of low status because it was small scale and used inferior techniques, because as a result it could not compete with organized market producers, and because its practitioners did not have comparable control over the resources of production, distribution, and consumption.

But many of the jobs available to women in developed urban market economies were not part of this weakened sphere of petty commodity production. Instead, they were part of the new wage economy, and most of them were in piecework. Although this kind of work expanded in the early modern European market economy, bringing with it places for both married and unmarried women, it granted its practitioners only low labor status, for these women, possessing neither training nor technology equivalent to their competitors', did not control the resources of production and distribution.

In summary, women's loss of high-status occupations in urban market production, therefore, was related to structural changes in production, specifically to the metamorphosis of the family production unit under the new institutions of market production. Women continued to hold their place in lower-status work on the periphery of the economy because this work could still be contained within the family. There is much we still do not know about urban women's work in this period, and we will surely find that other factors helped determine women's place in urban market production. Nevertheless, these two case studies leave little doubt that the family production unit and the metamorphosis it underwent will feature importantly in the full history of women's work in late medieval and early modern market production.[43]

## Notes

The research on which this essay is based was conducted over several years and was supported at each of its stages by different organizations: the Social Science Research Council; the Institute of International Education (through the Fulbright-Hays Program); the Ministerie van Onderwijs en Wetenschappen (Netherlands); and the Deutscher Akademischer Austauschdienst (West Germany). Both this essay and a shorter version of it that was delivered at the Annual Meeting of the American Historical Association in December 1982 were prepared while on leave from Rutgers University as a Mellon Fellow at the University of Pennsylvania. Both Professor Barbara Hanawalt and Dr. Susan Cahn offered helpful criticisms and editorial suggestions. I wish to thank all these organizations and individuals.

I would particularly like to thank Professor J. W. Smit for his valuable help with the research for and conceptualization of the investigation summarized in this essay as well as for his assistance with the essay itself.

1. Geoffrey Chaucer, *The Canterbury Tales*, trans. Nevill Coghill (Harmondsworth, Middlesex, and New York, 1951), p. 31; William Langland, *The Vision of William concerning Piers Plowman*, ed. W. W. Skeat (Oxford, 1886), p. 51.

2. Studies exploring the history of women's work from the late Middle Ages into the modern period have not employed the notion of labor status to distinguish among the varieties of women's (or men's) work, but it is nevertheless the case that the work they describe as essentially unchanging is what this essay calls low-status. The best English-language survey of the material available is Louise A. Tilly and Joan W. Scott, *Women, Work and Family* (New York, 1978). Some more recent studies focusing on shorter time spans within the centuries during the development of modern Europe confirm that urban women were visible and important in this sort of market production; see, for example, Natalie Davis, "Women in the Crafts in Sixteenth-Century Lyon," chap. 9, this volume; Alice Kessler-Harris, *Out to Work: A History of Wage-Earning Women in the United States* (New York and London, 1982); Merry Wiesner Wood, "Paltry Peddlars or Essential Merchants? Women in the Distributive Trades in Early Modern Nuremberg," *The Sixteenth-Century Journal* 12, no. 2 (Summer 1981): 3–13; Eric Richards, "Women in the British Economy Since about 1700: An Interpretation," *History* 59 (1974): 337–57; Gay Gullickson, "The Sexual Division of Labor in Cottage Industry and Agriculture in the Pays de Caux," *French Historical Studies* 12, no. 2 (Fall 1981): 177–99.

3. Basic readings on the meaning of work in market economies and its relationship to status in other spheres include John Hicks, *A Theory of Economic History* (London, Oxford, and New York, 1969); Karl Polanyi, *The Great Transformation* (New York, 1944); idem, "Aristotle Discovers the Economy," in *Trade and Market in the Early Empires*, ed. Karl Polanyi, Conrad M. Arensberg, and Harry W. Pearson (New York, 1957); Karl Marx, "The Power of Money in Bourgeois Society," in *The Economic and Philosophic Manuscripts of 1844* in vol. 3, Karl Marx and Frederick Engels, *Collected Works* (Moscow, New York, and London, 1975); idem, "Commodities," "The Buying and Selling of Labor Power," "Co-operation" and "Division of Labor and Manufacture," in *Capital*, 3 vols. (New York, 1967), Vol. 1, pp. 35–83, 167–76, 322–36, and 366–71.

4. These data are drawn from G[eorges] B[ernard] Depping, *Réglemens sur les arts et métiers de Paris rédiges au xiii^e siècle, et connus sous le nom du Livre des métiers d'Etienne Boileau*, vol. 31, *Collection de documents inédits sur l'histoire de France*, prémière série, histoire politique (Paris, 1837).

5. One of the first to draw attention to the place of women in late medieval urban market production was Karl Bücher, *Die Frauenfrage im Mittelalter* (Tübingen, 1910, rev. ed.). Important later studies include Wilhelm Behagel, "Die gewerbliche Stellung der Frau im mittelalterlichen Köln," *Abhandlungen zur mittleren und neuren Geschichte* 23 (1910); Margret Wensky, *Die Stellung der Frau in der stadtkölnischen Wirtschaft im Spätmittelalter* (Cologne and Vienna, 1980); Julius Hartwig, "Die Frauenfrage im mittelalterlichen Lübeck," *Hansische Geschichtsblätter* 14 (1908): 35–94; Helmut Wachendorf, *Die wirtschaftliche Stellung der Frau in deutschen Städten des späteren Mittelalters* (Cologne and Vienna, 1980); Jenneke Quast, "Vrouwenarbeid omstreeks 1500 in enkele nederlandse Steden," in *Jaarboek voor Vrouwengeschiedenis* (Nijmegen, 1980) pp. 46–64; idem, "Vrouwen in gilden in Den Bosch, Utrecht en Leiden van de 14e tot en met de 16e eeuw," in vol. 1, *Fragmenten vrouwengeschiede-*

*nis*, ed. Wantje Fritschy (The Hague, 1980) pp. 26–37; Bruno Kuske, "Die Frau im mittelalterlichen deutschen Wirtschaftsleben," *Zeitschrift für handelwissenschaftliche Forschung* 11 (1959): 148–56.

6. Eileen E. Power, *Medieval Women*, ed. M. M. Postan (Cambridge, 1975); Alice Clark, *The Working Life of Women in the Seventeenth Century* (New York, 1920); A. Abrams, "Women Traders in Medieval London," *Economic Journal* 26 (1916): 276–85.

7. Frances and Joseph Gies, *Women in the Middle Ages* (New York, 1978), pp. 174–77, 183.

8. The evidence for Douai and Bruges comes primarily from Georges Espinas and Henri Pirenne, *Rècueil de documents rélatif à l'histoire de l'industrie drapière en Flandre, des origines à l'epoque bourguignonne*, 4 vols. (Brussels, 1909); for Leiden, see Martha Congleton Howell, "Women's Work in Urban Economies of Late Medieval Northwestern Europe: Female Labor Status in Male Economic Institutions" (Ph.D. diss., Columbia University, 1979); for Cologne, see Wensky, *Die Stellung der Frau*; Hondschoote, see E. Coornaert, *Un Centre d'autrefois: la Draperie-sayetterie d'Hondschoote (xivme–xviiime siècle)* (Paris, 1931); for Lübeck, see Hartwig, "Die Frauenfrage"; for London, see Abrams, "Women Traders," Clark, *The Working Life of Women*, and Power, *Medieval Women*; for Utrecht, see Quast, "Vrouwenarbeid omstreeks 1500" and "Vrouwen in gilden"; for Paris, see Madeleine Guilbert, *Les fonctions des femmes dans l'industrie* (Paris, 1966), p. 23. Because very few systematic examinations of women's roles in market production have been done, the evidence indicating both that women had positions granting high labor status in some sectors (see notes 4, 5, and 6 above) and that they did not have such jobs in other sectors or were losing the jobs they had cannot be accepted as conclusive. In some cases, as in Paris, where the evidence consists simply of a count of the ordinances that treat organized trades practiced by women, the evidence should be used especially cautiously. In some places, women were deliberately excluded from high-status trades, as in 1367 in Ghent when a dyer's daughter was forbidden entry to the craft (Espinas and Pirenne, *Récueil de documents rélatifs à l'histoire de l'industries drapière en Flandre*, vol. 2, doc. no. 479) or when in 1508 the dry finishers of Leiden ordered that women no longer train for the craft (N. W. Posthumus, ed., *Bronnen tot de Geschiedenis van de Leidsche Textielnijverheid*, 6 vols., Rijksgeschiedkundige Publicatiën, vols. 8, 14, 18, 22, 39, 49 [The Hague, 1910–22], vol. 2, doc. no. 810). More often, however, women's access to such work was gradually restricted as widows' rights were limited or as the informal training programs through which women had often acquired their skills were ended. That women left certain sectors of commerce and craft production during the early modern period is widely accepted; see, for example, Schlumbohm's comments, p. 195 and n. 3 in Peter Kriedte, Hans Medick, and Jürgen Schlumbohm, *Industrialisierung vor der Industrialisierung: Gewerbliche Warenproduktion auf dem Land in der Formationsperiode des Kapitalismus* (Göttingen, 1978).

9. Tilly and Scott, in *Women, Work and Family*, provide a specific and sophisticated definition of the family economy, distinguishing between a family economy producing goods and services for use or for sale into the market, and a family wage economy, in which all family members worked for wages that they contributed to the family. In the former, all family members might be involved in the same business, but husbands and wives might also practice different trades. As Tilly and Scott emphasize, the family production unit was the center of production in preindustrial Europe and was regarded as such. Only the family (through the male

head-of-household or his widow), not its individual members, had independent status in law; for example, property and inheritance law conceived of the family as the unit that must be served and taxes were directed at the family. In *Women, Work and Family*, see especially pp. 18–21 for a description of the family production unit. Many commentators, however, have used looser and less useful definitions. Some, like Clark, *The Working Life of Women*, p. 7, or Gullickson, "The Sexual Division of Labor," have made no apparent distinction between the family production unit and the family wage economy. Others, like Guilbert, *Les fonctions des femmes dans l'industrie*, pp. 27–36, refer to the family production unit as if defined by a household in which work takes place. In fact, of course, the family production unit was not necessarily physically located in the household, although it always had the family and its coresidents as its producers; for example, Cologne's butchers and retail cloth merchants (*Gewandschneider*) had shops away from their residences. Moreover, in capitalist Europe, households were quite often the sites of wage work, but they cannot be considered *production* units. Medick, "Die proto-industrielle Familienwirtschaft" in Kriedte, Medick and Schlumbohm, *Industrialisierung vor der Industrialisierung*, discusses the rural family economy and its role in the creation of capitalist industry. Although his comments concern the peasant household and its transformation as capitalist wage relations were introduced, he offers important theoretical concepts of use in analyzing the urban family production unit. In particular, he explains that the family as an economic unit responded to market incentives in ways that seem "irrational"; for example, the family sought first to meet consumption needs and thus worked to achieve a certain minimal income—at whatever cost in terms of labor and capital—rather than to maximize unit profits. Although many commentators—Tilly and Scott as well as Medick among them—have regarded women's place in market production as having been linked to the family's place in market production, none has explained how it was that urban market production and the family production unit could coexist only temporarily and why the new structures of market production could not accommodate female labor.

10. This argument is presented in detail in Robert S. DuPlessis and Martha C. Howell, "Reconsidering the Early Modern Urban Economy: the Cases of Leiden and Lille," *Past and Present*, no. 94 (February 1982): 49–84.

11. For a description of the "crafts" in medieval Leiden, see N. W. Posthumus, *De Geschiedenis van de Leidsche Lakenindustrie*, 3 vols. (The Hague, 1908 and 1939), vol. 1, pp. 365ff.

12. The argument is developed in DuPlessis and Howell, "Reconsidering the Early Modern Urban Economy," pp. 49–84.

13. The supporting data for these conclusions come from municipal court cases, tax rolls, and administrative records and are summarized in Howell, "Women's Work," chap. 4.

14. Posthumus, ed., *Bronnen tot de Geschiedenis van de Leidsche Textielnijverheid*, vol. 2, doc. no. 810 (dated 1508).

15. A regulation of 1466 required a quarterly oath from dyers, their wives, and their master journeymen, and similar oaths were required in subsequent editions of the drapery ordinances. The 1541 edition made the partnership especially clear: "It is always to be understood that a man and his wife who have given the aforesaid oath shall be considered a single person." Ibid., doc. nos. 263, 440, 1034, and 1114 (dated 1453/72 to 1551); the quotation is from doc. no. 1034 (dated 1541).

16. The data on suburban women are from N. W. Posthumus, *Een zestiendeeu-*

*wche Enqueste naar de Buitenneringen rondom de Stad Leiden, Bijdragen en Mededelingen van het Historisch Genootschap,* 33 (Amsterdam, 1912); those on urban women come from *Corrextieboeken* A, B, C, D, F, H, Oude Rechterlijke Archief 4, Gemeente Archief, Leiden. Both analyses are contained in Howell, "Women's Work," chap. 4.

17. Others have previously suggested that there was an inverse correlation between women's access to a trade and the trade's place in the political hierarchy; in particular, see G. K. Schmelzeisen, *Die Rechtsstellung der Frau in der deutschen Stadtwirtschaft* (Stuttgart, 1935); more recent commentators include Quast, "Vrouwen in gilden," p. 27, Guilbert, *Les fonctions des femmes dans l'industrie,* pp. 21–31, and Power, *Medieval Women,* pp. 62–65. But none has traced the links between a trade's move into politics and women's exit from the trade in specific cases. The idea that women are denied a place in economic production when it is linked to politics has been developed, in a more general formulation, by theoreticians who distinguish between private and public realms and argue that women are by definition excluded from the public, in which politics, of course, resides. For two quite different examples of this reasoning, see Eleanor Leacock, "Women, Power and Authority," in Leela Dube, Eleanor Leacock and Shirley Ardener, *Papers from the Women's Commission of the International Congress of the Anthropological and Ethnological Sciences,* Delhi, 1978 (forthcoming) and Talcott Parsons, *Essays in Sociological Theory* (New York, 1954). Others have quite rightly pointed out that the content of neither realm is constant and that no single human activity—including political activity—belongs exclusively to a private or a public realm. Joan Kelly's "The Doubled Vision of Feminist Theory: A Postscript to the Woman and Power Conference," *Feminist Studies* 5 (Spring 1979): 221, for example, argues in part that

> *woman's place is not a separate sphere or domain of existence but a position within social existence generally.* It is a subordinate position, and it supports our social institutions at the same time that it serves and services men. Women's place is do women's work—at home and in the labor force. And it is to experience sex hierarchy—in work relations and in personal ones, in our public and private lives. Hence our analyses, regardless of the tradition they originate in, increasingly treat the family in relation to society; treat sexual and reproductive experience in terms of political economy; and treat productive relations of class in connection with sex hierarchy. [Italics in original.]

Zillah Eisenstein, *The Radical Future of Liberal Feminism* (New York and London, 1981), p. 26, makes a similar argument: "Nevertheless there is no constant meaning to the terms *public and private* other than their sexual identification, and even this identity takes on particular meaning within the specific culture and society one is examining." Thus, it seems we cannot place women in a private sphere where one kind of activity is located and place men in a public sphere where different activities take place. Nevertheless, it seems reasonable to regard formal participation in government as a public activity, perhaps the quintessential public activity, and it seems foolish to disregard the abundant evidence we have that argues that women were usually absent from this sort of public activity in western Europe.

18. These activities are amply documented by Posthumus, *Geschiedenis,* vol. 1.

19. These activities are described in ibid.

20. The extent of the participation of drapers in Leiden's government during the fifteenth and early sixteenth centuries has not been precisely measured. For some indicative statistics, see DuPlessis and Howell, "Reconsidering the Early Modern Urban Economy," p. 57; for the mid-sixteenth century, see Sterling A. Lamet,

"Men in Government: The Patriciate of Leiden, 1550–1600" (Ph.D. diss., University of Massachusetts, 1979).

21. Posthumus, *Bronnen tot de Geschiedenis van de Leidsche Textielnijverheid*, vol. 2, doc. no. 1118 (dated 1572).

22. Ordinances of this sort abound in the six separate editions of the *Draperie-keurboeken* first issued between 1363 and 1568, and records of fines imposed for their violations indicate that they were enforced. The ordinances have been printed in Posthumus, *Bronnen tot de Geschiedenis*. For examples of both ordinances and records of their enforcement, dating from 1363/84 to 1568/85, see doc. nos. 12, 103, 263, 440, 525, 603, 763, 773, 1041, and 1214.

23. Ibid., doc. no. 29 (dated 1470).

24. Ibid., doc. no. 508 (dated 1478). Also see, however, the drapers' reply, doc. no. 509 (dated 1478), in which it is argued that "it has always been the custom here in Leiden that the fullers and their wives, their domestic servants and helpers take cloth from the frames."

25. Based on sampled data from *Corrextieboeken*, A, B, C, D, F, H.

26. Two male potters and one female; one male cobbler; one male tailor and two seamstresses; seventeen men skilled in woodworking; one man in leatherworking; one male shipper; three male bakers and one female; one male butcher; seven male pub keepers and eight female; one male "surgeon" and one midwife; one male toll collector and one female: Posthumus, *Een zestiendeeuwsche Enqueste*.

27. The details of the history, while the product of the work of many historians over the last century, are available in a few recently published studies: Franz Irsigler, *Die wirtschaftliche Stellung der Stadt Köln in 14. und 15. Jahrhundert* (Wiesbaden, 1979); Wolfgang Herborn, *Die politische Führungsschicht der Stadt Köln im Spätmittelalter* (Bonn, 1977); idem, "Verfassungsideal und Verfassungwirklichkeit in Köln während der ersten zweijahrhunderte nach inkrafttreten des Verbundbriefes von 1396 dargestelt am Beispiel des Bürgermeisteramtes," in *Städische Führungsgruppen und Gemeinde in der werdenden Neuzeit*, ed. Wilfried Ehbrecht (Vienna, 1980); Klaus Militzer, *Ursachen und Folgen der innerstädtischen Auseinandersetzungen in Köln in der zweiten Hälfte des 14. Jahrhunderts* (Cologne, 1980).

28. The best general history of the guilds in Cologne remains that provided in the Introduction to Heinrich von Loesch, *Die Kölner Zunfturkunden nebst anderer Kölner Gewerbeurkunden bis zum Jahre 1500*, 2 vols. (Bonn, 1907).

29. The information on silk makers is from Wensky, *Die Stellung der Frau*, chap. 5.

30. Ibid., chaps. 3 and 4.

31. Ibid., chap. 5.

32. Wensky, *Die Stellung der Frau*, p. 105, emphasizes that these guilds, exemplified by the silk makers, had the structure and functions of men's guilds and therefore were their equals. She also points out that the men who governed the silk makers' guild were husbands of silk makers and thus dependent on their wives for entry to the guild. Wensky's points are well taken, for the women's guilds were certainly not bogus organizations; nevertheless, it cannot be denied that the women members did not have the full rights of men in similar circumstances. She also notes, p. 15, that the guild of silk makers, which was first established in 1437, was not assigned to a *Gaffel*, its (male) members already having memberships in various other *Gaffeln*.

33. See von Loesch, *Die Kölner Zunfturkunden*, Introduction.

34. Ibid., vol. 1, doc. nos. 53A and 53B.

35. See ibid., Introduction, for Cologne's brotherhoods.

36. Ibid., vol. 1, doc. no. 109, and Wensky, *Die Stellung der Frau* (with corrections to von Loesch), p. 35, n. 30.

37. These figures are based on my reading of the documents published by von Loesch, *Die Kölner Zunfturkunden*, and of Wensky's *Die Stellung der Frau*, summary of her reading of documents from this collection and from a few unpublished dossiers.

38. For the hat makers, see von Loesch, *Die Kölner Zunfturkunden*, vol. 1, doc. no. 38; for the cloth retailers, ibid., doc. no. 74; for the sword makers, ibid., doc. no 648.

39. See Irsigler, *Die wirtschaftliche Stellung der Stadt Köln*, pp. 116–18.

40. For details on the needle makers and the belt makers, see Irsigler, *Die wirtschaftliche Stellung der Stadt Köln*, esp. pp. 116–18.

41. Information about the trade on the Staple was obtained from records of outstanding excise taxes, *Akzisestundung*, available for trade over one of Cologne's major markets for a good portion of the late fifteenth and early sixteenth centuries. Part of the records have been published in Bruno Kuske, *Quellen zur Geschichte des Kölner Handels and und Verkehrs im Mittelalter*, 4 vols. (Bonn, 1917–34), vol. 3; the remaining records are summarized in Irsigler, *Die wirtschaftliche Stellung der Stadt Köln* and in Wensky, *Die Stellung der Frau*. The records of cloth sales are reproduced in Irsigler and Wensky. Those of wine sales are in the same two studies, but for the late fourteenth century, see the more detailed records in Wolfgang Herborn and Klaus Militzer, *Der Kölner Weinhandel: Seine sozialen und politschen Auswirkungen im ausgehenden 14. Jahrhundert* (Sigmaringen, 1980).

42. Many scholars have suggested that the difficulty of adapting family schedules to the pace of market production explains why women typically operated on the periphery of market production. For two examples, see Tilly and Scott, *Women, Work and Family*, especially pp. 123–29, and Medick, "Die proto-industrielle Familienwirtschaft," pp. 133 ff., in Kriedte, Medick and Schlumbohm, *Industrialisierung vor der Industrialisierung*.

43. The effects of changes in the political and business organization of work on the family economy were surely not solely responsible for changes in urban women's work during this period or even, more specifically, for the changes in women's access to high-status positions in market production. For a fuller discussion of how supply and demand factors or technological developments may have been related, see the fuller study from which this essay was drawn: Martha C. Howell, *Women's Work, the Structures of Market Production, and Patriarchy in Late Medieval Cities of Northern Europe* (forthcoming, University of Chicago Press).

# CONTRIBUTORS

**Judith M. Bennett** did her graduate work at the Pontifical Institute of Mediaeval Studies and the University of Toronto. An assistant professor of history at the University of North Carolina at Chapel Hill, she has a book forthcoming from Oxford University Press on women in the medieval countryside.

**Natalie Zemon Davis,** Henry Charles Lea Professor of History at Princeton University, is author of *Society and Culture in Early Modern France, The Return of Martin Guerre,* and numerous essays on the social and cultural history of women in the early modern period. Her new book, *The Gift in Sixteenth-Century France,* is forthcoming from the University of Wisconsin Press.

**Barbara A. Hanawalt** is a professor of history at Indiana University. She is the author of two books, *Crime and Conflict in Medieval England, 1300–1348* and *The Ties That Bound: Peasant Families in Medieval England.* She has also written articles on the history of crime, medieval women, and the medieval family.

**Martha C. Howell** received her Ph.D. from Columbia University in 1979 and is now an associate professor of history at Rutgers University. Her publications include "Reconsidering the Early Modern Urban Economy: The Cases of Leiden and Lille" (with R. S. DuPlessis) and *Women's Work, the Structure of Market Production, and Patriarchy in Late Medieval Cities of Northern Europe* (University of Chicago Press, forthcoming 1986).

**Christiane Klapisch-Zuber** is a professor at the École des Hautes Études en Sciences Sociales, Paris. She is coauthor, with David Herlihy, of *Tuscans and Their Families,* and author of *Women, Family and Ritual in Renaissance Italy.*

**Maryanne Kowaleski** received her Ph.D. in Medieval Studies from the University of Toronto in 1982 and is currently an assistant professor of history at Fordham University. She has published several articles on various aspects of medieval English economic and urban history and is completing a book on the local markets and regional trade of late medieval Exeter.

**Leah L. Otis,** who received her doctorate in medieval history from Columbia University in 1980, currently lectures at the University of Montpellier I and for the University of Minnesota's Montpellier Program. She is the author of *Prostitution in Medieval Society: The History of an Urban Institution in Languedoc.*

**Kathryn L. Reyerson** received doctorates from Yale University and the Faculté de Droit et des Sciences Economiques de Montpellier. She has published a number of articles on the social, economic, and legal history of Montpellier and a monograph, *Business, Banking and Finance in Medieval Montpellier.* She is currently associate professor of history at the University of Minnesota.

**Susan Mosher Stuard** is an associate professor of history at SUNY Brockport and a 1984–85 member of the School for Historical Studies, The Institute for Advanced Study, Princeton. She is the author of numerous articles and edited *Women in*

*Medieval Society.* Her chapter in this volume is part of a larger study on Ragusa, soon to be published.

**Merry E. Wiesner** is currently teaching at the University of Wisconsin–Milwaukee, after teaching many years at Augustana College. She has recently completed a book, *Working Women in Renaissance Germany,* which will appear in the spring of 1986 from Rutgers University Press.

# INDEX

Abandoned children. *See* Foundlings
Abortion, 107–108, 109
Abram, Annie, 145
Accidents: among English peasants, 7–8, 9, 10, 11, 18 n.24, n.25
Administrators of estates: women as, 134
Age of consent, 118
Agricultural societies, xv
Agricultural trade. *See* Commodity trade
Agricultural work, 1, 10, 85–86
Agriculture: open-field farming, 26–27
Alberti, 58–59
Albrecht of Saxony, Duke, 98
Ale: in peasant diet, 20
Ale fines, 21–23, 25–26, 31 n.4, 33–34 n.21
Ale-tasters, 21, 22, 29
Ale-wives, 2, 20–30, 148, 151; use of term, 32 n.13. *See also* Brewing
Alms: in Nuremberg, 105
Ambassadorial missions: male slaves used on, 45, 54 n.28
Anabaptists, 106, 107
*Ancilla babiça*, 43–44, 49
*Ancillae. See* Slaves
Animals, domestic, 10, 13, 18 n.24; trade in, 124 (table), 128
Apprenticeships, 97, 146, 191 n.9; in drapery trade, 206, 207; in Lyon, 169–70, 175, 178, 181, 185–86, 191 n.7, n.9; for midwives, 98–99, 100, 106; in Montpellier, 120–21, 132; for women, 59, 115, 163 n.56, 200
Apulia: slave traders from, 47
*Arme Kindbetterin Almosen*, 105, 107–108, 112 n.37
Armorers: in Cologne, 210
Artisans, 120, 203; in Cologne, 209–10, 212, 213, 214; in Exeter, 148 (table), 151–53; in Lyon, 167, 168, 172–87; in Ragusa, 41, 43, 45
Assarting, 23, 27
Assize of Bread and Ale, 20–30
Augment (marital gift), 140 n.17; return of in will, 173
Aumône Générale, 170–71, 177, 185

Autopsies: of infants, 108
Avicenna, 100, 102

*Baiula* (governess), 44
Bakers, 85, 119, 182, 208; in English villages, 8, 11, 20, 31 n.4; female apprentices to, 115, 120
Baking guild, 213
Ball, John, 6–7
"Ballad of the Tyrannical Husband," 9
Banking: women in, 132–34
Baptism: registration of, 106, 112 n.38; role of midwives in, 100, 106–107; of slaves, 40
Barberino, Francesco da, 58–59
Barber-surgeons, 108, 175, 186
Barley: use in brewing, 21
Bastelieres de Lyon, les (the boatwomen of Lyon), 180
Bedlinens: as part of dowry, 68
Beer, 21, 35 n.32
Beer-brewing guild, 213
Beggars: in Lyon, 177
Belt makers, brotherhood of, 213
Belt-making guild, 213–14
Bennett, Judith, 6
Birthing. *See* Delivery
Birthrate: in Nuremberg, 96–97
Black Death, 12, 65, 117, 153
Blanche of Castile, 139 n.3
Boatwomen of Lyon (Les bastelieres de Lyon), 180
*Bona paraphernalia* (personal property), 118
Bonuses: for midwives, 99
Borrowers: in Montpellier, 133
Bosnia, 39, 40, 42–43, 47, 48
Bread, 11, 20, 24 n.24
Bread fines, 21, 31 n.4
Bread riots, 12
Brewing, 2, 8, 11, 20–21, 31 n.4, 32 n.12; in Exeter, 148, 151, 156, 160 n.27; and labor status, 215–16. *See also* Ale-wives
Brigstock, 30; brewing in, 22–29, 31 n.4, 32 n.11, n.12, 33–34 n.21, 34 n.24
Britton, Edward, 11
Brothel keepers: in Exeter, 148 (table), 154, 157, 162 n.53

225

Barbara A. Hanawalt is a professor of history at Indiana University and author of *Crime and Conflict in Medieval England, 1300–1348* and *The Ties That Bound: Peasant Families in Medieval England.*